The Art of Immersion

Also by Frank Rose

The Agency

West of Eden

Into the Heart of the Mind

Real Men

The Art of Immersion

How the Digital Generation Is Remaking Hollywood, Madison Avenue, and the Way We Tell Stories

Frank Rose

W. W. Norton & Company
New York London

Printed in the United States of America
First Edition

For information about permission to reproduce selections from this book, write to Permissions, W. W. Norton & Company, Inc., 500 Fifth Avenue, New York, NY 10110

For information about special discounts for bulk purchases, please contact W. W. Norton Special Sales at specialsales@wwnorton.com or 800-233-4830

Manufacturing by Courier Westford
Book design by Lovedog Studio
Production manager: Anna Oler

Library of Congress Cataloging-in-Publication Data

Rose, Frank.
The art of immersion : how the digital generation is remaking Hollywood, Madison Avenue, and the way we tell stories / by Frank Rose.
p. cm.
Includes bibliographical references.
ISBN 978-0-393-07601-1 (hbk.)
1. Internet entertainment industry—Social aspects. 2. Internet entertainment—Social aspects. 3. Internet marketing—Social aspects. 4. Entertainment computing—Social aspects. 5. Internet—Social aspects. I. Title.
HD9696.8.A2R67 2011
306.4'802854678—dc22

2010038676

W. W. Norton & Company, Inc.
500 Fifth Avenue, New York, N.Y. 10110
www.wwnorton.com

W. W. Norton & Company Ltd.
Castle House, 75/76 Wells Street, London W1T 3QT

1 2 3 4 5 6 7 8 9 0

For Susan, Jeff, and Nick,
and in memory of Bill

Contents

I thought I should turn back; a coyote's range is large and one can trot for hours. What if his trail went on ad infinitum? What if the story had no end? Why are we so unsatisfied by tales that don't conclude, that have no gun, no knife, no corpse, that leave us hanging? What if this sentence just. . . . . !!! How much does our following words across a page engage the old neural pathways, and recapitulate the need to follow game and find . . . the food?

—Brad Kessler, *Goat Song*

The Art of Immersion

Prologue

What is it about stories, anyway? Anthropologists tell us that storytelling is central to human existence. That it's common to every known culture. That it involves a symbiotic exchange between teller and listener—an exchange we learn to negotiate in infancy. Just as the brain detects patterns in the visual forms of nature—a face, a figure, a flower—and in sound, so too it detects patterns in information. Stories are recognizable patterns, and in those patterns we find meaning. We use stories to make sense of our world and to share that understanding with others. They are the signal within the noise.

So powerful is our impulse to detect story patterns that we see them even when they're not there. In a landmark 1944 study, 34 humans—Massachusetts college students actually, though subsequent research suggests they could have been just about anyone—were shown a short film and asked what was happening in it. The film showed two triangles and a circle moving across a two-dimensional surface. The only other object onscreen was a stationary rectangle, partially open on one side. And yet, only one of the test subjects saw this scene for what it was: geometric shapes moving across a plane. Everyone else came up with elaborate narratives to explain what the movements were about. Typically, the participants viewed the triangles as two men fighting and the circle as a woman trying to escape the bigger, bullying triangle. Instead of registering inanimate shapes, they imagined humans with vivid inner lives. The circle was "worried." The circle and the little triangle were "innocent young things." The big triangle was "blinded by rage and frustration."

But if stories themselves are universal, the way we tell them changes with the technology at hand. Every new medium has given rise to a new form of narrative. In Europe, the invention of the printing press and movable type around 1450 led to the emergence of periodicals and the novel, and with it a slow but inexorable rise in literacy rates. The invention of the motion picture camera around 1890 set off an era of feverish experimentation that led to the development of feature films by 1910. Television, invented around 1925, gave rise a quarter-century later to *I Love Lucy* and the highly stylized form of comedy that became known as the sitcom. As each of these media achieved production and distribution on an industrial scale, we saw the emergence of twentieth-century mass media—newspapers, magazines, movies, music, TV. And with that, there was no role left for the consumer except to consume.

Then, just as we'd gotten used to consuming sequential narratives in a carefully prescribed, point-by-point fashion, came the Internet. The Internet is a chameleon. It is the first medium that can act like all media—it can be text, or audio, or video, or all of the above. It is nonlinear, thanks to the World Wide Web and the revolutionary convention of hyperlinking. It is inherently participatory—not just interactive, in the sense that it responds to your commands, but an instigator constantly encouraging you to comment, to contribute, to join in. And it is immersive—meaning that you can use it to drill down as deeply as you like about anything you care to.

At first, like film and television in their earliest days, the Internet served mainly as a way of retransmitting familiar formats. For all the talk of "new media," it functioned as little more than a new delivery mechanism for old media—newspapers, magazines, music. The emergence of peer-to-peer file-sharing networks encouraged a lot of people to get their deliveries for free. But as disruptive as the Net has been to media businesses, only now is it having an impact on media forms.

Under its influence, a new type of narrative is emerging—one that's told through many media at once in a way that's nonlinear, that's participatory and often gamelike, and that's designed above all to be immersive. This is "deep media": stories that are not just entertaining, but immersive, taking you deeper than an hour-long TV drama or a two-hour movie or a 30-second spot will permit. This new mode of storytelling is transforming not just entertainment (the stories that are offered to us for enjoyment) but also advertising (the stories marketers tell us about their products) and autobiography (the stories we tell about ourselves).

We have seen the results all around us. ABC's *Lost*, which ran from 2004 to 2010, told a story so convoluted that the audience had little choice but to work together to decipher it communally online. The 2010 season of the BBC's *Doctor Who* was made up of 13 television episodes and 4 subsequent episodes that came in the form of downloadable video games. James Cameron's *Avatar* was a phenomenally immersive movie—but when game developers tried to translate it to interactive form, they failed. The 2008 Hollywood blockbuster *The Dark Knight* was preceded by

Why So Serious?, an "alternate reality game" that played out over a 14-month period and engaged some 10 million people worldwide. Ads introducing a new burger from Carl's Jr. unspooled not as 30 second spots to be avoided on TV but as Web videos that were sought out on YouTube. Nike+, a Web service that doubles as a marketing platform, functions as a branded corner of cyberspace where runners can keep their stats and tell their own stories.

ALL THIS EXPERIMENTATION IS taking place against the backdrop of a stark and uncomfortable fact: conventional entertainment isn't working the way it used to. *The Dark Knight* broke box office records, and 17 months later *Avatar* blew them out the door. But while the movie industry's total box office take for 2009 was a record $10.6 billion in the United States and Canada, the total number of tickets sold in North America peaked at 1.6 billion in 2002 and hasn't reached that level since. There was a slight uptick in 2009, but in general, people are paying more for movies and seeing them less.

And it isn't just movies. The number of DVDs and videotapes sold has been falling since 2005. Spending on music, which hit $39 billion worldwide in 1999, sank to $25 billion in 2009. As for television, young people in the US are deserting the four commercial broadcast networks so fast that in the 2007–08 season, for the first time ever, the median age of viewers in prime time hit 50—which isn't even inside the 18–49 demographic that advertisers want to reach. (The median age of US households is 38.) Even video games, which pulled in nearly $12 billion in the US in 2008—more than double the amount of a decade before—declined in sales in 2009.

There have been times when entertainment lost its audience before. Generally, these moments have signaled a major shift in the industry. The classic example was the generational divide of the late 1960s. The music business at the time was still nimble and entrepreneurial enough to accommodate rapid changes in taste. Hollywood was not. The studios were still dominated by the men who had built them through the Silent Era and the Great Depression—Adolph Zukor of Paramount, then in his nineties; Jack Warner of Warner Bros., well into his seventies; Darryl F. Zanuck of 20th Century-Fox, a veritable youngster at sixty-something. Now, having delivered big-budget box office turkeys on the order of *Camelot*, *The Bible*, and *Tora! Tora! Tora!*, these once-great enterprises were on the verge of collapse. *Easy Rider*, the drug-saturated hippie biker flick that Dennis Hopper and Peter Fonda made for $500,000, was more what audiences wanted. "What we're doing is fucking with the rules," Fonda told one studio executive. Only with the emergence of the young directors of the "New Hollywood"—rebels like Francis Ford Coppola, George Lucas, and Martin Scorsese, who were ready to scrap the rules entirely—would the movie industry be saved.

The previous dislocation, in the early 1950s, was technological. Television started to get big in the US in 1948 with the incredible success of Milton Berle's *Texaco Star Theater*, which was so popular that the reservoir levels in Detroit dropped every Tuesday night at 9:00 PM because everyone waited until the show was over to go to the toilet. Before then, many in the broadcasting business had regarded television as a fad—and a dangerous fad at that, since it was too small to generate decent ad revenues, yet it was cannibalizing the extremely profitable business of radio. It seemed equally threatening to Hollywood, because as soon as people had free entertainment in their living rooms, they lost interest in the cheap, run-of-the-mill B pictures the movie studios had always depended on for profits. As with radio, television shows were broadcast live from New York. Hollywood was stymied until MCA, the most aggressive talent agency of the era, demonstrated that money could be made by taping TV shows to be shown later. Only then did the studios take the obvious next step: instead of churning out B pictures, churning out TV shows.

Today the dislocation is technological and generational both. The Internet is cannibalizing television at a fearsome rate, but it shows no sign yet of generating comparable advertising revenues. The couch potato, introduced in a 1987 *New York* magazine cover story as the inevitable result of "marriage, children, and home video (not necessarily in that order)," is now history. Even the concept of audience is growing outdated; participants would be more like it. And as the people formerly known as the audience begin to take part in their own entertainment, what they're experiencing changes in a fundamental way. *Grand Theft Auto IV* has been compared more than once to a Scorsese film. *Lost* was told in a deliberately obscure manner because its producers had the expectation that viewers would treat it as a vast, collective puzzle to be solved—which they did. Stories become games, and games become stories.

Neuroscientists are only beginning to understand how games work on the brain. But all indications are that they have a powerful effect on the reward system, the neurochemical mechanism behind both learning and addiction. As the once-clear delineations between story and game become a blur, gaming's more addictive aspects are being copied willy-nilly. They turn up in online extensions of *The Office*. They turn up in ad campaigns. They turn up on Facebook.

Like games, stories are rehearsals for life. We create a world in microcosm, an alternate reality, a world we wish were true or fear could become so. And then we immerse ourselves in it. This much never changes. But our ability to indulge that impulse grows with each new medium, and with it, the stakes we're playing for.

WE'VE GOTTEN TO THIS POINT only gradually. A critical inflection point was the 2000 dot-com bust. At the time, skeptics interpreted the bursting of an investment bubble as a sign the Internet fad was over. In fact, the Internet and its dominant format, the World Wide Web, were just beginning to assume their true function.

The Web, introduced in 1991, was what made the Net accessible to ordinary people. A decade later—the elimination of a host of ill-considered, mostly superfluous, me-too e-businesses notwithstanding—the Web began its transition from a simple delivery mechanism to the cornucopia of participation (blogs, wikis, social media) known as Web 2.0. More and more people were moving to broadband, and new software tools were making it easy to build platforms that would enable those people to connect with one another online. Flickr, YouTube, Wikipedia, MySpace, Facebook, eBay—Web 2.0 was all about connecting people and putting their collective intelligence to work.

Now, another decade on, the harnessing of collective intelligence goes far beyond sharing photos, videos, and too much information. "An artistic movement, albeit an organic and as-yet-unstated one, is forming," David Shields writes in *Reality Hunger: A Manifesto*, a book whose truth to its time is underscored by the gleeful way it samples from other sources. "What are its key components?" Shields names several: randomness, spontaneity, and emotional urgency; reader/viewer participation and involvement; anthropological autobiography; a thirst for authenticity coupled with a love of artifice; "a blurring (to the point of invisibility) of any distinction between fiction and nonfiction: the lure and blur of the real."

We stand now at the intersection of lure and blur. The future beckons, but we're only partway through inventing it. We can see the outlines of a new art form, but its grammar is as tenuous and elusive as the grammar of cinema a century ago.

We know this much: people want to be immersed. They want to get involved in a story, to carve out a role for themselves, to make it their own. But how is the author supposed to accommodate them? What if the audience runs away with the story? And how do we handle the blur—not just between fiction and fact, but between author and audience, entertainment and advertising, story and game? A lot of smart people—in film, in television, in video games, in advertising, in technology, even in neuroscience—are trying to sort these questions out. This is their story.

1.

The Dyslexic Storyteller

ONE DAY TOWARD THE END OF 2007, SEVERAL THOUSAND people received a cryptic and, it must be said, highly inappropriate email from humanresources@whysoserious.com. The email read, "Heads up, clown! Tomorrow means that there's one last shifty step left in the interview process: Arwoeufgryo."

The people who got this missive had applied to serve as henchmen of Batman's perpetual nemesis, the Joker. Some recipients—the savvier ones—realized they had just gotten a tip-off to go to www.whysoserious.com/steprightup ("arwoeufgryo" shifted one letter over on the keyboard). There they found a carnival game in which a series of ratty-looking stuffed animals appeared a few at a time, each with a different street address pinned to its belly.

Since Whysoserious.com was known to be associated with weird occurrences involving the upcoming Batman movie *The Dark Knight*, word of the new Web page quickly spread among those who gravitated to online discussion forums about the film.

There they learned from those who had googled the addresses that each one was for a bakery. A note on the Whysoserious.com carnival game bore instructions to go to each address and pick up a "very special treat" that was being held for someone named Robin Banks. The race was on.

In Boston, a local couple and a friend from the Netherlands went to an address on Salem Street in the North End and found themselves at an old-fashioned Italian American pastry shop. It was empty except for a handful of employees. When they announced they were there to pick up a package, they were met with a curt response. "Name?"

"Robin Banks."

They were given a box. Opening it, they found a cake inside. Written on top in lurid purple and green icing was a phone number and the words "Call Me Now." So they called—and the cake started ringing.

Borrowing a knife from the bakery, they cut into the cake and found a sealed evidence pouch inside. The pouch contained a cell phone, a charger, and a note with instructions to call another number—which in turn triggered a text message to keep the phone turned on and charged at all times. Also in the pouch was a single playing card—a joker. To anyone attuned to the mythology of Batman, the message was clear: from now on they were accomplices of the Joker—in robbing banks. The cake was chocolate and, they reported, quite good.

This scenario was repeated in 21 other cities across the United States. City by city, minute by minute, the reports came in. Los Angeles, Las Vegas, St. Louis, Miami—each time someone phoned in from one of the cake phones, another stuffed animal disappeared from Whysoserious.com. When all the animals were gone, people could click on the strength bell next to the empty animal display and be taken to another page on the site. There they would find an evidence pouch, a set of keys, and a pair of jokers. But what did this mean?

The week before, another page on Whysoserious.com had shown a police evidence vault, together with a nonsensical set of instructions that turned out to contain a code that would get them inside. There they had found, among other things, a set of keys and an ID card stolen from one Jake Karnassian, an employee of the Gotham Unified School District who had apparently been mugged. On the school district's Web site they had seen Karnassian listed as "Mgr. Buildings and Grounds (on hiatus)," along with a notice announcing that school bus service had been rerouted in District 22. Over the next few days they had been led to a series of other pages on Whysoserious.com, culminating in a page that showed Karnassian's ID to be missing from the evidence vault, along with one of his keys.

So the two jokers they were looking at now were a sign that the Joker had been there. Clicking on the card on the left unveiled a new poster for the film. The card on the right led to tickets for IMAX screenings a couple days later in New York, Philadelphia, Toronto, Chicago, and LA. There was no indication of what was being screened. When ticket holders got to the theaters, however, they discovered it was footage from *The Dark Knight*. Christopher Nolan, the film's director, introduced it at the New York theater by saying, "I wanted to make the Joker's introduction a mini film. That's what this footage is."

What followed was the first six minutes of the movie—six minutes during which a gang of robbers shoot up a bank. The scene begins with a sweeping view of Gotham City, the camera slowly zooming in on a black glass tower, just as two guys in clown masks shoot a grappling hook to the roof of the next building. This is the start of an elaborately choreographed heist. Five robbers, each wearing a grotesque clown mask, rough up the bank employees, break into the vault, and kill each other one by one, apparently on the boss's orders.

In the midst of the mayhem, a bright yellow school bus bursts through the bank's front doors, rear end first. The sole surviving robber hurls bags full of cash into its interior, and then casually shoots the bus driver. Then he turns back to confront the bank manager, who's lying wounded, yet defiant, on the floor. "Whadda you believe in, huh?" the manager demands. "WHADDA YOU BELIEVE IN?"

Calmly, deliberately, the clown-faced robber kneels down, pulls a concussion grenade from his pocket, and places it in the bank manager's mouth. It's a fair question, and he answers it. "I believe," he says, in a preternaturally quiet tone, "whatever doesn't kill you, simply makes you"—and here, fully five minutes into the film, he finally removes the mask, revealing a face smeared with red and white makeup—"*stranger.*" It's the world's first glimpse of Heath Ledger as the Joker.

Shuffling back to the school bus, the Joker hops in the back and drives off. The bus, "District 22" emblazoned on its side, pulls into a long line of identical buses filled with happy, squealing children. For many in the audience, this was the big reveal: So that's why they had broken into the evidence vault—so the Joker could take Karnassian's key and ID and use them to steal a school bus. They were accomplices in the getaway of a psychotic criminal. An agent of chaos with a bent for destruction. A nihilistic cartoon supervillain rendered in larger-than-life, high-definition digital flesh. Heath Ledger—the brilliant and promising young actor who seven weeks later, at the age of 28, would be found dead in his New York loft, apparently from an overdose of the pills he had swallowed in a vain attempt to get some sleep.

FOR LEDGER, WHO HAD INHABITED his role in *The Dark Knight* with a vengeance, the fiction became all too real. But to a (fortunately) far lesser extent, the line between fiction and reality could also become blurred for anyone with an Internet connection. The cake phones were a mechanism that enabled thousands of people to step into the fiction long before the movie's July 2008 premiere. The 12-hour cake hunt involved only a few dozen people on the ground, but some 1.4 million gathered online to see what would happen. And that episode was just a small part of the larger collective experience known as *Why So Serious?*, which played out intermittently for 14 months before the movie's release. Ultimately, more than 10 million people across the planet took part in a cascading sequence of riddles, puzzles, and treasure hunts that sucked them into the latest chapter in the 69-year-old story of Batman. Not coincidentally, *The Dark Knight* grossed $1 billion worldwide during its 33-week run—far more than any previous Batman movie, and enough to make it the number one film of 2008.

On one level, *Why So Serious?* was an enormously successful marketing stunt, not just for the movie but for Nokia (which supplied the phones) and for other brands that had cut product-placement deals with Warner Bros., the studio behind the production. This is what won it a Grand Prix at the 2009 Cannes Lions, the world's largest and most prestigious advertising festival. But it was also a new kind of interactive fiction, one that blurred the line between entertainment and advertising, as well as between fiction and reality, in ways barely imagined a decade earlier.

Alternate reality games, as these experiences are known, are a hybrid of game and story. The story is told in fragments; the game comes in piecing the fragments together. The task is too complicated for any one person. But through the connective power of the Web, a group intelligence emerges to assemble the pieces, solve the mysteries, and, in the process, tell and retell the story online. Ultimately, the audience comes to own the story, in ways that movies themselves can't match.

Staged for Warner Bros. by 42 Entertainment, a small Pasadena company headed by a former Walt Disney Imagineer named Susan Bonds, *Why So Serious?* was essentially an experiment in the future of narrative. There are many such experiments, and though they vary wildly in form, most share a few essential characteristics.

Crucially, *Why So Serious?* was nonlinear. Like hypertext—text that has embedded within it links to other texts, an essential feature of the Web—it could lead you along different paths. Links can carry you deeper and deeper into a story, revealing levels of detail that would be impossible to convey in a single, two-hour movie. Or they can take you into alternate story lines, showing what would happen if you, or the author, made different choices along the way.

Why So Serious? also assumed that the participants would be connected. The game wasn't restricted to the Internet or to any other medium, but it certainly relied on the connective tissue of the Web. In a networked world, information doesn't just travel from author to audience, or in a closed loop from author to audience and back again; it spreads all over the place, and more or less instantly. Fans can collaborate with each other, as they did in the search for the cake phones. This is what generates the hive mind, the spontaneous joint effort that transformed *The Dark Knight* into an experience anyone could take part in.

At the same time, *Why So Serious?* was a fusion of game and narrative. Conventional narratives—books, movies, TV shows—are emotionally engaging, but they involve us as spectators. Games are engaging in a different way. They put us at the center of the action: whatever's going on is not just happening to a character on the page or an actor on the screen; it's happening to us. Combine the emotional impact of stories with the first-person involvement of games and you can create an extremely powerful experience.

An immersive experience, you might say. And that immersiveness is what blurs the line, not just between story and game, but between story and marketing, storyteller and audience, illusion and reality.

For most of its 69 years, Batman existed as a series of comic books—printed artifacts that followed certain well-defined rules of narrative and graphic art. It stayed within the lines. You picked it up, you put it down. You could read it or not, but it would not read you. It wouldn't bleed into your life. As a television series in the sixties, Batman remained very much, as they say, inside the box. When Tim Burton brought the story to movie theaters in 1989, it got larger than life, but it didn't try to jump the screen. No longer.

THE FORCES THAT TOOK BATMAN to new dimensions were at work long before most people experienced the Internet or even heard about it. They could be felt decades earlier at a summer camp deep in the north woods of Wisconsin. Jordan Weisman, a 14-year-old from the Chicago suburbs who would grow up to more or less invent the concept of alternate reality games, was back for his sixth summer—this time as a junior counselor. Camp Shewahmegon fronted on a remote and pristine lake, its thousand-foot shoreline dotted with sugar maples, yellow birches, white pines, and balsam firs. But for Jordan the fun started after dark, when the little kids were asleep and the older ones had the evening to themselves. That's when the camp's senior counselor brought out a new game he'd just discovered in college. The game was *Dungeons & Dragons*. The year was 1974.

When he was in second grade, Jordan had been diagnosed as severely dyslexic. In a way, he was lucky. Dyslexia had been identified by European physicians in the late nineteenth century, but American schoolteachers had only recently been introduced to the idea that otherwise normal kids might be unable to read because their brains couldn't process words and letters properly. Jordan's teacher had just attended a seminar on the disorder, and a nearby teachers' college was one of the few places in the country that tested for it. Since then, years of daily tutoring had given Jordan a way to cope, but reading was still difficult—so difficult he found it almost physically painful.

Dungeons & Dragons gave him a different kind of story—one he could act out instead of having to read. The first commercial example of what would become a long line of fantasy role-playing games, *D&D* provided an elaborate set of rules that guided players through an imaginary adventure as they sat around a table together. Each player got to pick a character with certain characteristics (human or elf, fighter or wizard) and abilities. The game started with the lead player, the "Dungeon Master," describing the setting and the plot to all the others. As the game progressed, the Dungeon Master determined the outcome of the players' actions, often with a roll of the dice. For those few hours, they weren't a bunch of knock-kneed mall rats in a cabin in the woods; they were axe-wielding warriors fighting goblins and orcs. The images that played out in Jordan's head during these sessions were so vivid, and the socialization with the other boys so intense, that decades later he remembered thinking, Wow—my life is going to be changed.

As he told me this story, Weisman and I were sitting in his lakeside guesthouse in the Seattle suburb of Bellevue, the snow-covered peaks of the Cascade Range rising in the distance beyond the water. Bellevue's downtown has the raw look of an insta-city, but here on the shores of Lake Sammamish it felt secluded in an upscale, north woods kind of way. Now in his late forties, Weisman was slender and soft-spoken, with dark, curly hair and a salt-and-pepper beard that gave him an almost Talmudic appearance.

"Here was entertainment that involved problem solving and was story based and social," he recalled, taking a sip of coffee. "It totally put my brain on fire." Ultimately, it led him to fashion a career in game design and social interaction—two fields he sees as intimately connected. "Games are about engaging with the most entertaining thing on the planet," he added, "which is other people."

On his way home from Camp Shewahmegon that summer, Jordan convinced his parents to stop at Lake Geneva, Wisconsin, a small resort town near the Illinois border. He wanted to buy his own copy of *Dungeons & Dragons*, and the only way you could do that was to see Gary Gygax, the local insurance underwriter who had invented it with a friend. Gygax had a passion for games, but no publisher was interested in taking this one on, so he had published it himself and was selling it out of his house.

Jordan started a *Dungeons & Dragons* club when he went

back to school that fall—the beginning of what would become a lifelong pattern of entrepreneurship. After graduation he attended the Merchant Marine Academy and then the University of Illinois, but before long he dropped out and started a company he called FASA Corporation—short for Freedonian Aeronautics and Space Administration, after the fictional nation in the Marx Brothers' film *Duck Soup*.

Building on the role-playing game genre that Gygax had started with *Dungeons & Dragons*, FASA created games like *BattleTech*, a science fiction title inspired by Japanese anime—the animated films and television shows that were beginning to turn up on videocassette in the United States, usually with English-language subtitles provided by fans. Launched in 1984 as a board game, *BattleTech* existed in an elaborate fictional "universe" of warring feudal states set centuries into the future. Over the years it morphed into a PC game, a console game, an online game, a series of novels, and an immersive simulation in Chicago that enabled players to sit in a virtual cockpit and engage in combat with other players.

In 1999, Microsoft acquired a spin-off company called FASA Interactive and moved it from Chicago to the woodsy Seattle suburb of Redmond, not far from corporate headquarters. Weisman became creative director of Microsoft's new entertainment division, which was about to launch the Xbox—the console that would pit the company against Sony and its best-selling PlayStation in the video game business.

Weisman's new role gave him creative oversight of everyone developing video games for the Xbox. One such group was Bungie Studios, another Chicago-based game developer that Microsoft had bought and moved to Seattle. Bungie's big project was *Halo*, a shooter that had generated rave reports after being demonstrated at game shows in prototype form. In 2000 and 2001, as the Bungie team was retooling *Halo* to be a game that could be played exclusively on the Xbox, Weisman helped the Bungie crew create a backstory for the game, like the universe he had devised for *BattleTech*.

"You need characters," he explained. "You need plotlines that can be extended and moved to other media to create a more robust world." Weisman's team put together a *Halo* "bible," a compendium of information about the characters in the game and the universe in which it takes place. They made a deal with Del Rey Books to publish a series of novels that would flesh out the *Halo* story. But while Weisman was spending most of his days thinking about *Halo* and other new Xbox titles, on his own time he was thinking about an entirely different kind of game.

In truth, Weisman didn't really care that much about video games. He liked storytelling, and game developers at the time were far too busy trying to deliver gee-whiz computer graphics to pay much attention to story. Ever since his days at camp, he'd loved telling stories through interaction with other people. Now he was starting to think about how interactive stories could be told in a way that was organic to the Internet.

"What do we do on the Net?" he asked. "Mainly we search through a ton of crap looking for information we care about, like an archaeologist sifting through dirt." Gradually, after months of midafternoon rambles through Microsoft parking lots and 3:00 a.m. phone calls with a young protégé named Elan Lee, this line of thought evolved into the notion of a deconstructed narrative. They could write a story, fabricate the evidence that would have existed had it been real, and then throw the story out and get an online audience to reconstruct it. That was the theory anyway—that we humans would forage for information the same way other species forage for food, and use it to tell ourselves a story. Now all he needed was some way to try it out.

One of the video games Weisman was supervising at Microsoft was based on the upcoming Steven Spielberg movie *Artificial Intelligence: AI*. Originally developed by Stanley Kubrick in the 1970s, then taken over by Spielberg after Kubrick's death, the film was meant to be a futuristic retelling of the Pinocchio legend, with an android in place of the wooden puppet that dreamed of becoming an actual boy. Personally, Weisman had his doubts about the appeal of a video game centered on a boy who longed for his mother's love, even if the boy in question was a robot. But he also figured that the kind of deconstructed narrative he wanted to create could be used to establish a context for the game, and for the movie as well.

While overseeing development of the video game, Weisman worked closely with Spielberg and his producer, Kathleen Kennedy. One day he sat in Spielberg's headquarters at Universal Studios, a grandly appointed "bungalow" just down the hill from *Jurassic Park—The Ride*, and told them he wanted to explore a new way of telling stories.

Much as the theme park ride was designed to give the sensation of being hurled headlong into *Jurassic Park*, Weisman wanted to create an experience of being plunged into the world of *AI*. But there the similarities stopped. The *Jurassic Park* ride was Hollywood's idea of participatory entertainment: a five-and-a-half minute boat trip past some robotic dinosaurs, with a scream-inducing 85-foot drop at the end. It was an expensively produced theme park attraction that sought to match the public's desire for more *Jurassic Park* entertainment with Universal's desire for more *Jurassic Park* profits. Weisman's idea was to use the Internet to go beyond the very personal narrative of Spielberg's new film to tell the story of the world the movie was set in.

Weisman is a persuasive guy. At the end of the meeting, Kennedy called the head of marketing at Warner Bros., which was making the picture. As Weisman recalls it, she made an announcement: "I'm sending Jordan over. I want you to write him a very big check. And don't ask what it's for."

"It's good to be king," Weisman remarked when the call was over.

"Yes," she said, "it is."

The experiment began in April 2001, 12 weeks before the release of the movie, when a credit for something called a "sentient machine therapist" appeared among the myriad other credits listed in trailers and posters for the film. The clue was so tiny you could easily miss it, but that was the point. Marketers were already encountering a growing problem: how to reach people so media saturated that they block any attempt to get through. "Your brain filters it out, because otherwise you'd go crazy," Weisman told me. So he opted for the subdural approach: instead of shouting the message, hide it. "I figured that if the audience discovered something, they would share it, because we all need something to talk about."

He was right. Within 24 hours, someone posted the discovery on the movie fan site Ain't It Cool News. Googling the therapist's name, people found a maze of bizarre Web sites about robot rights and a phone number that, when called, played a message from the therapist saying her friend's husband had just died in a suspicious boating accident. Within days, a 24-year-old computer programmer in Oregon had organized an online discussion forum to investigate. More than 150 people joined the forum in its first 48 hours. By the time the movie came out in June, some 3 million people around the planet were involved at one level or another.

Whatever they were experiencing seemed to know no boundaries. Clues were liable to appear anywhere—on Web sites, on TV, in fake newspaper ads. Phone calls, faxes, and emails could come at any time, day or night. Almost the weirdest part was that no one announced or even acknowledged that anything unusual was going on.

One day a Warner Bros. marketing executive asked Elan Lee, who was essentially running the *AI* game, for a single line of text to go at the end of an *AI* movie trailer being made for TV. He needed it in 20 minutes. Lee was desperate. He wanted to make people feel good, or at least not silly, about responding to emails from a fictional character. So he came up with the line "This Is Not a Game." It was flashed for a few seconds on TV. This cryptic missive quickly became a mantra among the players, a neat summation of the mystique generated by a game that refused to acknowledge its own existence. It was the closest Lee or Weisman or any of them ever came to speaking publicly about the experience as it was happening.

They made mistakes, of course. When he and Lee were planning the game, Weisman had argued that no puzzle would be too hard, no clue too obscure, because with so many people collaborating online, the players would have access to any conceivable skill that would be needed to solve it. Where he erred was in not following that argument to its logical conclusion.

"Not only do they have every skill set on the planet," he told me, "but they have unlimited resources, unlimited time, and unlimited money. Not only can they solve anything—they can solve anything instantly." He had dubbed his game *The Beast* because originally it had 666 items of content—Web pages to pore over, obscure puzzles to decipher. These were supposed to keep the players busy for three months; instead, the players burned through them in a single day. With people clamoring for more, the name took on a different connotation: Weisman had created a monster.

It's little wonder that the game's success took Weisman by surprise. Its mix of real-world and online interaction violated every notion of what futuristic digital entertainment was expected to be. For years, science-fiction novels like Neal Stephenson's *Snow Crash* had conditioned readers to think the future would bring some swirling electronic phantasm so vivid that the real world could never compete. But Weisman didn't do virtual reality; he trafficked in alternate reality. *The Beast* wasn't about retreating into some digitally synthesized head space. It was about interacting with other humans in response to an alternate sequence of events.

The world in the spring of 2001 might have been trying to cope with the sudden deflation of the Internet bubble, but people caught up in the *AI* game had to deal not only with that issue but with the furor over civil rights for sentient machines in the year 2142. This was, if anything, more radical, and perhaps ultimately more in sync with the current direction of technology, than the gloves and goggles that kept popping up in the media's breathless reports about virtual reality. "What we're doing is a giant extrapolation of sitting in the kitchen playing *Dungeons & Dragons* with our friends," Weisman told me as we sat at the table in his guesthouse, gazing out across the placid surface of the lake. "It's just that now, our kitchen table holds three million people."

In commercial terms, however, Weisman was years ahead of his time. Three million people engaging with *The Beast* was a lot for something that had never been tried before, but by Hollywood standards it was a negligible figure. The film itself was a dud—ticket sales in the US and Canada came to only $79 million, a fraction of the box office take for *E.T.* or *Jurassic Park*. Microsoft canceled the *AI* video game while it was still in development, so no one at his own company paid much attention to what Weisman was doing. Executives in Redmond were fixated on *Halo*, which quickly became the must-have title that gave traction to the Xbox.

Nonetheless, Weisman wasn't the only person to try his hand at an immersive entertainment experience. Electronic Arts, the San Francisco Bay Area video game giant, had *Majestic*, an online computer game that likewise attempted to create an alternate reality experience. Developed by a 31-year-old EA production executive named Neil Young, it was introduced in July 2001, not long after the conclusion of *The Beast*. Players were thrust into a story that was described at the time as "interactive, immersive and invasive." Five minutes into the tutorial, your computer would crash. Then your cell phone would ring with a cryptic missive regarding a fire at Anim-X, the fictional Oregon studio that had purportedly built the game. For $9.99 a month, you could continue to delve into the mystery of Anim-X and the government conspiracy it was said to have uncovered—a mystery that unfolded through an unpredictable sequence of faxes, phone calls, emails, and instant messages. "Whenever your phone rang," Young says now, "I wanted the next thing in your head to be, Oh my God—is that part of the game?"

Even though *Majestic* had been highly anticipated before its release, it garnered only about 15,000 subscribers. Young sees several reasons why it didn't gain traction. One is the linear structure of the story: "If you got interrupted, it became harder to get back into it. It would have been better to allow the users to consume episodes in any sequence, so they could explore the characters versus exploring the story." There was another structural issue as well: the game designers installed brakes to keep players from running through the game's content the way they had done with *The Beast*, but players complained about being forced to wait for the next step rather than being allowed to proceed at their own pace. And then there was timing: the game was put on hiatus for several weeks following the September 11 attacks on the World Trade Center and the Pentagon. It never recovered. Eleven months after introducing it, EA pulled the plug, calling it "a noble experiment that failed." It would be a long time before anyone tried something like this again.

Young went on to produce two *Lord of the Rings* games for EA before leaving to become founder and CEO of the iPhone gaming company ngmoco. Weisman left Microsoft to run WizKids, a company he had started that built games around collectible action figures. But then Chris Di Cesare, a Microsoft Game Studios executive who had worked with him on *The Beast*, approached him about doing an alternate reality game for the November 2004 launch of *Halo 2*.

Del Rey had published three *Halo* novels by this time, the latest of which showed the series' space aliens at the point of invading Earth. At the E3 gaming conference in Los Angeles, Bungie had unveiled a *Halo* 2 trailer that showed Master Chief, the humans' faceless supersoldier, looking down from a spacecraft as the invasion begins. Di Cesare wanted to create a *War of the Worlds*–like experience that would end with Master Chief's arrival on Earth to lead the resistance—the point at which *Halo* 2 begins. Using an accounting sleight of hand, he got $1 million from the game's marketing budget to pay Weisman up front. "I honestly thought there was a risk I'd get fired," Di Cesare recalls. "No one invests a million dollars in an unproven medium for a marketing effort you won't admit exists. Especially when its success is measured in PR."

Weisman took the bait, launching a boutique marketing firm—42 Entertainment—to develop alternate reality games full-time. The name was a cosmic in-joke: in *The Hitchhiker's Guide to the Galaxy*, the answer to the ultimate question of life is revealed, after tremendous buildup, to be . . . 42. "I figured if we were going to set up a consulting company, we ought to offer people the answer to the secret of the universe," Weisman quips.

The game Weisman and his team created, *I Love Bees*, was *The War of the Worlds* told over pay phones. It had people answering phones around the world in the weeks leading up to the game's release. One player braved a Florida hurricane to take a call in a Burger King parking lot. Each call provided a clue that made sense only later, after all the clues had been pieced together online.

When *Halo* 2 racked up $125 million in sales on its first day, people in marketing took notice. Soon alternate reality games were being used to market all sorts of things. In 2005, an Orlando company, GMD Studios, even staged a fake auto theft at a Park Avenue auto dealership as part of a game to promote Audi's A3 premium compact. The stunt launched a three-month alternate reality game called *The Art of the Heist* that caused a huge spike in traffic to Audi Web sites and was said to have generated more than 10,000 sales leads for US Audi dealers.

To Weisman, it was a case of the Internet transforming the nature of marketing. For centuries, Western commerce had been built on a clear proposition: I give you money, you give me something of value. But like a rug merchant who invites the customer in for tea before discussing his wares, marketers were now beginning to sense that the customer had to be engaged and entertained—whether with a free single on iTunes or an alternate reality game that could run for months. "I believe all marketing is heading in that direction," he said. "But for artists, it's a different thing. To them, this is a new way of telling stories."

THAT'S CERTAINLY THE WAY Trent Reznor thought. Reznor is the singer, songwriter, and sole permanent member of Nine Inch Nails, the industrial-rock project he started in Cleveland in 1988. He spent much of 2006 recording *Year Zero*, a grimly futuristic song suite evoking an America beset by terrorism, ravaged by climate change, and ruled by a Christian military dictatorship. "But I had a problem," he recalled when I saw him the following year, lounging on the second-floor deck of the house he was remodeling in the vertiginous terrain above Beverly Hills.

The problem was how to provide context for the songs. Reznor had spent a long time imagining his future dystopia. Now he wanted to make sure the story he was telling got through to his fans. In the sixties, concept albums came with extensive liner notes and lots of artwork. MP3s don't have that. "So I started thinking about how to make the world's most elaborate album cover," he said, "using the media of today."

Years earlier, Reznor had heard about the strange game that tied into the Spielberg movie *AI*. He wanted to give people a taste of what life would be like in a massively dysfunctional theocratic police state, and with a game like that he could do so in a visceral way. A little googling took to him to 42 Entertainment's Web site. He filled in the contact form he found there and clicked Send.

Weisman had barely heard of Nine Inch Nails, but Alex Lieu, 42's creative director, was a major fan. Over the next few weeks, he and 42's president, Susan Bonds, spent a lot of time talking with Reznor at Chalice, the Hollywood recording studio where he was mixing the album. Reznor and his art director, 28-year-old Rob Sheridan, had already constructed a wiki describing in great detail the dystopia Reznor envisioned 15 years into the future and explaining how things had gotten that way. With Weisman already preparing to launch his next project, a kid's entertainment company called Smith & Tinker, it was up to Lieu to figure out how to translate the wiki into something people could experience firsthand. Rather than write a narrative for the players to reconstruct, he approached it as a songwriter might—by creating a series of poignant emotional moments that people would seize and make their own. By the end of January, as Nine Inch Nails was about to start a European tour, he had a plan.

The initial clue was so subtle that for nearly two days, nobody noticed it. On February 10, 2007, the first night of the tour, T-shirts went on sale at the nineteenth-century Lisbon concert hall where the group was playing. The shirts had what looked to be a printing error: random letters in the tour schedule on the back seemed slightly boldfaced. Then a 27-year-old Lisbon photographer named Nuno Foros realized that, strung together, the boldface letters spelled "i am trying to believe."

Foros posted a photo of his T-shirt on the message boards of The Spiral, the Nine Inch Nails fan club. People started typing "iamtryingtobelieve.com" into their Web browsers, which led them to a site denouncing something called Parepin, a drug apparently introduced into the US water supply. Ostensibly, Parepin was an antidote to bioterror agents, but in reality, the page declared, it was part of a government plot to confuse and sedate citizens. Email sent to the site's contact link generated a cryptic autoresponse: "I'm drinking the water. So should you." Online, fans worldwide debated what this had to do with Nine Inch Nails. A setup for the next album? Some kind of interactive game? Or what?

A few days later, a woman named Sue was about to wash a different T-shirt from one of the Lisbon shows when she noticed that the tour dates included several boldface numbers. Fans quickly interpreted the sequence as a Los Angeles telephone number. People who called it heard a recording of a newscaster announcing, "Presidential address: America is born again," followed by a distorted snippet of what could only be a new Nine Inch Nails song.

Next, a woman named Ana reported finding a USB flash drive in a bathroom stall at the hall where the band had been playing. On the drive was a previously unreleased song, which she promptly uploaded. The metadata tag on the song contained a clue that led to a site displaying a glowing wheat field, with the legend "America Is Born Again." Clicking and dragging the mouse across the screen, however, revealed a much grimmer-looking site labeled "Another Version of the Truth." Clicking on that led to a forum about acts of underground resistance.

For Nine Inch Nails fans, the unfolding of the *Year Zero* game was as puzzling as it was exciting. Debates raged online as to whether all this had anything to do with the science fiction of Philip K. Dick or with the Bible, and why the *Year Zero* Web sites kept referring to something called the Presence, which appeared to be a giant hand reaching down from the sky. The band's European tour dates became the object of obsessive attention. Fans were so eager to find new flash drives that they ran for the toilets the moment the venue doors opened. With every new development, the message boards were swamped. By the time the album hit store shelves in April, 2.5 million people had visited at least one of the game's 30 Web sites. "I don't know if the audience was ready for it to end," says Susan Bonds. "But we always expected to pick it up again." Reznor, after all, had conceived *Year Zero* as a two-part album. "Those phones are still out there," she adds. "The minutes have expired. But we could buy new minutes at any point."

2.

Fear of Fiction

SEVERAL YEARS AFTER HE AND JORDAN WEISMAN STAGED *The Beast*, Elan Lee went to visit his parents at the antique shop they own in Los Angeles. The shop, which goes by the name Aunt Teek's, occupies a modest storefront on Ventura Boulevard, a commercial strip that lies like a fault line between the winding lanes and bougainvillea-clad homes of the Hollywood Hills and the sunbaked sprawl of the San Fernando Valley. When Lee walked in, his father pulled out a rare treasure: a first edition of *Robinson Crusoe*, published by Daniel Defoe in 1719 and generally regarded as the earliest novel in the English language. The author's name was nowhere on the book; the title page identified it as *The Life and Strange Surprizing Adventures of Robinson Crusoe, of York, Mariner: Written by Himself.* As Lee carefully examined the volume, which was falling apart yet strangely beautiful, he was struck by the disclaimer he read in its preface:

> If ever the Story of any private Man's Adventures in the World were worth making Pvblick, and were acceptable when Publish'd, the Editor of this Account thinks this will be so. . . . The Editor believes the thing to be a just History of Fact; neither is there any Appearance of Fiction in it . . . ; and as such he thinks, without farther Compliment to the World, he does them a great Service in the Publication.

This might seem a rather elaborately defensive justification for a work that today, nearly three centuries later, is considered a major landmark in English literature. With hindsight, we can see that *Robinson Crusoe* and the novels that followed it—Henry Fielding's *Tom Jones*, Samuel Richardson's *Pamela*, Laurence Sterne's *Tristram Shandy*—led to a fundamental shift in our view of the world. Where earlier forms of literature had been expected to hew to history, myth, or legend, novels were judged by their "truth to individual experience," as the critic Ian Watt put it. They gave readers for the first time a window onto other people's lives. Yet in the early 1700s, nearly three centuries after the invention of movable type in Europe, prose fiction remained highly suspect: it was categorized with history but had the flaw of not being true.

Defoe himself was equally suspect. Nearly 60 at the time of the book's publication, he was a failed businessman, chronic debtor, political pamphleteer, and occasional spy. Even his name was false; he'd been born Daniel Foe, the son of a tradesman, but had changed his name in an attempt to pass as an aristocrat. In 1703, despite years of propagandizing for king and government, he'd been jailed and pilloried for sedition. In 1704, after his release, he had started one of England's first periodicals, a proto-newspaper on political and economic affairs that he continued to write and publish for the next nine years. And then, after that, he somehow used his imaginative powers to channel the tale of a shipwrecked sailor forced to live by his wits for 28 years on a remote Caribbean island.

Robinson Crusoe was an instant success. After its publication, Defoe went on to write other novels—*Moll Flanders, The Journal of the Plague Year*—that vividly dramatized the lives of very different people: a prostitute and thief, a witness to the epidemic that killed 20 percent of London's population in 1665 and 1666. By this time, a modest rise in literacy and leisure was starting to create what seemed by contemporary standards to be an explosion of reading, and of writing as well. As Samuel Johnson wrote, "There never was a time in which men of all degrees of ability, of every kind of education, of every profession and employment, were posting with ardour so general to the press."

Yet decades would pass before the novel became a generally accepted literary form in England. And even after it did, literary figures would argue about its function. Is fiction merely a personal "impression of life," as Henry James maintained in "The Art of Fiction," an 1884 essay in *Longman's Magazine*, the London literary journal? Or is it something more fundamental—an abstraction of life, a simulation we use to help us understand our existence? "Life is monstrous, infinite, illogical, abrupt and poignant; a work of art in comparison is neat, finite, self-contained, rational, flowing, and emasculate," Robert Louis Stevenson wrote a few months later in response. Life is true; art is a construct. But Defoe was writing long before this particular type of construct became accepted as art. So never mind that every story is by definition a fiction of some sort—what Defoe was saying in his preface was, This is not a novel.

It was certainly a statement that resonated with Lee. In

March 2002, nearly a year after he and Weisman had staged *The Beast,* Lee had given a talk about the experience at the Game Developers Conference, an annual expo that was held that year in San Jose, in the heart of Silicon Valley. He called his talk "This Is Not a Game"—the same enigmatic statement that had been flashed at the end of the TV trailer for *AI*—and in it he set out to explain their goal. They wanted to tell a story that would blend into your life—a story that would send you email, page you when you were in business meetings, transmit secret messages through ringtones. They weren't building a game; they were building an experience that was capable of, as he put it, "transforming your life into an entertainment venue."

But of course it was a game, just as *Robinson Crusoe* was a novel. And as he sat in his parents' shop reading that preface from 300 years before, Lee had a sudden jolt of insight. By denying that they had created a game, he realized, he had fallen into a pattern that had been repeated many times before, whenever people were trying to figure out a way of telling stories that was new and unformed and not yet accepted. He was trying to make it seem okay.

"WHAT DEFOE WAS SAYING WAS, 'Take this seriously,'" Lee said as we sipped espresso at a café in a century-old commercial building in downtown Seattle, around the corner from the bustling, tourist-friendly waterfront. "Novels didn't exist yet, and he needed to justify this experience"—and what better way to justify a new medium than by pretending it's not new at all? Early moviemakers, Lee figured, were making the same plea with the proscenium arch shot—filming the story as if it were a play, with a single, stationary camera from the perspective of a spectator in the center row. "That's them screaming, 'This is not a game.' It wasn't until later that they took the camera and started doing zooms and pans."

That sort of thing began around 1903, a decade after films were first shown publicly. In *The Great Train Robbery*, generally considered to be the first Western, Edwin S. Porter, a director at the Edison Manufacturing Company, used crosscutting to link parallel events. It took years for such practices to become commonplace. But by the time D. W. Griffith made *The Birth of a Nation* in 1915, directors had developed a grammar of film, abandoning stage conventions in favor of dramatic close-ups and sophisticated editing techniques—flashbacks, crosscuts, point-of-view shots—that took full advantage of the new medium's possibilities. Even before sound and color, film conveyed a degree of realism viewers had never encountered before.

Television, too, began by mimicking familiar forms. America's first big hits—Milton Berle's *Texaco Star Theater* and Ed Sullivan's *Toast of the Town*—were pure vaudeville, the variety format that a half century before had lured people to theaters to see a bill of singers and dancers and novelty acts. Popular dramatic series—*Man Against Crime*, *Philco Television Playhouse*, *Kraft Television Theatre*—were broadcast live from New York, just as radio dramas had been. So were comedy series like *The George Burns and Gracie Allen Show*. Not until the 1951 debut of *I Love Lucy*—shot on film in the now-classic, then-revolutionary sitcom format—did television begin to find success on its own terms.

The demise of live drama and comedy brought with it the end of the so-called Golden Age of Television, the brief period when broadcasters were as likely to challenge the audience as to pander. But by inviting viewers into Lucy and Desi's living room, producers found a far more dependable and cost-effective way to get audiences to turn on the tube. Inadvertently, as Clay Shirky has pointed out, they also found a way of soaking up all the free time created by vacuum cleaners, automatic dishwashers, and post–World War II prosperity. Now, two decades into the development of the Web, the sitcom in its classic form—three cameras and a laugh track—has given way to more psychologically involving comedies like *The Office* and *Curb Your Enthusiasm*, even as the concept of leisure time has all but evaporated in a constant bombardment of information.

But no new medium's attempt to cloak itself in familiar garb has succeeded in rendering it immune from attack. Janet Murray made this point in her 1997 book *Hamlet on the Holodeck*, a prescient look at narrative in cyberspace: Every new medium that has been invented, from print to film to television, has increased the transporting power of narrative. And every new medium has aroused fear and hostility as a result.

Ray Bradbury's *Fahrenheit 451*, written in the early fifties—the dawn of the television era—concerns a man named Montag whose job is burning books. Montag's wife, like her friends, is enthralled by the weirdly nonlinear yet mesmerizing video transmissions on the giant "televisors" on her living room walls. Lulled by their narcotic effect, Mildred and most of the rest of the population are too distracted to register the coming nuclear holocaust. "My wife says books aren't 'real,'" the book burner tells Faber, the former English professor who gradually transforms him into a preserver of books. Faber replies,

> "Thank God for that. You can shut them and say, 'Hold on a moment!' But who has ever torn himself from the claw

that encloses you when you drop a seed in a TV parlor? . . . It is an environment as real as the world. It becomes and is the truth. Books can be beaten down with reason. But with all my knowledge and skepticism, I have never been able to argue with . . . those incredible parlors."

A claw that encloses you. An environment as real as the world. That was Bradbury's beef with television—it was just too immersive. Logical, linear thought was no match for its seductively phosphorescent glow. It became and was the truth.

Before television came along, the same danger could be found in the movies. In Aldous Huxley's *Brave New World*—published in 1932, five years after talkies finally gave motion picture actors a voice—young John the Savage is taken to the "feelies." There, viewing an "All-Super-Singing, Synthetic-Talking, Coloured, Stereoscopic Feely," he is revolted by the sensation of phantom lips grazing his own as the actors kiss. "Suddenly, dazzling and incomparably more solid-looking than they would have seemed in actual flesh and blood, far more real than reality, there stood the stereoscopic images, locked in one another's arms, of a gigantic negro and a golden-haired young brachycephalic Beta-Plus female. The Savage started. That sensation on his lips!"

Too real. Dangerously, immersively, more-real-than-reality real, Huxley would say. Better to curl up with a good book.

But once upon a time, books, too, had seemed more real than reality. They offered a passport to imaginary worlds. They triggered delusions. They were new, and not to be trusted. More than a century before *Robinson Crusoe,* Don Quixote went tilting at windmills because he'd lost his mind from reading:

> [He] so buried himself in his books that he read all night from sundown to dawn, and all day from sunup to dusk, until with virtually no sleep and so much reading he dried out his brain and lost his sanity. He filled his imagination full to bursting with everything he read in his books, from witchcraft to duels, battles, challenges, wounds, flirtations, love affairs, anguish, and impossible foolishness, packing it all so firmly into his head that these sensational schemes and dreams became the literal truth. . . . Indeed, his mind was so tattered and torn that, finally . . . he decided to turn himself into a knight errant, traveling all over the world with his horse and his weapons, seeking adventures and doing everything that, according to his books, earlier knights had done.

So Don Quixote was a book geek, and an embarrassing one at that. It's little wonder Defoe felt need of a disclaimer.

Books, movies, TV—and now the Internet. William Gibson introduced the concept of cyberspace in a short story and popularized it two years later in *Neuromancer,* the 1984 novel in which he describes it as a powerful electronic delusion, immersive and immaterial. Case, the main character, is a crime refugee in Chiba, a swath of gray industrial blight on the east side of Tokyo Bay. But where he really lives is in the gossamer construct Gibson calls cyberspace: "A consensual hallucination experienced daily by billions. . . . A graphic representation of data abstracted from the banks of every computer in the human system. Unthinkable complexity. Lines of light ranged in the nonspace of the mind, clusters and constellations of data. Like city lights, receding."

Right around the time this passage appeared, a strange mutation began to overtake the Japanese word "otaku." In its original form, "otaku"—written in kanji, Japan's traditional characters, as お宅—was an extremely formal and polite way of saying "you." It was an archaic form of address connoting distance and respect. It meant in a literal sense "your house," reflecting the fact that in traditional Japanese culture it was difficult to imagine anyone as an individual independent of family, household, or station in life. But during the eighties, "otaku" came to take on an entirely different meaning. It became a slang term meaning "geek, nerd, obsessive." And in that sense it is written not in kanji, but in the informal script known as kana: おたく.

The difference between otaku お宅 and otaku おたく is the difference between the Zen serenity of the seventeenth-century Nanzenji temple at the foot of Kyoto's Eastern Mountains, say, and the pulsing energy of Akihabara, the high-rise electronics district in central Tokyo. Akihabara is ground zero for otaku in the slang form. In that sense, "otaku" referred to a sudden, spontaneous, and, to most Japanese, inexplicable eruption of extreme obsessiveness among the country's youth. One day, Japanese in their teens and twenties were normal, well-adjusted young people. The next day, or so it seemed, they were hopeless geeks who had forsaken all social skills in favor of a deep dive into—whatever. Manga (comics). Anime. Super-hard-core deviant anime porn in which tender young schoolgirls are violated by multi-tentacled octopi. Trains. It could be anything really.

In Gibson's novel *Idoru*, a Japanese character describes her otaku brother as a "pathological-techno-fetishist-with-social-deficit." That works.

The simultaneous coinage of "otaku" and "cyberspace" on different sides of the planet seems in retrospect like an almost inevitable coincidence. "Understanding otaku-hood," Gibson once wrote in an essay, "is one of the keys to understanding the culture of the web." Otaku was the prequel—a glimpse of the future a connected world would bring. Passion. Obsession. A yearning to immerse oneself in stories that transpire in a fictional universe. The desire to experience that universe through as many different media as possible. A need to extend and embrace that universe by telling new stories within it.

To be otaku was long considered shameful. The nadir came in 1989, when a 26-year-old schizophrenic was arrested for sexually molesting, murdering, and then mutilating four little girls. When the police found his home stuffed to the ceiling with thousands of videocassettes, some of them anime productions of the underage "lolicon" (short for "Lolita complex") variety, the media promptly dubbed him the Otaku Murderer. His crimes were portrayed as the natural outcome of the dangerously immersive otaku lifestyle. But even though otaku were considered something between hopeless geeks and murderous deviants, their cult kept growing.

Although it's possible to be otaku about almost anything, the emergence of Japan's techno-fetishist culture was closely tied to the rise of anime (a Japanization of the English word "animation") and manga. The celebrated pop artist Takashi Murakami traces the origins of otaku to *The Super Dimension Fortress Macross*, a seminal 1982 anime TV series created by students at Tokyo's elite Keio University. He cites Toshio Okada, a noted anime producer who for many years lectured in otakuology at Tokyo University—a sort of otaku of otaku, if you will—as saying the creators of *Macross* used the term when addressing one another. The anime's hero, a brash young fighter pilot, even says "otaku" when addressing other characters. Fans picked it up as a way of showing their respect.

Macross—the name is a bizarre mashup of the Japanese words for "megaload," "megaroad," and "MacBeth"—was itself inspired by a pioneering seventies anime, *Space Battleship Yamato*, the television series that redefined anime as an adult genre capable of dealing with epic themes. It shows the proud battleship *Yamato*, sunk in real life by US bombers and submarines in the final months of World War II, resurrected and rebuilt as a spacecraft by the twenty-second-century survivors of an alien radiation-bomb attack. But "Yamato" refers to more than an ill-fated ship; it's an archaic and poetic synonym for Japan, as "Albion" is for England. Other cultures have creation myths; Japan, for understandable reasons, has a nuclear destruction myth. Like many anime and manga, the *Yamato* and *Macross* series represent an obsessive telling and retelling of that primal story.

In *Macross*, an alien spacecraft crash-lands near Iwo Jima and is rebuilt as the most advanced ship in the fleet of UN Spacy, the embattled humans' space navy. Key to the story are shape-shifting "mecha"—walking armored vehicles, which in this series transform themselves into fighter planes. The elaborately designed mecha fed a strong demand for action figures, which were supplied by Bandai and other companies. Big West Advertising, a Tokyo ad agency, became both the owner of the franchise and its main commercial sponsor. And while the original television series lasted for just a single season, the *Macross* saga has since played out in all sorts of media, including anime films and videos, manga, and video games.

This is Japan's "media mix" strategy, based on the idea that a single story can be told through several different media at once. Media mix emerged in Japan in the seventies, decades before Western publishers or producers saw the potential for any kind of synergistic storytelling—indeed, for anything more ambitious than a licensing deal that gave a movie studio, say, the right to make its own version of a story. The idea of telling a single story through multiple media didn't win official recognition in Hollywood until April 2010, when the Producers Guild of America—prodded by such people as James Cameron and his former wife and producer, Gail Anne Hurd—approved a credit for "transmedia producer." But media mix was not a product of established companies in Japan either. It came from manga publishers like Kadokawa Shoten, a family-controlled firm whose president was eventually forced to resign after being convicted of cocaine smuggling.

One of the most important media mix franchises in Japan is the mecha series *Gundam*, which began in 1979 as a TV anime and has since morphed into manga, novels, video games, and action figures. So popular is the *Gundam* series in Japan that the 2007 video game *Gundam Musou*, a title exclusive to Sony's PlayStation 3, sold 100,000 copies the day it was released. But what familiarized the rest of the world with media mix and otaku culture was *Pokémon*, the global manga/anime/trading card/video game phenomenon from Nintendo.

Introduced in Japan in 1996 and in North America two years later, *Pokémon* was a new kind of kids' media franchise. It was meant to be enjoyed communally rather than individually; it was meant to be inhabited rather than consumed. In the West, this was almost revolutionary. "In traditional Disney narratives, they didn't think about communication between viewers," says Mimi Ito, a cultural anthropologist at the University of California at Irvine. "But with *Pokémon*, you can't even play unless you have friends who are into it. And in order to play, you have to make your own *Pokémon* deck."

Media mix is one outgrowth of otaku culture. Another is

the tacit understanding—"anmoku no ryokai" in Japanese—that manga publishers have made with fans. Otaku like to live in alternate realities, and sooner or later this means they want to start telling their own stories in the worlds that others have built. The unspoken agreement leaves fans free to do what they want with popular manga characters. At expos like Comic Ichi and Super Comic City, thousands of amateurs sell slickly produced, self-published manga in which well-known characters express forbidden desires and otherwise behave in clear violation of intellectual property laws. Yet commercial publishers show no inclination to send out their copyright attorneys and shut the markets down. Instead they've learned to look the other way, because they know that the fervor these fan-created manga generate can only lead to increased sales for everyone.

IT'S BEEN MORE THAN A QUARTER CENTURY since the idea of cyberspace began to filter into the collective consciousness. In the meantime, works like Neal Stephenson's *Snow Crash* and the Wachowski brothers' *Matrix* series have celebrated and extended Gibson's vision even as they've paid homage to Japanese pop culture. The Wachowskis cited anime as a major influence on their work; they were also among the first artists in the West to embrace Japan's media mix strategy, augmenting the story that's told in the films with anime, comics, and video games in which they had a hand. Japanese audiences returned the favor: Shortly after the 2003 premiere of *The Matrix Reloaded* (the second in the series), more than 100 fans converged on Tokyo's Shibuya Station to reenact the "burly brawl" scene—a martial-arts sequence in which Agent Smith, the black-suited villain of the series, replicates himself a hundredfold to take on Neo, the hacker hero. Similar fan-organized events took place in Kyoto and Osaka. Cosplay (short for "costume play") is a staple of otaku culture, and in dressing up as Agent Smith and reenacting the burly brawl, Japanese fans were taking the story of *The Matrix* and making it their own.

For all the initial excitement, however, *The Matrix* was ultimately a disappointment. The final film, *The Matrix Revolutions*, struck many as the supreme letdown: if you weren't a *Matrix* adept, there was little to distinguish it from the heavy-duty mayhem of the average Michael Bay flick. And as the saga grew in ambition and complexity, major plot points were developed not in the movies, which naturally had the largest audience, but in media that reached only the most committed fans. "For the casual consumer, *The Matrix* asked too much," Henry Jenkins, the leading academic proponent of transmedia storytelling, concluded in his influential book *Convergence Culture*. "For the hard-core fan, it provided too little."

But mistakes are inevitable. Like early novelists, early motion picture directors, and early television producers, the people who would actually create Gibson's consensual hallucination have had to ask for patience as they try to make it work. We think we live on Internet time, but the Internet is no more in a hurry to reveal its possibilities than other media were—something would-be cybermoguls like Jerry Levin, who sold Time Warner to AOL at the tail end of the dial-up era, have discovered to their shareholders' chagrin.

"All media start with the author saying, 'Please take this seriously,'" Elan Lee said that morning as we sat above the Seattle waterfront. "And what we're doing is the same thing. It's the first in a long series of steps in the birth of a new medium. It's not movies on the Web. It's not interactive TV. It's the way the Internet wants to tell stories."

The waitress brought another round of espresso. Despite the lack of cigarette smoke, or maybe because of it, we were in the perfect Pacific Northwest simulacrum of an old Parisian café.

"No one has a clear definition of what that is," Lee continued. "But the Internet is trying very, very hard to tell us. And the only way to figure it out is to try."

3. Deeper

Some people have stories that are too big for the Internet to handle. In September 2006, I stood next to James Cameron on a Montreal soundstage as he discussed what he was about to take on with *Avatar*. "It's an epic," he said. "It's an entire world that's got its own ground rules, its own ecology. It's the kind of fantasy that, as a geek fan, you can hurl yourself into. And even though it's not a sword-and-sorcery-type fantasy, it's like *The Lord of the Rings* in that it's immersive."

What Cameron had in mind was moviemaking on an unprecedented scale: a $200-million-plus Hollywood spectacular that would revolutionize movie production—live action and computer-generated imagery combined, in 3-D, all in service of an aliens-versus-humans saga that aimed to blur the line between the audience and the movie.

We were at Mel's Cité du Cinéma, a movie production complex in an industrial zone between a rail yard and the autoroute, on the set of the 3-D remake of *Journey to the Center of the Earth* starring Brendan Fraser. Directed by Eric Brevig, a 3-D enthusiast who had spent years at George Lucas's digital-effects house, Industrial Light & Magic, *Journey* was the first feature film to employ the stereoscopic 3-D camera system that Cameron had spent years developing after his triumph with *Titanic*. Next to us were Cameron's producer, Jon Landau, and Vincent Pace, the inventor he had teamed with to create the new camera system. They were there that day to see how it performed, but what was really on Cameron's mind was *Avatar*.

At that point the story of Jake Sully, the paraplegic ex-marine recruited into an avatar program that enables humans to function on the distant moon Pandora, existed solely in Cameron's head. Pandora would be a rain forest world, home to bizarre plants, exotic beasts, and a primitive species of humanoids who are 10 feet tall and blue. But the story that audiences would see onscreen was only a fraction of the world Cameron had imagined. He planned to create a "bible" that explained life on Pandora—its economy and technology, its flora and fauna, its social structure and mores—down to the smallest detail. He would prepare renderings and character studies and models of the place and its inhabitants. He would engage Paul Frommer, a linguist and management professor at the University of Southern California, to devise a Pandoran language with its own vocabulary and grammar and syntax for the actors to learn. He would invent hundreds of plants and dozens of animals. "I love science fiction," he said. "I love the idea of creating another world—another ecosystem of amazing creatures." Yet of the animals he made up, only eight or so seemed likely to make it into the finished film. "That's just the limitation of movies."

Cameron is hardly the first director to go to a lot of trouble imagining the backstory for a film. But most of the time, all that work remains hidden in notebooks and drawings that no one outside the production ever sees. He didn't want that to happen with *Avatar*. He would make *Avatar* for the otaku.

"I think the role of this type of film should be to create a kind of fractal-like complexity," he went on. "The casual viewer can enjoy it without having to drill down to the secondary and tertiary levels of detail. But for a real fan, you go in an order of magnitude and, *boom!* There's a whole set of new patterns. You can step in in powers of 10 as many times as you want, and it still holds up. But you don't need to know all that stuff to enjoy it—it's just there if you want it. To me, that's the best science fiction."

"This is not just a movie," Landau put in. "It's a world. The film industry has not created an original universe since *Star Wars*. When one comes along so seldom, you want to realize it to the fullest possible extent."

CAMERON HAS WANTED TO BUILD a universe ever since *Star Wars* came out in 1977. He was 22 back then, a college dropout living in Orange County, California. He had dreamed of making movies as a teenager growing up on the Canadian side of Niagara Falls. The family had moved to Orange County when his father got a job there, but that put him no closer to Hollywood, realistically speaking, than he'd been in Ontario. So now he was married to a waitress, working as a truck driver, and spending a lot of time with his buddies, drinking beer and smoking pot. Hollywood could wait.

Then he saw *Star Wars*. From the moment he walked out of the theater, he was obsessed. This was the kind of movie he had always wanted to make. He quit his job and started spending all his free time at the USC library in Los Angeles, reading about special effects and anything else about moviemaking he could find. He teamed up with a friend to write a script for some dentists who wanted to invest in movie production as a tax shelter. The project went nowhere, but he learned enough while working on it to land a job working for Roger Corman, Hollywood's king of low-budget productions. After apprenticing for a few years on movies like *Battle Beyond the Stars* and *Galaxy of Terror*, he managed to get backing to direct a movie he had written called *The Terminator*. It came out in 1984, and suddenly his career was launched.

Eleven years later, after the success of *Aliens*, *The Abyss*, and *Terminator 2: Judgment Day*, Cameron wrote the treatment for *Avatar*. By this time he was head of Digital Domain, Hollywood's newest visual-effects house, and it struck him that computer-animated characters were going to be the next big thing in movies. With the slithery alien water snake in *The Abyss* and the shape-shifting cyborg in *Terminator 2*, he had already pushed computer-generated effects to new limits. Now he wanted to take them even farther—and, by the way, establish Digital Domain as the go-to shop for creature animation. "But I went too far," he said.

Cameron's partners at Digital Domain were two of the top people in digital effects: Scott Ross, the longtime general manager of Industrial Light & Magic; and Stan Winston, who had won three Oscars for his work with Cameron on *Aliens* and *Terminator 2*. "I came in and I said, 'Okay, guys, I've got the ultimate character animation movie,'" Cameron recalled. "'Let's break it down and see how much it would cost to make.' And they didn't even give me a number. They just said, 'Are you out of your mind? We can't do this movie. We'll die as a company. Our heads will explode. Are you *kidding*?'

"And you know what?" he added. "They were right. So I basically just threw it in a drawer. And then, when Peter Jackson proved you could get a powerful, completely photo-realistic performance from a humanoid character"—the treacherous Gollum in *The Lord of the Rings*—"I dusted it off."

IN THE MEANTIME, CAMERON made *Titanic*, broke every box office record, collected 11 Oscars (including Best Director and Best Picture), declared himself "king of the world" at the awards ceremony, and promptly disappeared for the better part of a decade. "After *Titanic*, I realized I could do what I'd always wanted to do," he said. "Not in a self-indulgent sense, but I could take a break and do all the things I had turned away from earlier—when I wanted to be a scientist, when I wanted to be an explorer."

In 2000 he began writing an IMAX film about a Mars expedition, but he didn't like the IMAX camera rig. So he started fiddling with high-definition video cameras with Pace, a videocam specialist and deep-sea-diving expert who had first worked with him shooting the extensive underwater sequences of *The Abyss*. "And then I decided, Hey, let's not do a fictional story about exploration," he recalled. "Let's go exploring! So we went off on a five-year detour, and out of that came this tool set"—the 3-D camera system Brevig was using here in Montreal.

Hollywood first pinned its hopes on the third dimension in the early 1950s. Desperate to win back audiences from television, studio chiefs tricked out B pictures like *Bwana Devil* and *It Came from Outer Space* with what was then the latest gimmick. The novelty of 3-D quickly faded, however, as the herky-jerky analog technology behind it sent moviegoers home with throbbing headaches and queasy stomachs. Decades later, 3-D was revived as a theme park attraction, but even then the technology that made it work was almost hopelessly clunky. In 1996, when Cameron shot his first stereoscopic picture, the 12-minute *T2 3-D: Battle across Time*, for Universal Studios, he had to use a camera rig so massive that Arnold Schwarzenegger's stunt double had to run at half-speed so it could keep up.

Ten years after that, Cameron was one of a handful of A-list directors pushing the industry—film studios and theater chains alike—to move to 3-D. Robert Zemeckis had been considering an IMAX 3-D version of his 2004 Christmas movie *The Polar Express* when he visited Cameron and came back a convert. Peter Jackson, in Santa Barbara to receive a film festival award, visited Zemeckis there and was impressed with what he saw. Steven Spielberg, a close friend of Zemeckis, had a similar experience. They all saw 3-D as a new tool for storytelling. It can still be a gimmick—the sword that leaps out from the screen and makes you duck. But for Cameron in particular, the point was depth. He wanted to use 3-D to draw you into his world.

How well would Cameron's stereoscopic camera system work? "This is an interesting beta test," he said, referring to the *Journey 3-D* shoot unfolding before us. Eric Brevig had put the brains of the system—the optical units from a pair of souped-up Sony F950 high-definition video cameras—on top of a golf cart, with a huge loop of fiber-optic cable connecting them to the remainder of the cameras (the bodies, so to speak) in a tent nearby. Affixed to the wall at the other end of the soundstage was the bottom half of an enormous, toothy, fiberglass dinosaur skull, with Brendan Fraser and a pair of child actors strapped inside. The script called for the skull to be shot like a rocket from inside a volcano, and then just as quickly to fall back in again. To capture this on tape, Brevig decided to leave the skull in place and have someone drive the golf cart full-speed toward the wall, then shift into reverse to simulate the fallback.

On cue, the cart hurtled forward. Fraser and the kids screamed and thrashed about. At the last possible instant, the cart jerked to a stop and began to pull back. All the while, the camera operator was adjusting not just the focus but also the convergence—the point at which the images from the left and right camera lenses come together. To anyone schooled in 3-D, this was revolutionary.

Just as the perception of depth comes from seeing with two eyes, the impression of 3-D comes from shooting with two cameras—in stereo, in other words. But what 92 percent of us find perfectly normal in life—seeing in three dimensions—requires a feat of illusion in art. In the past, directors using analog film cameras (including the refrigerator-sized units used to shoot in 3-D for theme parks and IMAX releases) couldn't see where the dual images converged until the film was developed. As a result, shots had to be mathematically plotted far in advance.

The point of the math was to preserve what's known as the screen plane—the surface on which the movie appears. In 2-D, that's the screen itself; in 3-D, it's an imaginary surface somewhere near the screen. But with digital video cameras, the camera operator can see the convergence in real time. Now there's no need for the math—and arguably no need for the screen plane as well.

When he set out to understand how people perceive 3-D, Cameron concluded that his twin cameras should converge on the main actor's face—just as your two eyes would do if you were looking at a person in front of you. As the actor moves nearer or farther, so does the point of convergence—and the idea of an arbitrary screen plane goes away. "The viewer doesn't think there's a screen plane," he declared with a snort. "There's only a perceptual window, and that perceptual window exists somewhere around arm's length from us. That's why I say everything that's ever been written about stereography is completely wrong."

"3-D is about immersing the audience in your story," said Jon Landau, a large man in black jeans and an electric-green tropical shirt. "And the screen plane has always been this subconscious barrier." By removing it, Cameron hoped to make his story more immersive. He had other ideas for accomplishing the same thing.

When I saw them on the *Journey* set, Cameron and Landau were already talking with video game developers about translating the world of *Avatar* to a console game. "Why do people turn to entertainment? Escapism," Landau said. "To get away from whatever it is in this world they want to get away from. And if you give them a unique universe, they will seek that out beyond just the cinema experience." So before 20th Century Fox had even given the film a green light, he invited several game developers to the Santa Monica headquarters of their production company, Lightstorm Entertainment. There, in a modest, white-brick office building several blocks from the beach, he presented the concept.

Everyone in the room knew the problem: for all the cross-fertilization between the two forms, movies and video games had never meshed. Electronic Arts and other leading game publishers had licensed countless Hollywood films, but with very few exceptions—among them Peter Jackson's *King Kong* from Ubisoft and the two *Lord of the Rings* titles that Neil Young produced for EA—the games that resulted were little more than cynical attempts to exploit a film franchise for some extra dough.

Even with Jackson, things didn't exactly go smoothly. EA worked closely with him on the *Lord of the Rings* titles, but afterward he let it be known that they didn't work closely enough—so for *King Kong* he picked a designer at Ubisoft's studios in Montpellier, in the south of France. Then, in 2005, it was announced that he would be partnering with Fox and Universal as executive producer on a movie version of *Halo*—a project that dragged on for more than a year before collapsing in a welter of egos.

Cameron, Landau maintained, had a better idea of how movies and games could work together. By creating the movie and the game in tandem, he hoped to have a game that would explore elements of the story the movie could not. He also wanted a home for some of those extra creatures he was coming up with.

A few months after the first round of meetings, the game developers returned one by one to present their ideas. This time, Cameron and Landau were both present. A few minutes into the presentation by Ubisoft, they began to think they'd found the right team.

Ubisoft is the world's third largest game publisher. Started in 1986 by five brothers in Brittany, now a €900 million company based in the outskirts of Paris, it's responsible for megaselling franchises ranging from Tom Clancy to the *Prince of Persia* series. Yannis Mallat, who heads the company's flagship studio in Montreal, won Cameron and Landau over with the first slide in his PowerPoint presentation. The real star of *Avatar,* he declared, was Pandora itself—Cameron's world.

"Usually, game developers just stick to concrete facts," Mallat recalled one afternoon in his office, in a rambling nineteenth-century red-brick mill building in Montreal's newly hipsterized Mile End district. "Who's starring in the movie? What is the plot? But when we approached *Avatar,* the first question we had was, What is the meaning? What does Jim want to express? The true meaning as we understood it—" He looked about, grasping for the word. "*Cupidité en anglais?* Greed. Greed is the cancer of life. In one sentence we defined it: What are humans doing on Pandora?"

Colonialism and exploitation, the moral issues in *Avatar,* are topics Mallat knows firsthand. A native of France, he graduated from secondary school in the Ivory Coast and then spent three years as an aid worker in West Africa. After receiving a master's degree in international agronomy and economic development from an elite engineering school in Paris, he returned to Africa to work on rural development projects. His other interest was gaming, and in 2000, after receiving an MBA from the University of Montreal, he joined Ubisoft's studio there. His breakthrough success came when he headed the production of *Prince of Persia: The Sands of Time*, a best-selling update of an early action-adventure game. He was named head of the Montreal studio—home to 1,400 employees, the majority of them French Canadian—in 2006.

Ubisoft saw *Avatar* as key to its emerging core strategy: to bring games and movies together. In March 2008, with *Avatar* development already well under way, the company purchased the rights to the Tom Clancy brand in all media. A few months later it bought Hybride Technologies, a digital-effects house tucked away among the ski resorts of the Laurentian Mountains, north of Montreal. Ubisoft's ambition is to rival Peter Jackson's Weta Digital in the top ranks of digital effects, producing computer-generated imagery for the likes of Cameron and Spielberg. Ultimately, the company wants to make movies of its own. In the meantime, said Mallat, "I need to learn from Jim and Jon, and they need to learn from us."

Because they're viewed on a television screen and need to be rendered on the fly by a game console, video games can't hope to rival the sensory wallop of a motion picture. But games offer something movies can't: the ability to insert yourself directly into the story. As a player, you're making choices, not watching actors follow a script. "The best stories in video games are the stories the player tells himself," said Mallat. "In French we say '*son propre film*'—the movie in his head."

As with the movie itself, the movie in your head during *Avatar: The Game* would pit the Na'vi, Pandora's indigenous population, against the mercs, the human mercenaries who've been hired to mine Pandora's resources, laying waste to the place in the process. You wouldn't play Jake, but you would play a character who's confronted by the same issues Jake faces. At a certain point in the game, you'd have to choose whether to throw in your lot with the mercs or the Na'vi. "You're confronted with two different cultures," said Mallat. "And in the end, you have to decide. What do you battle for—harmony or greed? That's the meaning of the movie—but only in the game will you be able to answer it your way and live with the consequences."

In a distant part of the building known as the bunker, Cameron's game world was taking shape behind a double set of locked doors. For security reasons, everyone working on *Avatar* had dual PCs—one connected to the Internet, and another connected only to an internal network that had no link to the outside world. On these computers was Pandora itself—its flora, its fauna, its weaponry: the giant thanator, its name inspired by the Greek spirit of death. The fearsome sturmbeest. The razor-toothed viperwolf, which seemed a cross between a hyena, a greyhound, and a meat shredder. The powersuit, an enormous version of a Japanese mecha—a single-person armored vehicle that walks on two legs.

At Ubisoft's suggestion, Landau had hired writers to collect all this information in a "Pandorapedia," an encyclopedic compendium of all things Pandora. The Pandorapedia would tell you the cost of a phone call from Pandora to Earth, four light-years away ($78,000 per minute). It would even offer an explanation of the science that makes such calls possible. It was the key to Cameron's fictional universe—the repository of everything he had created in all its obsessive detail.

To all outward appearances, the Ubisoft-Lightstorm partnership seemed likely to redefine the relationship between movies and video games. Even then, however, problems might have been apparent to anyone who looked closely enough. Was Pandora really the star of Cameron's movie? George Lucas had generated an elaborate world for *Star Wars*, yet there was never any question that his movie was about something far bigger: a mythic struggle between good and evil. *Avatar* was about good and evil as well, but by emphasizing locale over character, the game developers risked undermining their own point.

Inside the bunker, however, confidence ruled. "What can James Cameron do that's bigger than *Titanic*?" quipped Antoine Dodens, the game's producer, as we gazed at the bestiary on his computer screen. "*Star Wars*."

• • •

MEANWHILE, IN A VAST, WINDOWLESS, black-walled space in Los Angeles, Cameron was struggling to bring his universe to life. His soundstage was a former aircraft hangar in Playa Vista, the lonely oceanside district where Hughes Aircraft had churned out parts for fighter planes during World War II. Next door was the even bigger hangar where Howard Hughes had constructed his "Spruce Goose," the mammoth H-4 Hercules flying boat, a transport plane that never saw action because by the time it was finally completed the war had been over for two years. Cameron seemed bent on constructing a movie of similar proportions.

A silver-haired figure in worn jeans and a New Zealand Stunt Guild T-shirt, he was standing on the soundstage holding a small, flat-panel computer screen with handles and knobs attached. "Come on over here," he said between takes, waving me in his direction. "I'll show you what this is."

He was holding a "virtual camera"—a window onto a performance that couldn't be seen with the naked eye. The soundstage was set up for performance capture—a souped-up version of motion capture, which uses an array of cameras overhead to capture actors' movement through space. Once the data is recorded, digital-effects specialists can use it to animate any creature they like. They can transform Andy Serkis into Gollum in *The Lord of the Rings* or the giant ape in *King Kong*. But just as the infrared cameras strung across the ceiling of Cameron's soundstage registered the actors' movements from markers on their bodies, the cameras also picked up any movement of his screen from markers on its frame. Pointing it toward his two stars, Sam Worthington and Zoe Saldana, he could tilt and pan as if it were an actual camera.

Even more remarkable was what he saw on the screen. Not Sam Worthington and Zoe Saldana, standing a few feet away in their body-hugging black performance-capture suits; not the hollow gray risers on the soundstage; not the overarching blackness all around us. What the screen displayed was Jake Sully's blue, catlike, 10-foot-tall avatar standing next to Saldana's equally blue, catlike alien in the deep jungle of Pandora. Cameron's universe, in real time.

In the scene he was about to capture, Jake and Neytiri, the alien love interest played by Saldana, are playfully chasing fan lizards, a Cameron-invented species unique to Pandora. Ugly at rest, the creatures turn strangely beautiful when they lift up their whirligig wings and fly. At this point in the movie, Jake has become lost and separated from his unit. He met Neytiri a short time before, when she saved him from a charging thanator and a vicious pack of viperwolves. Soon he will face a fundamental test of loyalties—but for the moment, he's just having a blast chasing fan lizards.

For Worthington and Saldana, that meant leaping across the flimsy plywood risers, wearing not only standard-issue motion-capture tights but large fake ears (so they would know where their Na'vi ears were) and head rigs that kept a tiny high-definition camera pointed back at their faces. By getting video close-ups of the actors' eyes and features and mapping them to their characters' faces, Cameron hoped to avoid the "uncanny valley"—the creepy sense that the computer-generated humanoids onscreen aren't quite real.

If the screen plane was an impediment to the immersiveness Cameron wanted to achieve, the uncanny valley was a roadblock.

Zemeckis had pioneered performance capture while Cameron was inventing his 3-D camera rig, but his inability to get past the uncanny valley made the figures in *The Polar Express* and *Beowulf*, the 3-D picture that followed it, unnerving to watch. Zemeckis, Cameron explained, "used a completely different kind of facial capture. They used the same type of marker system that we use for the body, and then they captured the facial performance with mocap cameras." He shook his head in wonderment. "Really a bonehead idea."

AT THE FAR END OF THE SOUNDSTAGE, three tiers of computer monitors rose like bleachers toward the ceiling. This was *Avatar*'s "brain bar," the domain of its digital production team—the people who made all this work. Each tier was manned by five or six people—performance-capture specialists on the lower rung, animation and visual-effects supervisors from Cameron's Lightstorm Entertainment and Jackson's Weta Digital up above. It looked like mission control, only scruffier.

On their monitors, the brain bar people were watching different iterations of the fan lizard scene as it was being captured. One screen mapped skeletal data points on a grid. Other screens could toggle from Worthington and Zaldana on the risers to Jake and Neytiri in the jungle.

The brain bar was command central for a bit of software they had dubbed the simulcam. Using the simulcam, the crew could mix performance-capture data with footage from the live-action, 3-D shoot that Cameron had recently completed in New Zealand. The simulcam generated a real-time composite of performance-capture data and live-action photography on the fly, compressing into seconds a job that would normally take weeks.

That's how Cameron could hold a computer screen in his hands and see Jake and Neytiri with the fan lizards.

Getting there wasn't easy. "A movie like this had not been done," said *Avatar*'s virtual production supervisor, Glenn Derry—a hybrid of live action and performance capture, in 3-D, with a scale differential that makes 6-foot-tall actors look 10 feet, and not just in one or two scenes, but for almost every scene in the picture. To make it work, Derry and his team had to create what they called a virtual production system—the virtual camera, the simulcam, and a digital pipeline to feed it all together. "It just kind of evolved," he said. "We kept adding features and adding features, and then we got to the point where we couldn't keep track of them all." He laughed, a little too wildly for comfort. "We've been doing this for two years!"

"It always started with Jim going, 'What if I could do *this?*'" put in Richie Baneham, the animation supervisor.

While Derry was building the virtual production system, Baneham had to replicate the feat that had won him this job—bringing Gollum to life in *The Lord of the Rings*. Before Gollum, digital animators seeking to create a smile would just dial the mouth a little wider. Inevitably, it looked fake. So for *The Lord of the Rings*, Baneham and his team at Weta had gone back to basics: What muscles fire to produce a smile, and in what order? How much light does the skin absorb, and how much does it reflect? How deep is the pupil, the opening at the center of the eye? "We as human beings will process an image to see if there's something we need to look at," he explained, "with an emphasis on finding eyes. And all those things we unconsciously notice about other people, we notice immediately when they're wrong."

This, of course, is the definition of the uncanny valley—the pitfall Cameron wanted almost desperately to avoid. But the details that made Gollum so convincing had been provided by digital animators working frame by frame to Baneham's specifications. Cameron wanted this done for multiple characters throughout the movie. The solution was the head rigs that Worthington and Saldana were wearing down on the soundstage.

There, Cameron was about to capture a very different scene. Standing astride a gray plywood hump, longbow in hand, Worthington took his position. Despite the reflector-spotted leotard and the fake ears and the head rig sticking out in front of his face, he somehow managed to cut a commanding figure. At this stage of the story, relations between the humans and the Na'vi have come to the breaking point, and Jake is at the point of no return. Arrayed in front of Worthington on the set was an invisible throng of Na'vi warriors—invisible to all but Cameron, who panned away from Worthington to a spot in front of him on the empty soundstage. As he panned back to Worthington, his virtual camera displayed Jake's avatar in a pose straight out of *Braveheart*.

"This movie is ultimately about a guy finding his purpose," Cameron said after the take. "Jake falls into this situation because his twin brother had acted as the donor for the DNA to generate this genetically engineered body—so they were going to have to trash this $40 million avatar when his brother got killed by a mugger. They picked Jake because it was convenient and they thought he was this discountable human being. What they didn't realize is that he's a warrior in the classic, historical, mythological sense."

For Cameron, that meant a US marine. "I like the Marines," he went on. "My brother was a marine—fought in Desert Storm." But no one joins the Marines to become a mythological warrior. "So many people show up because they're looking for a sense of purpose," Cameron said. "It's like, I've been through high school, all my friends are drunks and stoners, none of the things I see make sense. So I join the Marine Corps because I know I'll be challenged."

Drunks and stoners? That's who Cameron's friends were after he'd been through high school, when he dropped out of college, got a job as a truck driver, and spent half of his time getting high. But Cameron didn't need to join the Marines to find purpose; he saw *Star Wars*. George Lucas, speaking to him from the multiplex, challenged him to do what he really wanted. Which is what brought him here to Playa Vista to make a $250-million-plus movie. In the age of YouTube, with everyone an uploader, Cameron was attempting what no one else had managed. He was reinventing cinema as overwhelming spectacle.

"I like the way they think," he said, still talking about the Marines. "The way they think is, they're not doing it because it's easy. They're doing it because it's hard. They're doing it because *you can't*."

TO ME, THERE IS ONE PARTICULAR scene in *Avatar* that perfectly captures Cameron's achievement. It comes early in the movie, when Jake's avatar, lost and alone at night in the hostile Pandoran jungle, finally succeeds in lighting a pitch-dipped stick—and realizes to his horror that staring back at him are dozens if not hundreds of eyes. Where there are eyes there are teeth, and these eyes belong to a pack of viperwolves. Barring a miracle, Jake is not going to survive the night. Naturally, this is when Neytiri appears.

When I first saw this scene, as part of some footage Landau screened while Cameron was still finishing the movie, I marveled at Jake's avatar's eyes—the way they darted wildly across the jungle as the viperwolves were menacing him. But months later, when I saw the entire movie at a Times Square screening shortly before its release, I actually forgot to notice. That's how good the effect is.

Cameron's focus isn't only on his actors' eyes; it's also on ours. The stereoscopic camera system he helped invent is an incredibly elaborate attempt to mimic what human eyes do naturally, which is to see in three dimensions. With *Avatar* he delivered on his goal of using 3-D not as a gimmick but as a way of drawing you into his world. "I couldn't tell what was real and what was animated," Josh Quittner gushed in *Time* magazine after his advance look. "The following morning, I had the peculiar sensation of wanting to return there, as if Pandora were real." I understood what he meant. Cameron's use of 3-D makes *Avatar* seem almost infinitely deep—a fractal experience, just as Cameron had promised, as if you really could jump in in powers of 10.

All of which made *Avatar: The Game* even more disappointing than it might otherwise have been. Despite the resources Cameron had made available during its development, despite his efforts to bring the development team and the movie production together, the game ended up playing more like a poorly executed promotion for the movie than a deep dive into Cameron's world. Players were plopped down on Pandora with little explanation of why they were there or what to expect. They found themselves in a mindless, generic shooter that actually told them less about Pandora than they needed to know to enjoy the game. As for the moral choice described by Ubisoft's Yannis Mallat—do you fight with the mercs or with the Na'vi?—the contrast between greed and harmony was too obvious to make it feel like much of a choice at all. Watching the movie (at least in 3-D) was such an overwhelming experience that audiences could ignore the simplistic plot and the one-dimensional characters. Gamers didn't have that option.

There's a reason the *Avatar* game felt generic: because it was. Video games are built around a game engine—software that provides such basic functionality as physics (what happens when objects collide), artificial intelligence (how characters behave), sound, animation, and graphics. In an effort to save money or time or both, developers often reuse old game engines with varying degrees of modification. That's what happened with *Avatar*: it was built around a modified version of the engine that powered *Far Cry* 2, a popular shooter created at Ubisoft Montreal and released in 2008. In the end, so much attention was lavished on Pandora and its creatures that, even though the developers had had nearly three years to work on it, the gameplay seemed like an afterthought.

The video game was not the only opportunity people had to connect with *Avatar* outside the movie theater, but it was one of the few that was more than a marketing attempt. As part of a tie-in with McDonald's, Big Mac boxes in the US carried a "Thrill Card" that led to an augmented reality experience of Pandora. Developed by a French company called Total Immersion, the Thrill Card and its associated McD Vision software enabled users to explore the world of Pandora on their computers simply by holding the card up to a Webcam. "The Big Mac is all about the thrill of your senses," McDonald's chief marketing officer for the US explained in an online press conference announcing the campaign. "We think it's a perfect match for the movie."

Not to be outdone, Coca-Cola worked with Total Immersion to create its own augmented reality experience, this one activated by holding an *Avatar*-branded Coke Zero can up to a Webcam. This enabled fans to deepen their *Avatar* experience, in the words of a Coke marketing director, by taking them to a specially built Web site where they could access "authentic and exclusive content"—a chance to fly one of the movie's Samson helicopters, for example, or live reports from Pandora by "online journalists."

McDonald's, Coca-Cola—these were deals the people at Fox could understand. The Ubisoft game was not. Landau, speaking at a gaming conference in Los Angeles months after *Avatar*'s release, blamed the game's failure largely on the studio. "There wasn't a common ground of interest," he said. "What we tried to say to Fox is, you can take Coke, you can take McDonald's, you can take Panasonic or other partners on the film, and the video game value of exposure is more than any of those promotional deals. And just like they focus on, hey, we have to support those promotional partners, you have to support Ubisoft!"

Landau isn't the only person to suggest that Fox executives were shortsighted in their approach. The idea of taking Cameron's story beyond the movie screen seemed as alien to them as Pandora itself. Yet part of the fault also sems to be with the film's producers. No one expects Cameron to know as much about video game design as he does about movie making. But for all his efforts to bring the two teams together, there wasn't the direct engagement that Peter Jackson had with the developers of his *King Kong* and *Lord of the Rings* games. "I think Peter Jackson is a remarkably committed gamer," says Neil Young. "I just don't see James Cameron going home and playing video games."

Avatar did well enough at the box office that we can expect to see new immersion opportunities for years to come. Hopefully they'll be more satisfying than "authentic" fake journalism from Pandora and a video game that takes the whole experience down several notches. But so far, the lesson of *Avatar* is just how difficult it is to create not just a fictional universe, but the kind of deep, fractal experience of it that Cameron had in mind.

• • •

In 1977, when Fox released *Star Wars*, it did not occur to anyone to create a science fiction universe that fans could explore in depth. It was all George Lucas could do to get his movie made. Lucas was a Hollywood renegade. His first film, the dystopian *THX 1138*, had been summarily recut by Warner Bros. His second film, *American Graffiti*, had been almost dumped to TV by Universal; the studio reluctantly released it, then watched as it became one of the most profitable box office hits of the seventies. Even so, the only studio that would take a chance on the space opera Lucas wanted to make was Fox—and so low were its expectations that Lucas was able to keep the sequel rights and the merchandizing rights as well.

Star Wars was accompanied by a cascade of spin-offs, but few of them had any direct connection with the movie. Del Rey Books published a novel, purportedly written by Lucas himself but in fact ghosted by a science fiction writer whose only guide was an early draft of the script. Marvel brought out a series of comics that began veering off in weird directions as early as episode 8, when Han Solo (played in the movie by Harrison Ford) and his Wookiee sidekick Chewbacca encounter Jaxxon, a giant rabbit that Marvel's writers dreamed up as an homage to Bugs Bunny. Only the toy line—hurriedly released by Kenner, a second-tier manufacturer, after bigger companies passed—maintained any faithfulness to the universe Lucas had conjured up in his head. Nobody—not Fox, not the fans, not Lucas himself—seemed to think this was odd. It was just the way things worked.

"The difference between then and now," explained Howard Roffman, the Lucasfilm executive in charge of what has become known as the *Star Wars* Expanded Universe, "is that we didn't know what we had."

We were sitting in a wood-paneled conference room at the Lucasfilm complex in the San Francisco Presidio, the decommissioned military post overlooking the Golden Gate. Lucasfilm is headquartered in a lotusland as lush as any Hollywood studio's. Its simple, loftlike buildings sit at the edge of a 1,500-acre park amid palms and fountains, vine-covered pergolas and flowering trees, the Golden Gate Bridge just visible above the eucalyptus, a statue of Yoda occupying pride of place at the entrance.

This is the house that *Star Wars* built. The last of the movies came out in 2005, but the flood of products continues unabated, generating an astonishing amount of income—some $15 billion by mid-2008, dwarfing the films' $4 billion worldwide box office take—along with an ever-proliferating cast of characters whose story now spans thousands of years. The entire complex is testament to the market power of the otaku consumer.

In the beginning, harnessing that power seemed easy. The studio licensed a spin-off, the licensee churned out a product and slapped the *Star Wars* name on it, and fans turned up in stores to buy it. Until they didn't—which is what happened in the mid-eighties.

There was no great mystery as to why: when *Return of the Jedi*, the last of the original trilogy, was released in 1983, Lucas had declared himself done. *Star Wars* had made him the top-grossing director of the seventies, wealthy enough to kiss Hollywood good-bye and start building his own studio in the hills north of San Francisco; but it had also wrecked his life and destroyed his marriage. Now it was over. For a lot of the fans it was over as well. Kids in 1977 were teenagers now, and *Star Wars* seemed a lot less cool at that age. Toys for boys accounted for roughly 80 percent of *Star Wars'* ancillary sales—"and by 1985," Roffman said, "you couldn't give the toys away." The year after that, Roffman was put in charge of licensing.

Short and slight, a wiry figure with close-cropped hair and an impish grin, Roffman had joined Lucasfilm as a young attorney in 1980, a week after the release of the second *Star Wars* film, *The Empire Strikes Back*. He handled merchandizing contracts for a couple years, then graduated to general counsel. Now, as head of licensing, he had to figure out how to revive a moribund business based on an expended franchise.

It didn't look promising. Kenner and other toy companies said *Star Wars* was dead. Friends said he should start looking for another job, since Lucas was obviously edging him toward the door. Instead, he retreated into a cave and tried to figure out what to do.

Lucas told him *Star Wars* wasn't dead, it was just taking a rest—the way Disney classics like *Snow White and the Seven Dwarfs* were left to lie fallow for 7–10 years before being rereleased for a new generation. The strategy made sense, but something was wrong with the comparison. Of all the animated classics Walt Disney produced over the decades, none added up to a saga like *Star Wars*. Nor did Sherlock Holmes really seem comparable, despite his intense following. Baker Street did exist in the real world, after all.

What *Star Wars* most resembled, it appeared, was *The Lord of the Rings*. J. R. R. Tolkien's fantasy novels told an extended story that took place in an entirely fictional universe complete with its own languages, pronunciation guides, humanoid species, and genealogical charts. But in the mid-eighties, Tolkien's saga of Middle Earth was still primarily a literary work, having spawned little more than a few radio adaptations and a none-too-successful animated film by Ralph Bakshi.

Star Wars had its own, unique problem. The licensees turned out tons of stuff—novels, comics, lightsabers, action figures, video games, radio adaptations, what have you. Some of it was great—like Boba Fett, the bounty hunter who started life onscreen as an obscure character in a 1978 TV special and ended up, thanks to the fans' response to the action figure that came out afterward, a significant figure in the movies. But try to put it all together and you had a confused jumble. If it wasn't Marvel conjuring up a giant bunny, it was Luke Skywalker in the 1978 novel *Splinter of the Mind's Eye* getting affectionate with Princess Leia—who five years later, in *Return of the Jedi*, would turn out to be his twin sister.

So Roffman set a new ground rule: from now on, any new installment in the *Star Wars* saga would have to respect what had come before. "It just seemed the logical thing," he said. "If you're going to tell stories beyond what you see in the films, the minute they contradict each other your house falls apart. If you kill off a character and then try to revive him, it's going to be bogus." The only other rule was set by Lucas himself: it said that Lucas didn't have to obey any rules.

With Roffman's decree, Lucasfilm not only found the instrument that would help reinvigorate the *Star Wars* franchise; it also created the prototype for the kind of deep, multilayered storytelling that's emerging today. It works because of a quality inherent in *Star Wars* from the beginning. "George created a very well-defined universe," Roffman said—a universe of fractal-like complexity. "But the movies tell a narrow slice of the story. You can engage on a simplistic level—but if you want to drill down, it's infinitely deep."

This complexity would be key. Lucas called it "immaculate reality"—entirely imaginary, and yet with such a level of detail as to feel instantly familiar. Every single utensil in the kitchen of Owen and Beru Lars, the humble moisture farmers who sheltered young Luke Skywalker on the arid planet Tatooine after his father became Darth Vader, Dark Lord of the Sith. The fully realized interior of the Death Star, the moon-sized Imperial battle station armed with a superlaser capable of destroying an entire planet. "You could zoom in on any section of any frame and have a hundred stories to tell," Roffman said. "But it wasn't because George ever imagined anybody would zoom in like that—he just wanted to make it feel real."

IN THE LATE EIGHTIES, as Lucasfilm was trying to get back into the merchandizing business, this immaculate reality provided the handhold. The first step was a novel. The original fans—the ones who were 8 or 10 when the first movie came out—would soon be in their twenties, so it made sense to give them something more grown-up than a comic. They made a deal with Bantam Books to bring out a story by the popular science fiction writer Timothy Zahn—the first part of a trilogy set five years after the events of *Return of the Jedi*. Published in 1991, it went to the top of the *New York Times* best-seller list and stayed there for months. With that, the rebirth of the franchise began.

Soon there were comics as well—not from Marvel but from Dark Horse, an Oregon-based independent, selected at least in part because *Star Wars* would be a much bigger piece of its business. And role-playing games. And a new line of toys. And yet more comics, now based on the novels. And videocassettes of the original movies, this time priced for sell-through rather than rental, to introduce a new generation of kids to the saga—and make them clamor for more comics, more toys, more games.

In addition to not contradicting the movies or each other, the new stories had to adhere to the core precepts of *Star Wars*: the struggle between good and evil, the role of mysticism and spirituality, the focus on family relationships, mythic depth beneath an apparently simple story. Working with a team of in-house editors, Roffman set the story arcs and decided, in consultation with Lucas, whether major characters would live or die. Years of discussion enabled him to channel Lucas on such questions as the nature of the Force and the power of the Jedi, as well as what parts of the story should be explained and what parts should be left deliberately untold—such as where Yoda comes from, or why Anakin Skywalker has no father.

In 1996, the Expanded Universe reached a new level of complexity with *Star Wars: Shadows of the Empire*. A multimedia production, it told a single story through a novel, a series of comics, a line of toys, a set of trading cards, and a video game for the new Nintendo 64 console. There was even a sound track and a making-of book, *The Secrets of Star Wars: Shadows of the Empire*. Together they filled in the gap between *The Empire Strikes Back* and *Return of the Jedi*, focusing on an attempt by the criminal overlord Prince Xizor to supplant Darth Vader as the Emperor Palpatine's chief lieutenant. They also paved the way for the 1997 rerelease of the first three pictures, which together grossed $250 million in the United States alone and were the number one box office draw for six weeks. And that in turn led to the three prequels, which grossed $2.4 billion worldwide and generated the sale of yet more novels, comics, toys, action figures, video games, trading cards, and sundry other items.

Ever since 2000, keeping that story straight has been the job of Roffman's deputy, Leland Chee. A fan turned employee, Chee is himself testament to the success of the Expanded Universe strategy: having seen the original film in 1977 at age six, he was lured back to the saga as a college student by the 1991 Timothy Zahn novel *Heir to the Empire*. At Lucasfilm, Chee has presided over the creation of the all-important Holocron. In *Star Wars*, a Holocron is a repository of mystical Jedi knowledge. In real life, it's a FileMaker database that Chee maintains as Lucasfilm's ultimate internal reference. Chee's Holocron contains more than 30,000 entries coded for levels of canonicity, with the highest level—"G" for George—standing as the word of God.

Lucas's obsessive accretion of detail has inspired an even greater obsessiveness among his devotees. Not all of them, of course; the audience for *Star Wars*, as for other deep media sagas, takes the form of an inverted pyramid. At the top are the hundreds of millions of people who've seen a couple of the movies and know *Star Wars* as a cultural icon. Just below them are the millions who respond to the story in different media—gamers who play the games, readers who love the books, collectors who obsess over the toys. And at the point of the pyramid are the otaku—the hundreds of thousands of superfans who are most deeply connected to the saga, who contribute to the online forums and belong to the official Hyperspace fan club and help construct the Wookieepedia, the fan-built knowledge base for true *Star Wars* otaku.

The Wookieepedia was started in 2005 by Chad Barbry, an Arkansas network administrator whose mania for *Star Wars* factoids provoked a purge on Wikipedia in which a series of entries he'd written were deleted. The new site is the ultimate resource for those who can't access the Holocron and aren't satisfied with the *Star Wars* Databank—a slimmed-down version of the Holocron that exists on the official Web site alongside the forums, the fan club, and various other resources. The Databank just doesn't go deep enough to satisfy the most committed fans, so they've taken it upon themselves to produce something more, well, encyclopedic. Where the Databank entry for Coruscant—a planet-sized city that first appeared in the initial Timothy Zahn novel—wraps it up in a mere 1,400 words, the Wookieepedia entry comes to nearly 9,000 words and includes links to every book, film, comic, and other artifact in which it's ever been mentioned (490 in all). Wookieepedia's Luke Skywalker article runs to an astonishing 31,000 words—about a third the length of this book.

Somewhere along the way, Lucas himself has been left behind. In December 2008, when Del Rey published *The Complete Star Wars Encyclopedia*—a three-volume, 1,224-page boxed set—Roffman gave it to him and joked that he probably didn't know 60 percent of what was in there. Lucas may have created *Star Wars*, but even he had to admit to Roffman that the fans own it now. He meant this figuratively, of course. In a literal sense, ownership is something else entirely. But it's all bound up with a much larger issue, which is control. Who controls a story—its creator or its fans?

4.
Control

One night in June 2009, Betty Draper, the frustrated suburban housewife married to sixties adman Don Draper, posted a poignant message on the three-year-old microblogging site Twitter:

> On back porch, opening jars of fireflies, releasing them into nite air. Beautiful things should be allowed to go free.

It is, of course, a small miracle that Betty Draper tweets at all. For starters, Betty is a fictional character in the television show *Mad Men*, then about to enter its third season, and fictional characters don't share their innermost thoughts online—or at least, they didn't used to. But more to the point, she's a fictional character from the early sixties, when Twitter was still decades in the future, along with the entire infrastructure that supports it—microprocessors, personal computers, the Internet, the World Wide Web, cellular telephones, text messaging, the lot of it. As one person in the growing audience for *Mad Men* tweeters observed, that must be some powerful IBM Selectric she's using.

Yet there's something fitting about *Mad Men* on Twitter all the same. An Emmy Award–winning television program that captures Madison Avenue on the cusp of radical social change, *Mad Men* is a show that explains who we are by reminding us how far we've come. It does this in a hundred subtle and not-so-subtle ways, from the blatant homophobia and over-the-top womanizing of its main characters to its repressed-to-bursting fashion sense—white shirts and narrow-lapelled suits for the men, hip-hugging sheaths for the women (at least, the sexier ones). What little nostalgia it delivers comes with a sting. At a time when advertising, like other industries, is trying to embrace what's known as the sense-and-respond model—anticipate change, be ready to adapt—it captures the old command-and-control model at its acme. The men in this show know what you want, and they get well paid to sell you on it. Having them on Twitter only exposes the yawning chasm between then and now.

But what really reveals the depth of the chasm is this: neither the producers of the show nor the network that carries it had anything to do with putting the characters on Twitter. *Mad Men* on TV may be all about command and control, but on Twitter it became a sense-and-respond case study: What happens when viewers start seizing bits of the story and telling it themselves?

That started to happen with *Mad Men* in August 2008, shortly after the beginning of the show's second season, when Paul Isakson, a brand planner at a small ad agency in Minneapolis, took it upon himself to start tweeting as Don Draper, Betty's husband. Don was the creative director of Sterling Cooper, the fictional

Madison Avenue agency in the show. Isakson began with an 11:00 a.m. aside about Don's fellow partner, Roger Sterling:

> drinking a scotch with Roger so he doesn't feel like an alcoholic.

A few days later, Carri Bugbee, who runs a marketing firm in Portland, Oregon, decided she wanted to tweet as Peggy Olson, Don's former secretary, recently promoted to the all-but-unprecedented position for a female of junior copywriter. An hour later, Bugbee phoned a friend, Michael Bissell, and told him he had to join in as well. Bissell, who runs a digital agency in Portland, decided he wanted to be Roger Sterling. Somebody else—they never found out who—started tweeting as Joan Holloway, the sexy office manager who had become Roger's playmate.

It didn't seem to matter that none of this was authorized by the show's creator, Matthew Weiner, or its network, AMC. Less than a month after the start of the second season, nine of the show's characters were on Twitter and the service was buzzing with *Mad Men* activity. Then, suddenly, it stopped. At 8:45 p.m. Pacific time on August 25, less than two weeks after Isakson started it all, Carri Bugbee logged into her Peggy Olson account and discovered it had stopped working. At first she thought Twitter had gone down—a likely enough occurrence, given the growing pains of the fast-growing site. Ten minutes later, she got an official Twitter email informing her the account had been suspended for suspicious activity. She took a deep breath and emailed her lawyer.

The next day, the Silicon Valley tech blog VentureBeat reported that "Don Draper" and "Peggy Olson" had been suspended. It soon emerged that Twitter, after being contacted by AMC, had shut down the accounts to avoid a violation of the Digital Millennium Copyright Act, the 1998 law that protects online services like Twitter and YouTube from being charged with copyright violation for anything their users post, as long as they remove any potentially infringing material at the request of the copyright holder. But no sooner were the accounts suspended than the *Mad Men* tweet stream—that is, comments about the show on Twitter—started going wild. And where "Don" and "Peggy" had been generating excitement about *Mad Men*, now the talk was all about how clueless the network was. Why would you choke off involvement from people who so clearly love the show?

Which is how Deep Focus, AMC's digital marketing agency, presented the situation to network execs. A small shop based in midtown Manhattan, Deep Focus works with clients like Samsung, Microsoft, and Electronic Arts to develop online promotional campaigns that seek to involve fans with the product. Ian Schafer, the agency's CEO, told AMC execs they shouldn't attempt to shut down something that was generating so much free publicity. "Sometimes the best thing to do in a situation like this is nothing," Schafer told me later. "But that takes a lot of self-control." Within 24 hours the accounts were back up, with AMC's tacit blessing but little in the way of explanation.

That's when Helen Klein Ross started tweeting as Betty. Ross had never met Carri Bugbee or the others, but she did know the ad business. She had started as a secretary in 1977 at the San Francisco office of Foote, Cone & Belding. After that she'd risen to copywriter and moved to New York, where she worked at a number of top agencies on accounts like Absolut, Dove, Nike, Revlon, and Volvo. Born around the same time as Betty's daughter Sally, she found admen in the seventies to be as casually misogynist as Peggy Olson had 15 years earlier. Tweeting as Betty gave her a way to reconnect with that period in her life.

It was not an easy job. For starters, someone else was already tweeting as Betty Draper. Ross tried to contact that person, got no response, and decided to start tweeting anyway. To get the details right, she spent hours watching previously aired *Mad Men* episodes and poring over cookbooks and housekeeping guides from the sixties. She needed to know her way around Betty's blue Formica kitchen, because as a homemaker Betty spent much of her life there. Ross put together page after page of background notes—on Betty, on Don, on life in New York's Westchester County suburbs in the early sixties. She made a point of responding to the more interesting questions she got from people who were following Betty's remarks, because on Twitter, as she put it when we met for coffee one day in New York, "you're interacting with the audience, not just with other characters." When Betty got unexpectedly pregnant at the end of season 2 and somebody asked how she was doing, Ross replied,

> Dr. Aldrich says I'm doing fine. He wants me to smoke as much as possible so the baby will be smaller and easier to deliver.

Ross is demure in appearance but unafraid to speak her mind. She wears her hair in a boyish bob and speaks in lilting tones, a slight smile playing across her face. As Betty, she never tweets out of character. Even so, Ross can't help but expose Betty's feelings online in ways the character is never allowed to on the show. "On *Mad Men*, so much is unspoken," Ross said. "Betty can't reveal her innermost thoughts. But people now don't want subtext, they want subtitles"—clear explanations of what's going on. And that's what the characters provide on Twitter.

Unofficially, Ross and the other tweeters have been accepted by the show. The AMC blog even ran a Q&A with Carri Bugbee a few months after the shutdown. Later, at the Clio Awards, an ad industry confab in Las Vegas, Ross met Matthew Weiner, the show's famously perfectionist creator, after he'd been honored for the program. Weiner told her he loved what she was doing as Betty. But not surprisingly, neither he nor anyone else connected with the show would reveal what was to come in season 3—like, would she keep the baby?

Well, so much for tweeting about Betty's pregnancy. To Ross, it was a missed opportunity—not just for "Betty," but for *Mad Men*. She viewed this whole Twitter thing as sort of an experiment in what entertainment could become. With this show, Weiner had created or, more correctly, re-created an entire world in incredible detail: the world of Madison Avenue in the early sixties. It was populated by humans and set on planet Earth, but as much as *Avatar* or *Star Wars* it had its own economy and technology, its own social structure and mores. And Weiner had done it brilliantly—so brilliantly that for many people, one hour a week for 13 weeks out of the year was simply not enough. "Now you get to live in that world from 10:00 to 11:00 on Sunday night," Ross said. "But I see the potential for telling that story in a different dimension—for bringing more of that world to an audience that has expanded because the world has expanded."

Several months after she started tweeting as Betty, Ross met Michael Bissell—"Roger Sterling"—for the first time. They were at South by Southwest Interactive, the digital-culture conference in Austin, to speak at a panel discussion on *Mad Men* and Twitter. As they were preparing for the panel, she and Bissell and Carri Bugbee compared notes. Before the shutdown, she told them, she had assumed that Weiner was somehow behind the *Mad Men* Twitter campaign and that she would be engaging in some kind of online tryout. "I thought he was casting for Twitter writers," she said. "He's so brilliant—why wouldn't he do that?"

"Because he's a control freak," Bissell replied.

IN A COMMAND-AND-CONTROL WORLD, we know who's telling the story; it's the author. But digital media have created an authorship crisis. Once the audience is free to step out into the fiction and start directing events, the entire edifice of twentieth-century mass media begins to crumble.

Mass media were an outgrowth of nineteenth-century technology—the development of ever more efficient presses and distribution networks, which made publishing such an expensive proposition that it made sense only on an industrial scale. Movies and television accelerated the trend. But now the Internet has reversed it. An author can still speak to an audience of millions, but the communication no longer goes just one way. Newspapers and magazines don't just report events anymore, they become forums for discussing them. Movies and TV shows cease to be couch potato fodder and become catalysts for the imagination. Ad people (they're not just men anymore) begin to realize they need to stop preaching to consumers and start listening to them. That's what "sense and respond" means—a dialogue.

In the late nineties I was in London reporting a story for *Wired* on Rupert Murdoch, a man who had built a global media empire largely on the basis of an epiphany he'd had when he was much younger. In 1945, Arthur C. Clarke had published a paper in *Wireless World*, a British journal for radio buffs, positing that a spacecraft in geosynchronous orbit 22,300 miles above the equator could beam a signal to a large, stationary footprint on the Earth below. Fascinated by Clarke's vision and by his prediction that the free flow of information would challenge the authority of national governments, Murdoch had embraced the power of satellite technology. Now BSkyB, the British wing of the vast satellite fleet Murdoch had assembled, was in the process of going digital and interactive.

As Clarke had predicted, satellites were ideal for broadcasting to the masses. They gave Murdoch a gigantic fire hose in the sky—but that's all they gave him. Satellites weren't designed for pinpoint delivery of billions of Web pages, nor did they make possible more than a rudimentary form of interactive TV. Murdoch wanted both. The solution seemed clear enough: partner with a phone company and run DSL lines to customers' homes. Those lines were designed to carry far more data into the home than out of it, but that didn't seem to be a problem. As Tony Ball, Sky's then CEO, offhandedly remarked, "There's not that many people sending streaming video back from their PC." It seemed almost too obvious to quote.

That was then. In June 2008, Michael Wesch, an anthropology professor at Kansas State University, pointed out in a talk at the Library of Congress that if the three leading US television networks had broadcast nonstop for the 60 years they'd been in business, that would have added up to more than 1.5 million hours of programming—which is a lot, but less than what Internet users had uploaded to YouTube in the previous six months.

By that time, Murdoch had abandoned his half-romantic

dream of a satellite armada circling the globe. He'd had it in his grasp when, after years of maneuvering, he won control of DIRECTV. This gave him a footprint that extended from Australia and New Zealand across China and southern Asia to India, blanketed much of Europe, and leaped across the Atlantic to cover most of North and South America. But by that time, his prize was worth more as a bargaining chip. In late 2006, after John Malone, the Denver-based cable mogul, bought up an uncomfortably large amount of stock in Murdoch's News Corporation, Murdoch gave him his satellite operations in the US and Latin America to go away.

By that time, Murdoch had made a deal that for $580 million gave him MySpace, the fast-growing social networking site, which already had 22 million members and was adding them at the rate of 2 million per month. MySpace was all about connecting people—to each other, to their favorite bands, to whatever identity they wanted to express. In early 2007, it drew 7 percent of the world's Internet users every month. And when that percentage started to decline—slowly at first, then precipitously—a few years later, it was only because Facebook emerged as a more appealing way of doing the same thing.

By the standards of mass media, the rise of the Web in general and social networking in particular seems to presage a revolution in human behavior—and a most unlikely one at that. "You aren't going to turn passive consumers into active trollers on the Internet," a senior executive at ABC condescendingly informed Kevin Kelly, a pioneer in the Bay Area's online community and one of *Wired*'s founding editors. This was in 1989, the golden age of the couch potato. With millions of humans voluntarily reduced to a vegetative state every night in front of the TV set, it seemed a safe enough assumption at the time. But even then the audience was starting to wake up, and not because of the Internet.

It started with the videocassette recorder. In 1975, when Sony introduced the notion of "time shift," as cofounder Akio Morita dubbed it, television was a staid and profitable business controlled in the United States by three national broadcast networks and in most other countries by one. *All in the Family,* America's most popular show, was watched in 30 percent of homes; cable was something you got for better reception. By 2010, 35 years later, the number one series in the US (Fox's *American Idol*) was being watched in less than 15 percent of households, hundreds of channels were available through cable and satellite, the broadcast networks were struggling to make a profit, and the entire apparatus of network television was beginning to break down.

The fundamental premise of broadcast television was its ability to control viewers—to deliver eyeballs to advertisers by the tens of millions. Because the networks had to attract those eyeballs and then hang on to them, programming—scheduling shows, creating effective lead-ins, countering the competition—became the network executive's highest art. The goal was to funnel eyeballs through the various day parts on the broadcasting schedule as if they were pinballs, from early evening through prime time all the way to late night—ka-ching! ka-ching! ka-ching! But the control that began eroding with the VCR has been eliminated by its successor, the digital video recorder, and blasted away entirely by the Web. Americans are watching more TV than ever—but, like their counterparts around the globe, increasingly they do it on their own schedule, and at the same time they're uploading their own videos to YouTube, posting their snapshots on Flickr, sharing their thoughts on Blogger or WordPress, and connecting with one another through MySpace and Facebook. The funnel is hopelessly, irretrievably busted.

But the media industry's loss of control extends far beyond what people watch and when. Movie studios and television networks are no longer even able to control what happens in the stories they present. As Matthew Weiner discovered when the *Mad Men* characters turned up on Twitter, the people who formerly constituted the audience are now capable of running off with the show. The same tools that enable people to spontaneously coalesce online make it easy for them to start telling the story their way, if they care about it enough to do so.

What's surprising is that anyone should find this surprising. That ABC exec notwithstanding, there's nothing inherent in humans that makes them want to be passive consumers of entertainment, or of the advertising that pays for it. The couch potato era, seemingly so significant at the time, turns out to be less an era than a blip—and a blip based on faulty assumptions at that.

In 2007, the American Association of Advertising Agencies and the Advertising Research Foundation, an industry think tank, issued a report asserting that the twentieth-century approach to advertising—the approach epitomized by *Mad Men*—had it all wrong. For decades, ad people had assumed that consumers thought in a linear and essentially rational fashion. All a television spot had to do to arouse desire for the product was get the viewer's attention and make a strong case. This "input-output engineering model," as the report described it, was enshrined in ad industry thinking by Rosser Reeves, the longtime chairman of Ted Bates & Company, in his 1961 book *Reality in Advertising*: if the ad people could define the "unique selling proposition" of the product they were pitching, be it an expensive new sports car or an over-the-counter medication for headache relief, consumers would get the message and act accordingly.

Alas for Madison Avenue, it wasn't that simple. In the 1980s and '90s, the idea that creative types could input a story and get output in the form of sales began to collapse. As cognitive researchers took a closer look at the workings of the human brain, they discovered that this isn't what happens at all. People don't passively ingest a marketing message, or any type of message. They greet it with an emotional response, usually unconscious, that can vary wildly depending on their own experiences and predispositions. They don't just imbibe a story; they imbue it with meaning. Which means that perceptions of a brand aren't simply created by marketers; they're "co-created," in the words of Gerald Zaltman of Harvard Business School, by marketers and consumers together.

To anyone outside the ad business, this may seem obvious: of course the audience brings something to the table. But it's a powerful idea all the same. If individuals in the audience "co-create" a story in some sort of give-and-take with the storyteller, then the whole notion of authorial control starts to get fuzzy. The author starts the story; the audience completes it. The author creates the characters and the situation they find themselves in; the audience responds and makes it their own. Matthew Weiner produces *Mad Men*; the viewers interpret it by empathizing with its characters and imagining themselves in that scenario. Given half a chance, at least a few of them will want to start tweeting as Betty Draper or Roger Sterling—and Weiner has no choice but to accept that. People have always wanted to in some way inhabit the stories that move them. The only real variable is whether technology gives them that opportunity.

• • •

NEARLY TWO CENTURIES BEFORE Twitter and Wookieepedia, there was the serialized novel. England in the 1830s was being transformed by technology as profoundly as the entire planet is today. Industrialization was drawing people to the cities in unimaginable numbers, crowding them together in often appalling conditions of filth and disease. Overflowing cesspools and cellars packed with "night soil"—a euphemism for human shit—were commonplace. So were cholera epidemics, which from 1831 on killed tens of thousands in an excruciating process that began with uncontrollable diarrhea and ended a day or two later with death by dehydration.

Yet the same forces of urbanization that generated such misery also led to the rise of literacy among the working and middle classes. Suddenly, there was a far bigger market for reading material than had existed even a few decades before, much less in Defoe's era. At the same time, improvements in paper manufacture, in printing, and in transportation were making it possible to print and distribute periodicals on a much greater scale. Book publishers saw a market for serial fiction—books released a few chapters at a time in flimsy paperback editions that sold for a shilling or so each (12 pence). Writers were lucky to stay one or two installments ahead of the deadline, so readers who wanted to share their thoughts could influence the plot as the books were being written—could participate, in other words.

Many authors were published in this manner, but one became identified with it above all. As a young boy, Charles Dickens had imbibed *Don Quixote* and *Tom Jones* and *Robinson Crusoe*; but when his father was sent away to a London debtor's prison, Charles, then 12, was pulled out of school and sent to work in a rat-infested boot-blacking factory near Charing Cross. Largely deprived of a formal education, he nonetheless found success as a teenage newspaper reporter in the House of Commons, quickly rising to an enviable position at the widely read London *Morning Chronicle*. In 1836, having just turned 24 and published a collection of short fiction, he was commissioned by the London publishers Chapman & Hall to write a series of sketches about life in the English countryside. The picaresque adventures that made up *The Pickwick Papers* appeared in monthly installments from March of that year until October 1837. They aroused little interest at first, but when Dickens introduced Sam Weller, valet to the aristocratic Mr. Pickwick, readers clamored for more and he gave it to them. The series took off.

Dickens quickly became the most popular novelist in England, and the acknowledged master of the serial. In February 1837, while still churning out *The Pickwick Papers*, he began writing *Oliver Twist* for *Bentley's Miscellany*, a new literary journal he'd just been hired to edit. The tale of an indigent boy forced into the miasma of crime and despair that was contemporary London, *Oliver Twist* spoke directly to the new audience that cheap serials had created. In scathing tones it charged the local religious authorities with attempting to starve the poor out of existence. Yet the same technological upheaval that gave rise to the workhouses that Dickens described also created a readership for his story, and a way of reaching those readers that was cheap enough to be practicable.

Inevitably, serialization changed the structure of stories. Dickens fashioned tales with cliff-hanger endings to keep readers coming back (though this technique wouldn't get its name until decades later, after Thomas Hardy literally left his hero hanging off a cliff at the end of the sixth installment of *A Pair of Blue Eyes*). More significant, however, was the way he improvised in response to his readers' reactions. Even as he was in the midst of writing *Oliver Twist*, *Nicholas Nickleby* began appearing in monthly installments. In 1841, "to shorten the intervals of communication between himself and his readers" (as he put it in a preface), he launched a weekly periodical, *Master Humphrey's Clock*, for which he wrote *The Old Curiosity Shop* and *Barnaby Rudge*.

The weekly deadlines of *Master Humphrey's Clock* proved a bit much even for Dickens, but communication with his readers remained paramount. Not that he always heeded their wishes. As he neared the end of *The Old Curiosity Shop* in 1841, it became increasingly apparent that the saintly Nell Trent, orphaned and pursued by predators, was doomed to die. As the suspense built, readers beseeched the author to be merciful. A ship from England sailed into New York Harbor to be greeted at the pier by a crowd of people shouting, "Is Little Nell dead?" When her inevitable demise came, it was greeted with near hysteria.

Dickens knew exactly what he was doing, of course: *The Old Curiosity Shop* was his most successful novel to date. On occasions when a story was faltering, he paid much closer attention to what his readers were saying. In 1843, when monthly sales of *Martin Chuzzlewit* failed to meet expectations, he moved the action to America; and when readers latched onto Mrs. Gamp, the novel's tipsy nurse, he obligingly wrote more scenes for her.

Scholars have come to see such give-and-take as crucial to Dickens's method. "Through serial publication an author could recover something of the intimate relationship between storyteller and audience which existed in the ages of the sagas and of Chaucer," John Butt and Kathleen Tillotson observed in their 1957 study *Dickens at Work*. Princeton's E. D. H. Johnson concurred: "The drawbacks of adhering to a rigorous schedule . . . were for Dickens more than counterbalanced by the sense of immediate audience participation."

In Dickens's own time, however, serialized novels were hugely controversial. Novels themselves were only beginning to find acceptance in polite society; for upper-class commentators, serialization was entirely too much. From our perspective, Dickens is a literary master, an icon of a now threatened culture. From theirs, he represented the threat of something coming. Not for him a celebration of the old ways so romantically alluded to in John Constable's paintings of the rural English landscape. Dickens's preoccupation with the unpleasant side effects of industrialization was of a piece with the serialized novel itself—clearly the product of mass manufacture, and highly suspect as a result.

Worse, the format seemed dangerously immersive. In 1845, a critic for the patrician *North British Review* decried it as an unhealthy alternative to conversation or to games like cricket or backgammon. Anticipating Huxley and Bradbury by a century, he railed against the multiplying effects of serialization on the already hallucinatory powers of the novel:

> The form of publication of Mr. Dickens's works must be attended with bad consequences. The reading of a novel is not now the undertaking it once was, a thing to be done occasionally on holiday and almost by stealth. . . . It throws us into a state of unreal excitement, a trance, a dream, which we should be allowed to dream out, and then be sent back to the atmosphere of reality again, cured by our brief surfeit of the desire to indulge again soon in the same delir-

ium of feverish interest. But now our dreams are mingled with our daily business.

Toward the end of the nineteenth century, as further advances in technology continued to bring down the costs of printing and distribution, books and periodicals evolved into separate businesses and book publishers gradually moved away from serialization. The threat of immersiveness moved with them, first to motion pictures, then to television. Books, movies, TV—all were mass media, and mass media had no mechanism for audience participation. But the reader's impulse to have a voice in the story didn't vanish. It went underground and took a new form: fan fiction.

FANS HAVE CREATED STORIES about their favorite characters for decades, but until recently those stories seldom circulated beyond a handful of friends. When Helen Ross, the ad woman who tweets as Betty Draper, was in seventh grade, she and her best friend wrote little stories about the Monkees, the sixties pop band and TV sensation. Helen, who aspired to be a writer, weaved her friend into stories about Mickey Dolenz, the drummer; her friend wrote Helen into stories involving Davy Jones, the lead singer. Fortunately for them, neither NBC nor Columbia Records became aware of their activities, so they were able to continue unchallenged.

Fans of *Star Wars* were a lot more public about their activities. By the early eighties the movies were giving rise to a raft of fanzines, most of them reproduced on Xerox machines and sold for a nickel at conventions. As Lucasfilm's general counsel, Howard Roffman had to figure out how to respond. "You've stimulated these people's imaginations, and now they want to express themselves," he told me. "But that expression very often finds itself becoming a copyright infringement. I would have a parade of people coming into my office in all kinds of tizzies—'Oh my God, they're showing Han Solo and Princess Leia screwing!' I tried to be the voice of reason—how much damage can it do? But we did draw the line at pornography."

As the linchpin of the Bay Area's rebel alliance against Hollywood, Lucasfilm tried to at least be more understanding than the studios, working to suppress the X-rated stuff while ignoring most of the rest. But with the arrival of the Internet, fan fiction could no longer be ignored. After an initial period of hesitation, Lucasfilm adopted an embrace-and-encircle strategy. The turning point was *Troops*, a 10-minute *Star Wars* parody that appeared in 1997. *Troops* got so much attention that the guy who made it, a 30-year-old animation-cel archivist for the Fox Kids Network named Kevin Rubio, was profiled in *Entertainment Weekly*. "We loved it," said Roffman. "It was a defining moment."

Instead of trying to shut such efforts down, Lucasfilm sought to channel them into forms that could be, to some degree at least, controlled. In 2000, the company offered free Web hosting for personal home pages on Starwars.com, but with a catch: anything put up there would become Lucasfilm's intellectual property. That same year, the company struck a deal that made AtomFilms the official site for fan productions. Actual fan fiction—that is, dramatizations of events in the *Star Wars* universe—was not allowed until years later, but parodies and documentaries were okay. In 2002, AtomFilms even launched an annual contest called the *Star Wars* Fan Film Awards, with the winners picked by AtomFilms and Lucasfilm employees, and Lucas himself selecting a personal favorite. Fans couldn't play in

Lucas's sandbox—but as long as their efforts were purely non-commercial, they could at least pay tribute to it.

Harry Potter fans didn't fare so well. Like *Star Wars*, the *Harry Potter* series is set in a richly imagined fictional universe that has proved deeply, almost compulsively engaging. The books' author, J. K. Rowling, has generally been supportive of fan contributions; and her publishers—Bloomsbury in the UK and Scholastic in the US—have tolerated them as well. But that attitude was not shared by Warner Bros., the Hollywood studio (owned by Time Warner) that bought worldwide rights from Rowling in 1998. In early 2001, young readers who had started *Harry Potter* fan sites found themselves targeted by Warner Bros. It was the beginning of what came to be known as the PotterWar.

Warner's idea of sharing the magic of the *Potter* stories was to spend hundreds of millions of dollars making and marketing a series of movies that stood to bring in billions. With all that money at stake, the studio felt compelled to protect its intellectual property rights. So it started sending cease-and-desist letters to kids around the world who had set up tribute sites that used the Harry Potter name or otherwise trespassed on studio property.

This action aroused the ire of Heather Lawver, a 16-year-old military brat who lived in the Virginia suburbs of Washington, D.C. Heather had started an online newspaper named after the *Daily Prophet*, the paper read by wizards in the *Potter* books. She herself wasn't threatened by Warner, but many other fans who had started *Harry Potter* Web sites were, and she took offense. "They attacked a whole bunch of kids in Poland," she told Henry Jenkins for his book *Convergence Culture*. "How much of a risk is that? They went after the twelve- and fifteen-year-olds with the rinky-dink sites. They underestimated how interconnected our fandom was."

Their fandom was in fact extremely interconnected, as Warner soon found out. Incensed, Heather started an online organization called Defense Against the Dark Arts and launched a boycott against *Harry Potter* merchandise. As she declared in the site's mission statement,

> We believe that what Warner Brothers is doing is just wrong. It is unethical, it is immoral, and it is downright nasty. A major corporation has been playing the bully on the playground, scaring innocent children into thinking that if they do not hand over a domain name, a website, or a few photos, that they will lose all their pocket-money and their families will go into debt. Is this the price for "corporate advancement"? Sacrificing children?

In December 2000, one such child, 15-year-old Claire Field of West Yorkshire, received a threatening letter demanding she close her fan site, Harrypotterguide.co.uk, and surrender the Web address to Warner. Instead, she and her father engaged a solicitor and launched a public campaign against the studio, beginning with an interview in the sensationalist London tabloid the *Daily Mirror.* A 33-year-old London councilman named Alastair Alexander started a fan empowerment site called PotterWar and took up her cause. Other kids started to go public with their own tales of harassment. Online bulletin boards buzzed with anti-Warner sentiment worldwide. Newspapers ran with the story. By Easter Sunday 2001, preachers in Britain were excoriating Warner for its campaign against children. Faced with a public relations disaster, the company had no choice but to call the whole thing a "miscommunication" and back down.

• • •

For entertainment corporations, the lesson should be obvious: don't threaten a bunch of Web-savvy teens who've done nothing wrong. The bigger lesson is, don't attack the audience for trying to connect with a story you hold the rights to. Actually copying and profiting from someone else's work is not at issue. What's at issue is the kind of behavior that's covered in the unspoken agreement that manga publishers in Japan have reached with their otaku fans. People tell and retell stories they love because that's what humans do. If the story is meaningful enough, a superficial encounter won't leave them satisfied. They'll want to go deeper. They'll want to imagine themselves in it, retell it, make it their own. And the more powerful the connection, the less likely they'll be to submit to a demand that they cease and desist.

A few companies are figuring this out. In 2008, when the Walt Disney Company released its 1959 classic *Sleeping Beauty* on Blu-ray Disc, the package included access to the studio's new BD-Live Network, which through an Internet connection enables little users in different locations to sync playback with one another, communicate via text message while watching, and even insert their own video into the film. Nonetheless, they have to accept a 58-page End User License Agreement before they can do any of this. And of course, you can't please everyone. "Has Disney decided that American youth suffers from an excessively long attention span?" a reviewer for the *New York Times* harrumphed. "Things have come to a curious pass when children have to be entertained during their entertainment."

A more accurate assessment would be that children want to

entertain themselves during their entertainment. But yes, things have come to a curious pass indeed. We live in a moment when two modes of popular culture are vying for supremacy: passivity versus participation. Mass media versus deep media. Mass media are industrial, manufactured by someone else and consumed by you. The deep-media experience is digital; it offers a way to participate.

The apotheosis of mass media is Hollywood, the place once known as the Dream Factory. At its peak, in the 1930s and '40s, the motion picture industry functioned as smoothly as Henry Ford's River Rouge plant outside Detroit. Its constituent parts, from the studios that made the films to the theater chains that showed them, were owned by a handful of vertically integrated corporations, Warner Bros. among them, that had evolved from the primordial muck in the early years of the century. At the "movie colony" in Hollywood, contract writers, directors, and actors labored to create films that would lure people to the theater chains. The glamour of Hollywood was manufactured along with the films. But much of the profit came from the theater chains, which were in business to rent seats by the hour. The entire motion picture industry was essentially a real estate operation, with mass-produced entertainment the come-on.

That changed in the fifties, after a 1948 Supreme Court decision in a long-running antitrust case forced the movie studios to divorce themselves from the theater chains. At the same time, television destroyed the audience for B pictures—Hollywood's bread and butter. When the studios stopped making B movies and started making TV shows instead, the product didn't change in any fundamental way; it just got smaller. It certainly didn't allow for little girls to play fast and loose with the characters.

Yet the impulse to do so—not just for little girls but for teenage boys and a great many grown-ups as well—is far from frivolous. It's closely tied to creativity—a point Wim Wenders made in a discussion at the Cannes Film Festival a few years back. We had come to the American Pavilion, an extremely fancy tent on the beach, to opine about the future of entertainment, and inevitably the subject of "piracy"—industry-speak for the unauthorized sharing of music or video—came up. For Wenders, the word brought up childhood memories:

> I am a little scared of it becoming too difficult, for one simple reason. I grew up as a pirating kid. It was even before television. I had inherited a crank projector and a box of eight-millimeter films from my dad, all Charlie Chaplin and Buster Keaton stuff. . . . And when they got too bad, because I showed them hundreds of times, I started to cut them up, and I found this little machine—my friend had one—that could paste them together and make new movies out of them. And it worked beautifully—Buster Keaton and Charles Lloyd suddenly interactive was fantastic!
>
> So I am very, very scared that for a contemporary generation of kids, that possibility to take it and use it and do what they want to with it is all of a sudden gone, because they block it all and it is out there, but you can't eat it any more and use it for your imagination.

In other words, what's bad for control can be good for creativity.

William Gibson once described his excitement on discovering that William Burroughs, "the least imitative of authors," was sampling other people's work with scissors and paste. Now there are scissors and paste in every computer. "The remix is the very nature of the digital," Gibson writes. "Today, an endless, recombinant, and fundamentally social process generates countless hours of creative product." But mashups have no place in the way industrial-age media companies do business. If the audience retells the story, then whose story is it? It's the media companies', according to lawsuits brought by the Motion Picture Association of America and the Recording Industry Association of America.

Ostensibly these suits are designed to deter people from downloading movies and music without paying. There's no question that piracy has hurt the recording industry. According to the market research firm NPD, American college students downloaded 1.3 billion songs illegally in 2006 alone. In the UK, a 2009 study of 14- to 24-year-olds found that 60 percent were downloading music illegally, most of them on a daily or weekly basis. Meanwhile, in the decade from 1999 to 2009, world music sales fell by more than a third.

There's a case to be made that piracy is largely a response to the music companies' greed and ineptitude. For years the labels resisted calls to make music available for legal download. After a couple of decades of selling cheaper-to-produce CDs at an even higher price than records, they didn't want customers downloading music for a dollar per song. Nor did they want to undercut the chains that sold CDs—companies like Tower Records, which eventually went bust anyway. By the time Apple dragged the labels into its iTunes store in 2001, piracy was already becoming entrenched. The lawsuits provoked a backlash that cemented it into place.

When you look carefully at what media companies are doing, however, you begin to realize that their piracy panic isn't simply a response to theft. It's also a reaction against participatory culture. Lawrence Lessig of Harvard Law School has been including in his talks a short video of 13-month-old Holden Lenz dancing across his parents' kitchen floor, a Prince song barely audible in the background. Holden's mom posted the video on YouTube so her friends and family could watch it, but in so doing she ran afoul of the copyright police. Within months, an attorney for Universal Music Group—the world's largest music company, responsible for everyone from U2 to 50 Cent to, yes, Prince—sent YouTube a takedown notice. The dancing-baby video, it seems, constituted an unauthorized performance of Prince's music.

This is a stance so absurd it can only be explained as a manifestation of group hysteria. The people who threaten Holden's mom imagine themselves as fighters against piracy, but what they're really doing is working to protect twentieth-century mechanized media from an onslaught of creativity that looks to them like theft. In their scheme of things, artists like Prince exist in a zero-sum world: I have it, you don't. But what if, as manga publishers came to realize years ago, stories and characters actually gain value when people share them? What if they come to mean more, and to more people?

In his 2008 book *Remix*, Lessig recalls the 1906 congressional testimony of John Philip Sousa, the composer of "Stars and Stripes Forever." Sousa was speaking at a time very different from ours, a time when the mass production of entertainment was still a novelty. Movie studios like Universal and Warner Bros. had yet to be formed; the recording industry was in its infancy. But even then the phonograph was becoming more and more popular, and Sousa was disturbed by the trend:

> When I was a boy . . . in front of every house in the summer evenings you would find young people together singing the songs of the day or the old songs. Today you hear these infernal machines going night and day. We will not have

> a vocal cord left. The vocal cords will be eliminated by a process of evolution, as was the tail of man when he came from the ape.

No one alive today has a conscious memory of the world Sousa described—a world before phonographs and movies and radio and TV. A world where everyone sang. Sepia-tone photographs and antique verbiage betray few hints of its existence. But maybe we don't need to remember. We're re-creating it anyway.

5. Forking Paths

NATURALLY, THERE HAVE BEEN MISSTEPS ALONG THE WAY. One of the stranger examples took place in the early nineties, when a company called Interfilm sought to bring interactive cinema to America. Interfilm was the brainchild of Bob Bejan, a young entrepreneur who had made a bundle by latching onto the Teenage Mutant Ninja Turtles craze, composing some songs for the crime-battling cartoon characters and sending four guys in turtle suits on a much-ballyhooed world tour. A smooth talker with a more-than-passing resemblance to the ubiquitous game show host Pat Sajak, Bejan was well dressed, suave, and—to some people at least—persuasive. With Interfilm he set out to create "a cinematic game" in which theatergoers could control the plot by voting at critical intervals: press green if you want the guy who's cornered on a roof to run for the open door, yellow if you want him to jump to the neighboring roof, or red if you want him to announce that he's actually a secret agent.

That was one of the plot choices in *I'm Your Man*, Interfilm's first release, a 20-minute picture that came out in December 1992. Made in six days at a cost of $370,000, it had its premiere in a lower Manhattan theater outfitted with pistol grips in the armrests, where the cup holders had been. Viewers had 10 seconds to register their choice by pressing color-coded buttons in the pistol grips.

Bejan wasn't shy about trumpeting his achievement; in his publicity notes he declared Interfilm "the most revolutionary technological development since the introduction of sound," not to mention a "new paradigm for the world of arts and entertainment." In marrying cinema and games, Bejan was in fact attempting to introduce branching story lines to motion pictures. The conventions of linear storytelling—and most movies at the time were quite linear—require that things be laid out in a continuous and sequential manner. But video games are both nonlinear and interactive. They have different outcomes depending on the actions players take at crucial inflection points. To Bejan, Interfilm was the next frontier of entertainment.

Remarkably, Bejan's first interactive movie was not also his last. With backing from Sony, which was still painfully new to Hollywood, he went on to produce two more. The first of these, a low-budget gross-out comedy written and directed by Bob Gale, who had written Robert Zemeckis's *Back to the Future* movies, opened in 1995 in 44 theaters across the United States. Called *Mr. Payback*, it starred Billy Warlock, best known for playing a lifeguard on the hit series *Baywatch*, as a guy with the power to punish miscreants. When a healthy man parked in a handicapped zone, audiences got to decide whether Mr. Payback should cripple his car or cripple him. Other times they got to vote on whether to put Mr. Payback in "flatulence mode," which was powerful enough that his sidekick would put on a gas mask.

Mr. Payback got scathing reviews ("moronic and offensive," Roger Ebert declared in one of his kinder moments) and played to mostly empty theaters. Moviegoers greeted Bejan's new paradigm with a yawn. But those who did turn up tended to respond by going into a frenzy, shouting for choices when none were offered and scrambling to reach the dials at empty seats when they were. Interfilm released a third picture a couple months later and then went belly-up. Bob Bejan went to Warner Bros. and then to Microsoft, where he spent several years developing programming for MSN.

Obviously, Interfilm was a mess—an ill-considered experiment that succeeded only in demonstrating how not to make interactive entertainment. One reviewer compared it to Smell-O-Vision, the technology that for a few brief moments in 1960 promised to revolutionize motion pictures in an equally misguided way. Another quipped that if Bejan and company had been more industry savvy, they would have realized that audiences already decide which way a movie goes; that's what test-marketing is all about. Bran Ferren, an entertainment industry technology consultant who would later become head of Walt Disney Imagineering, observed that if you're trying to tell a story, you don't really want the audience deciding where it should go: "That's why you have a director and producer."

Good point. As awful as Interfilm's movies were, the concept was worse. Interfilm is exhibit A for the choose-your-own-ending fallacy—the idea that in interactive entertainment, the storyteller has to abdicate responsibility. Today that notion seems remarkably simplistic, a relic of the early nineties, a time when people talked about the information highway and expected multimedia CD-ROMs to be the future of publishing. But none of this was obvious in 1992, or even 1995, because interactivity was still so new. The idea that audiences would begin to create their own entertainment was not even on the horizon. Branching narrative seemed the way to go.

THE COMMON THREAD THAT VIDEO GAMES, CD-ROMs, and the information highway all shared—and conventional movies did not—was hypertext. Because of hypertext—the links embedded within text that have become an everyday feature of the Web—linear progression was no longer required or even expected. It was an innovation that has come to define our era.

The basic idea was laid out by Vannevar Bush, the leading American technocrat of the World War II era, in a seminal essay titled "As We May Think." As head of the wartime Office of Scientific Research and Development, Bush had directed the efforts of thousands of scientists, including those engaged in developing the atomic bomb as part of the Manhattan Project. His paper—published in the *Atlantic Monthly* in July 1945, weeks after the surrender of Nazi Germany and shortly before the bombing of Hiroshima and Nagasaki—asked the question, "What are the scientists to do next?"

In Bush's view, the most pressing problem science would face was humankind's growing inability to remember what it already knew—to efficiently access, as the *Atlantic* observed in an editor's note, "our bewildering store of knowledge." Indexing systems were inadequate to the task because, as Bush pointed out,

> The human mind does not work that way. It operates by association. With one item in its grasp, it snaps instantly to the next that is suggested by the association of thoughts, in

accordance with some intricate web of trails carried by the cells of the brain.

Though it may not seem so today, this was an astonishingly revolutionary idea. Born in 1890, Bush was a product of an era when taxonomy—the hierarchical organization of knowledge—reigned supreme. Originally applied to the classification of flora and fauna, taxonomy itself was the product of an earlier information explosion: The 500 or so species of plants known to the ancient Greeks had become 18,000 by the time the Swedish naturalist Carl Linnaeus catalogued them in the eighteenth century. Of course, no hierarchy of knowledge was ever perfect; each one became an invitation for further refinement as new information was uncovered. Enough, Bush declared: "The summation of human experience is being expanded at a prodigious rate, and the means we use for threading through the consequent maze to the momentarily important item is the same as was used in the days of square-rigged ships."

So he proposed the "memex," a mechanism that would serve as a memory supplement. Oddly, given that he had spent years as dean of engineering at the Massachusetts Institute of Technology, where one of his grad students, Claude Shannon, did the work that ushered in the computer age, he did not suggest that the information in his memex be encoded in zeros and ones and transmitted electronically. He thought it would be miniaturized and stored on microfilm, a clumsy analog alternative. Yet he was decades ahead of his time when he wrote, "Wholly new forms of encyclopedias will appear, ready made with a mesh of associative trails running through them." Those associative trails are the links we now follow from one document to another on the Web.

Twenty years after Bush introduced the idea, Ted Nelson gave it a name: hypertext. The occasion was the annual conference of the Association for Computing Machinery, the planet's first and largest scientific computer society, in August 1965. An eccentric computer visionary who had begun toying with the concept as a graduate student at Harvard, Nelson combined Bush's idea of associative trails with digital technology to imagine embedded links that would enable readers to hopscotch from one text to another to another. Reading, that most linear of activities, would go nonlinear.

Though Bush had been right when he pointed out that all humans think by association, it should surprise no one that the inventor of hypertext was hyperactive. As Gary Wolf reported in a lengthy profile in *Wired*,

> "Attention Deficit Disorder was coined by regularity chauvinists," [Nelson] remarked. "Regularity chauvinists are people who insist that you have got to do the same thing every time, every day, which drives some of us nuts. Attention Deficit Disorder—we need a more positive term for that. Hummingbird mind, I should think."
>
> Xanadu, the ultimate hypertext information system, began as Ted Nelson's quest for personal liberation. The inventor's hummingbird mind and his inability to keep track of anything left him relatively helpless. He . . . needed a way to avoid getting lost in the frantic multiplication of associations his brain produced. His great inspiration was to imagine a computer program that could keep track of all the divergent paths of his thinking and writing. To this concept of branching, nonlinear writing, Nelson gave the name hypertext.

Nelson based his term on the Greek prefix "υπερ-," meaning "over" or "excessive." It's the equivalent of the Latin prefix "super-," which is why, when DC Comics wanted to introduce Superman's double from another planet, he was dubbed Hyper-Man. But Nelson has come up with any number of forgotten coinages over the years—"teledildonics," "transclusion," "intertwingularity"—and there was little reason at the time to think this one would be any different. He provided few technical details in the paper he presented before the ACM, and for good reason: his proposal would have required an amount of memory and processing power that in the mid-sixties seemed hopelessly out of reach. Computer professionals were dismissive of the idea. "Only Nelson's ignorance of advanced software permitted him to pursue this fantasy," Wolf declared in *Wired*.

But with rapid advances in microprocessor technology and memory storage, many things that once seemed in the realm of fantasy—personal computers, for example—became doable. By the late eighties, computer scientists were becoming increasingly interested in hypertext as a means of information retrieval. In 1989, when Tim Berners-Lee—then a research fellow at CERN, the European Organization for Nuclear Research—proposed the Internet service that eventually came to be known as the World Wide Web, he made hypertext central to its design. In the nonlinear structure of the Web, Ted Nelson's fantasy would find life—in bastardized form by his account, but life all the same.

THE INITIAL PROPOSAL FROM Tim Berners-Lee wasn't for some sort of global information system; it was for something much more specific to CERN. As he described it, the problem for the physicists there was how to keep track of information in an organization characterized by high turnover and a reliance on "corridor gossip." In such an environment, he observed, "the technical details of past projects are sometimes lost forever, or only recovered after a detective investigation in an emergency. Often, the information has been recorded, it just cannot be found." This was the same problem Bush had identified nearly 45 years earlier. Berners-Lee's solution was to encourage the development of "a pool of information" that could grow and evolve over time. "This," he added, "is why a 'web' of notes with links . . . between them is far more useful than a fixed hierarchical system."

A few years later, at a symposium held at MIT to celebrate the fiftieth anniversary of the publication of Bush's article in the *Atlantic*, Berners-Lee described what he was thinking. "I had (and still have) a dream that the web could be less of a television channel and more of an interactive sea of shared knowledge," he declared. "I imagine it immersing us in a warm, friendly environment made of the things we and our friends have seen, heard, believe or have figured out." Warm and friendly the Web has not always turned out to be. But shared, interactive, and immersive—here, Berners-Lee was clearly right.

In the same talk, he somewhat playfully asked what associations we might have with the word "link." His answers included: confusion ("or so it was for many when the web seemed at first to threaten the orderly, hierarchical world"); coolness; and readership, since "every link brought more readers." But the final connection he made was in many ways the most interesting: dollars.

That was in 1995. Since then, hyperlinks have given rise to a "link economy"—the product of an emerging realization that in a world defined by the Web, value resides not so much in information (much of which is redundant anyway) as in links to the bits of information that are most relevant and enlightening. It's not hard to see why this would be true. The "bewildering store of knowledge" that existed in 1945 has grown exponentially in the decades since. In 2002 alone, according to a study conducted at UC Berkeley, the world produced five exabytes of new information on print, film, tape, and hard drives—five billion billion bytes, the equivalent of a half-million copies of the print collection of the Library of Congress. That was double the amount produced three years earlier.

When people say the Internet is wreaking havoc on existing media businesses, they're really pointing to two things: this ever-growing cascade of information, and the emergence of hyperlinks as a means of dealing with it. On a planet that even in 2002 produced a new Library of Congress print collection every 57 seconds, most information is never going to command the premium it once did. But links to the right information can be extremely valuable—especially to companies that know how to use those links to their advantage.

Links change our relationship to information. They empower individuals and destroy hierarchies. Most media companies are still hierarchical in their mind-set. They are in business to deliver information to a hungry populace—except that the populace is no longer hungry, it's sated. But instead of trying to find a place for themselves in the link economy, they all too often view links as theft.

Then there's Google, which was started by two Stanford University grad students who had an idea for searching the Web that involved ranking the results by the number of links coming in. The more links a Web page had from other Web pages, and the more links those pages had in turn, the more relevant it was presumed to be. This was an idea they adapted from Eugene Garfield, a bibliographer who in 1960 had come up with a citation index for scientific papers. Garfield's scheme, which itself was inspired by Vannevar Bush's essay in the *Atlantic*, was designed to show in a simple and straightforward way who cited whom. Change "cite" to "link" and you have the essence of Google's formula.

Later, Google figured out how to auction ads on the basis of those search results—a process overseen since 2002 by its chief economist, Hal Varian, who happens to be one of two authors of the UC Berkeley information study. In 2009, just over a decade after it was incorporated, Google took in $24 billion, almost all of it from advertising related to links, and turned a profit of $6.5 billion—nearly 30 percent of its revenues.

That same year, more than six decades after Vannevar Bush, the *Atlantic* published an essay by Nicholas Carr titled "Is Google Making Us Stupid?" His complaint: "Even when I'm not working, I'm as likely as not to be foraging in the Web's info-thickets, reading and writing e-mails, scanning headlines and blog posts, watching videos and listening to podcasts, or just tripping from link to link to link. . . . Once I was a scuba diver in the sea of words. Now I zip along the surface like a guy on a Jet Ski." Memex be damned, Carr would say; hyperlinks are Swiss-cheesing my brain.

Carr has a point: hyperlinks, and electronic media in general, do change the way we read and the way we think. But will the effects really be as toxic as Carr predicts? People have worried about the effect of new information technologies at least since the time of Socrates—who, as Jonah Lehrer observed in a review of Carr's subsequent book, *The Shallows*, complained that books encourage forgetfulness. What Socrates could not see is that books also enable us to "remember" far more information than we could ever keep in our heads. This is why, when books threatened to make us stupid 2,400 years ago, we responded not by abandoning books but by redefining "stupid." I suspect we'll do the same with Google.

SAY WHAT YOU WILL ABOUT HYPERLINKS, they're certainly changing the way we think about narrative. In a 2005 *Film Comment* review of Don Roos's *Happy Endings*, Alissa Quart introduced the term "hyperlink cinema" to refer to movies in which scenes seem linked more through chance than by sequential plot development. With *Happy Endings*, Quart wrote, Roos has "stopped worrying and learned to love his web browser, connecting one scene to the next through happenstance and linking text. It's all very Google meets Robert Altman." This idea was popularized a few months later in a review of *Syriana* by Roger Ebert, though he couldn't cite the exact term or the person who had coined it because, "irony of ironies, I've lost the link."

Unlike hypertext, movies can't actually offer a branching trail; Interfilm certainly demonstrated that. Quart and Ebert were using "hyperlink" metaphorically, to refer to films that employ obliquely intersecting plotlines to reveal the hidden connectedness of things. Quentin Tarantino's *Pulp Fiction* (1994), arguably the most influential example of nonlinear storytelling in Hollywood history, presents three out-of-order stories involving a pair of hit men, a corrupt prizefighter, and a gangland boss. Paul Thomas Anderson's *Magnolia* (1999) tells nine interwoven stories that play out in a single day in Los Angeles. In Alejandro González Iñárritu's *Babel* (2006), a rifle bullet fired in jest by adolescent sheepherders at a Moroccan tour bus ricochets through people's lives in Tokyo, San Diego, and the outskirts of Tijuana, connecting them all.

Nonlinear narrative was around long before the Web introduced anyone to hypertext. Until Tarantino came along, however, it was mainly the playpen of the avant-garde. Akira Kurosawa told the story of *Rashômon* from multiple perspectives, offering contradictory accounts of a rape and killing from the point of view of the bandit, the woman, her murdered husband, and a witness. A few years later, in films like François Truffaut's *Shoot the Piano Player*, the New Wave directors started putting shots out of sequence. In a mid-sixties discussion with Jean-Luc Godard at Cannes, the idiosyncratic director Georges Franju became thoroughly exasperated with these unconventional techniques. "But surely, Monsieur Godard," he blurted out, "you do at least acknowledge the necessity of having a beginning, a middle, and end in your films." To which Godard famously replied, "Certainly. But not necessarily in that order."

Jorge Luis Borges made nonlinearity his subject in the 1941 short story "The Garden of Forking Paths." The story centers on a mysterious Chinese novel, also called *The Garden of Forking Paths*, that appears to be a heap of contradictory drafts. In one chapter the hero dies; in the next chapter he is alive. The novel's illustrious author, Ts'ui Pên, had retired from public life to write his book and "to construct a labyrinth in which all men would become lost," but he was murdered before he could finish his writing, and his labyrinth was never found. The narrator of Borges's story, who lives in England and happens to be Ts'ui Pên's great-grandson, is a spy for the Germans in World War I. In a desperate attempt to communicate the name of a town on the Somme in France to his handlers in Berlin, he resolves to kill a man whose last name is Albert. He takes a train to a nearby village, where by turning left at every fork in the road he eventually finds himself at the home of Stephen Albert, his chosen victim. Albert, it turns out, is a noted Sinologist.

Inviting the narrator inside, the unsuspecting Sinologist proceeds to clarify the mystery of the garden of forking paths. He has deduced that the labyrinth is Ts'ui Pên's novel itself—but it is a labyrinth of time, not of space. Rather than being a physical maze of forking paths, it is a maze of forking possibilities. As the Sinologist explains,

> In all fictional works, each time a man is confronted with several alternatives, he chooses one and eliminates the others; in the fiction of Ts'ui Pên, he chooses—simultaneously—all of them. He creates, in this way, diverse futures, diverse times which themselves also proliferate and fork. . . . In the work of Ts'ui Pên, all possible outcomes occur; each one is the point of departure for other forkings.

Borges's labyrinth of possibilities is what we would call a multiverse. Coined by William James in 1895, the term was applied much later to the "many-worlds interpretation" of quantum physics. Borges, in his story, described such fiction as an incoherent jumble. Yet by the 1980s, half of Hollywood had a multiverse going. Robert Zemeckis and Bob Gale, operating at a considerably lower level of cerebration than Borges, dabbled in alternate realities by having Michael J. Fox mess up his parents' courtship in the popcorn comedy *Back to the Future*. What Borges treated as a philosophical conundrum and Zemeckis as a movie gimmick has since become fodder for prime-time TV. As Sylar the brain thief asked in NBC's *Heroes*, "Haven't I killed you before?"

• • •

Clearly the idea of branching, nonlinear narrative has lodged itself in our brains. But has our consciousness been warped by hypertext? Or is hypertext a product of our consciousness—a natural representation of the way we think? That's the question that ultimately came up when I asked David Lynch why so many of his films employ nonlinear story lines.

"It's the nature of life now," Lynch replied. "In one day we are in Iraq, in Pakistan, in New York City, in a car. Memories are coming in and birds are flying. And some part of you is now thinking about other parts of the world and it's influencing your work."

We were talking on the phone, I in a room in New York, he in a room 2,500 miles away in Los Angeles, sharing for the moment a single auditory experience.

Lynch delights in the surrealism of the everyday. His signature moment as a director is the opening scene of *Blue Velvet*, when the camera pans in on a glistening, hyperreal suburban lawn and then burrows deeper and deeper to find it teeming with bugs. He frequently gives us scenes that rub against each other for reasons that become apparent only later, if at all. This of course only highlights the consuming oddness of his films.

Take *Mulholland Drive*, for which Lynch was named best director at Cannes in 2001 (an honor he shared with Joel Cohen). Here, lush imagery and fractured narrative combine to create a sinister yet otherworldly portrait of Hollywood as dreamland. Mulholland Drive itself, a remote and wooded road that winds across the summit of the Hollywood Hills, signifies the acme of show business success. For two hours the camera lavishes its gaze on Betty (Naomi Watts), a naïve and irrepressibly bouncy wannabe star, and a mysterious brunette who calls herself Rita (Laura Elena Harring). After narrowly escaping a hit man on a lonely stretch of Mulholland, Rita turns up in Betty's apartment with $50,000 in her purse and a bad case of amnesia. Meanwhile, mobsters pressure a young director to cast an actress named Camilla in his next movie, and a young man in a diner tells someone about a dream in which he saw a monster behind the diner—only to collapse when they go outside to investigate and find a homeless person. Betty and Rita, investigating Rita's mystery, go to an old Hollywood apartment complex looking for someone named Diane Selwyn. They break into her apartment and discover her body decomposing on the bed. Later, back at Betty's place, they have hot lesbian sex.

In its last 20 minutes, the film takes an abrupt turn. No longer slow and dreamy, it turns all too real. Betty has lost her luster and morphed into Diane Selwyn, who turns out to be a failed actress living in the shabby apartment where, in the first part of the movie, she was found dead. Rita, the amnesiac, is now named Camilla. She breaks away from Diane in the middle of sex and says, "We shouldn't do this anymore." Later, Diane masturbates but can't climax. At a party at the director's mansion on Mulholland Drive, she watches with increasing distress as he announces his engagement to Camilla. Diane meets a hit man at the diner and gives him $50,000 to kill her girlfriend. We see her in her apartment; on the coffee table is a blue key, the signal the deed has been done. She picks up a gun and shoots herself in the head.

Many people found all this puzzling, to say the least. Lynch, as usual, wasn't talking. But Stephen Holden was not far off when he described it in the *New York Times* as "a post-Freudian, pulp-fiction fever dream of a movie." And when *Salon* interviewed a Freudian dream analyst, he found it not terribly mysterious at all. The first two hours were a dream, he said, "about murder, money, and success." The final 20 minutes were the sad reality that gave rise to it.

"There's nothing wrong with a straight-ahead story," Lynch told me. "You could take a very linear story, like Alvin Straight going from one place to another place to meet his brother and things happen"—in *The Straight Story*, his movie about an elderly eccentric who takes a 240-mile ride on a lawn tractor—"and you could throw the pieces up in the air and put them back in random order, but it wouldn't be mysterious, it would just be confusing. But if it's not done as just some kind of a hipster thing, then I think you can feel it working."

Like *The Straight Story* itself, this seemed like a pretty straightforward observation. But as Lynch continued, I began to realize that his sense of nonlinearity is more complicated.

"Ideas are everywhere," he said. "You get ideas all day long, and once in a while you get an idea you fall in love with. That's a beautiful day. But you never get the whole thing at once. You get it in fragments. So many nonlinear things are happening in a day. We've got this thing called memories, and a picture forms from memories or from imaginary things. An idea can be conjured up by a little something you saw in Northern Ireland, and it swims in right next to something that's on the floor in front of you. The flow of all different kinds of things—if you were to put that together, it would be like a crazy film."

The unexpected juxtapositions, the startling elisions, the scenes out of sequence—asleep or awake, this is how we think, in a fast-dissipating vapor. Certainly it's the way we think now, and hypertext makes for both a convenient metaphor and a convenient scapegoat. But though the concept originated in the forties, it wasn't fully articulated until the sixties—when people had spent the better part of two decades watching TV.

Hyperlink films, like hyperlinks themselves, are really about simultaneity—the sense that you can be seeing one thing and instantly switch to something else that's occurring at the same time. At some basic level, the implication is that we exist in a multiverse. Simultaneity as the salient fact of our culture long predates the Internet. It was television that got people acclimated to the idea—especially after remote controls started to proliferate in the seventies. But simultaneity predates even broadcasting. It began with nineteenth-century inventors like Alexander Graham Bell, who gave us the telephone; and Nikola Tesla, who pioneered the development of alternating current.

"The greatest of all reversals occurred with electricity," Marshall McLuhan wrote in *Understanding Media*, "that ended sequence by making things instant." *That ended sequence*: from that point on, McLuhan was saying, the demise of sequential narrative was inevitable.

Motion pictures—that most mechanistic of media, image after image unspooled by metal sprockets at a uniform rate of 24 frames per second—were to McLuhan the apotheosis of the fragmented and sequential. And yet, paradoxically, their frame rate sped things up so much that they heralded a new reality. Just as still images fuse together at 24 frames per second to form a movie, so movies themselves usher us from "the world of sequence," as McLuhan put it, to a world of blur. The invention of cinema more or less coincided with the arrival of cubism, which sought to show every facet of an object at once, abandoning "the illusion of perspective in favor of instant sensory awareness of the whole." Borges, writing about 35 years after the birth of cubism in Paris, hypothesized a novel that tried to convey every possible reality at once. It was all of a piece.

"There's so much input—that's what's given birth to the non-linear thing," Lynch was saying. He hesitated, threw in a little laugh. "But I don't know for sure."

6.

Open Worlds

In 1993, not long after Interfilm tried to give moviegoers a say in the plot, gamers got a title that represented another approach to branching narrative. This game was called *Myst*. It was created by Rand and Robyn Miller, family men who had set up shop on the barren outskirts of Spokane, Washington, where their father, an itinerant preacher, had finally settled down. A few years earlier, the two brothers—one a computer programmer, the other still in college—had had modest success with a video game for kids. But *Myst* was not going to be a modest success. To the brothers' surprise, and just about everyone else's, it became the best-selling computer game of the decade.

Myst wasn't an action game. It wasn't a shooter. It was barely even a video game; it was almost static, an interactive slide show with highly stylized imagery and an atmospheric sound track. Through word and image it conjured up a dreamy, almost magical world for the player to explore. Much of what you did had to do with mazes and puzzles, but more than most games at the time, it also involved a story. People found it immersive.

In its original incarnation, *Myst* was created using HyperCard, an Apple program that was one of the first implementations of hypertext. Built by Bill Atkinson, a legendary programmer on Steve Jobs's handpicked Macintosh crew, HyperCard was released in 1987, well before Tim Berners-Lee applied the idea of hypertext to the Internet to create the World Wide Web. The game was constructed, as the Web would be, of individual documents linked by hypertext commands.

In this case, the documents were computer-generated visuals—some 2,500 of them, one for each view the player might see, all gorgeously rendered and accompanied by ambient sound—along with a handful of video clips to move the story along. Your goal as the player was to explore the island and solve the story of its mysterious past. To do this you would have to travel through a series of "ages," each of which required you to solve various puzzles in order to progress to the next. At the end you would be presented with several choices that would determine the outcome.

In a way, the game in its entirety resembled the mysterious Chinese novel in "The Garden of Forking Paths": it contained every eventuality you might encounter. Unlike the novel Borges described in his short story, of course, it didn't try to present them all at once. And while hardly a literary experience, it did win praise for its sophistication; the online edition of the *Atlantic Monthly* even said its emotional impact was "at times reminiscent" of such writers as Jules Verne, Edgar Allan Poe, and Franz Kafka. *Wired* was a bit closer to the mark when it said the game suggested a new art form in the offing, "a kind of puzzle box inside a novel inside a painting, only with music. Or something."

But for all its plaudits and its popularity, *Myst* turned out to be more a dead end than a harbinger of things to come. Its runaway success seemed to signal the arrival of a new kind of adventure game, more contemplative than what had been the norm. Instead, when its popularity faded, adventure games faded with it, forsaken for sports titles and first-person shooters such as *Halo*. Adventure games died off because they were expensive to build—and the reason they were expensive to build was that every possibility had to be scripted in advance.

Myst also seemed at first to herald the ascendance of interactive CD-ROMs, then a nascent format for computer discs. But after the 1994 debut of Netscape Navigator, the first widely adopted Web browser, and the wildly successful initial public offering that followed, it became apparent that the Web would provide a far more flexible environment for publishing than CD-ROMs could.

ROM stands for "read-only memory," and that's what CD-ROMs provided: preprogrammed CDs that could be read, but not written to. What interactivity they offered was limited to paths that had been set by the authors. In games like *Myst*, this kind of branching story line seemed innovative at a time when many popular titles gave you just one path to pursue, but after a while it, too, began to feel dated. In electronic publishing, where Microsoft launched a major CD-ROM effort with reference works like the Encarta encyclopedia, the format aged even more quickly.

With the demise of CD-ROMs and the rise of the Web, the limited form of hypertext that *Myst* embodied became dated as well. Within a few years, as more and more people began to access the Web through always-on broadband, hyperlinks would enable an entirely different level of involvement—one nobody had anticipated, not even the technological adepts of the Bay Area. Kevin Kelly captured the change:

> When I examine issues of *Wired* from before the Netscape IPO (issues that I proudly edited), I am surprised to see them touting a future of high production-value content—5,000 always-on channels and virtual reality, with a side order of email sprinkled with bits of the Library of Congress. In fact, *Wired* offered a vision nearly identical to that of Internet wannabes in the broadcast, publishing, software, and movie industries: basically, TV that worked. The question was who would program the box. *Wired* looked forward to a constellation of new media upstarts like Nintendo and Yahoo!, not old-media dinosaurs like ABC. . . .
>
> What we all failed to see was how much of this new world would be manufactured by users, not corporate interests. . . . Anyone could rustle up a link—which, it turns out, is the most powerful invention of the decade. Linking unleashes involvement and interactivity at levels once thought unfashionable or impossible. It transforms reading into navigating and enlarges small actions into powerful forces.

Online, the simple act of linking would help foment a culture of participation that manifests itself in blogs, YouTube, Wikipedia, and the whole host of user-generated media known as Web 2.0. "The hyperlink is one of the greatest inventions of mankind," Kelly reiterated when I saw him at his home in the oceanside village of Pacifica, just south of San Francisco. "But it's not recognized for what it is. Something as simple as making a hyperlink, when it's done 24 hours a day by billions of people, creates a structure of information that's not directed by anyone but"—as amplified by tools such as Google—"is shaping our society."

Rand and Robyn Miller never came up with a satisfying follow-up to *Myst*, but the game's popularity endured for years, long after the rise of the Web. It remained the world's best-selling computer game until 2002, when it was overtaken by *The Sims*. Here was an entirely different type of game—one that gave you a set of tools, laid down a few basic rules, and left you to your own devices. Instead of playing by someone else's script, you got to write your own.

As the name implies, *The Sims* is essentially a computer simulation. Like hypertext, simulations emerged as a way of dealing with too much information. The concept far predates the computer. But as with fiction, the word long had a connotation of falsehood. In 1625, Francis Bacon defined it as "when a man industriously and expressly feigns and pretends to be that he is not." Now simulations are a tool for problem solving. They're an outgrowth of cybernetics—the study of self-governing systems, be they living organisms, social structures, or mechanical constructs.

The basic principles were laid out by Norbert Wiener, mathematician and longtime colleague of Vannevar Bush at MIT, in his 1948 book *Cybernetics*. Though its success seemed limited at the time, *Cybernetics* ushered in an era of systems thinking—of viewing the world in terms of how the parts interact to form the whole. And where there are systems, there are simulations. Much as hypertext weaves a path of associative trails through a labyrinth of information, simulations of complex systems lead us through multiple variables of cause and effect. They can be used to model the behavior of everything from hurricanes to contaminants in the Earth's atmosphere to computer-generated proto-people in *The Sims*. They are tools to help us think.

In games, the rise of *The Sims* signaled a move away from pre-programmed scenarios like *Myst*'s toward more or less user-generated narratives that would themselves be shared online, linked to and commented on by hundreds if not thousands of other users. These virtual play spaces became known as "open worlds."

ALMOST THE ONLY ASPECT OF *MYST* that would live on, in fact, was its focus on narrative. But narrative and games are a tricky combination. Nearly 40 years after *Pong* launched the video game industry, people are still arguing not only about how to tell a story through games but whether it can be done at all. Stories carry not just information but emotion, and a lot of people maintain that games will never have the emotional impact of television or cinema. But that hasn't stopped game designers from trying.

When *Pong* came along, the technology was too primitive to even attempt a story: the game was just blips on a screen, set up so people would visualize it as an electronic Ping-Pong match. *Pac-Man*, the iconic video game of the eighties, was only slightly more advanced. All you had to do was gobble the dots in a maze and stay one step ahead of the things that would gobble you. Really basic, really fun. But during the eighties and nineties, as games moved from commercial arcades to home computers and to consoles like the Sony PlayStation and the Nintendo 64, they began to sprout stories.

"The days of *Pac-Man* are gone," says Phil Spencer of Microsoft. As head of Microsoft Game Studios, Spencer is in charge of developing games for the Xbox consoles. In the past, he says, "the mentality was about building a hit—trying to create a shiny object consumers would follow. It was a bunch of guys building games for guys and focusing on the tech. You ended up with something like *Doom*—a story anybody would laugh at."

Introduced in 1993, *Doom* was a wildly popular game that gave you an excuse to gleefully shoot vast hordes of the undead. "Meanwhile, companies like Nintendo were focusing on character—Mario and Zelda." That would be Shigeru Miyamoto's mustachioed little Italian American plumber—the central figure in the best-selling game franchise in history—and the princess Miyamoto created for another best-selling series, *The Legend of Zelda*. "Characters were becoming something companies would place great value in, because they knew people would follow. It was a precursor to the story arc."

The shiny-object fixation Spencer describes was true of most of the video games of the nineties. But with the arrival of Sony's PlayStation 2 in 2000 and Microsoft's Xbox in 2001, game consoles reached a level of sophistication that not only made narrative plausible but, in Spencer's view at least, almost demanded it. "As the technology has evolved, we have the opportunity to make the player the hero. That's something movies and television can't do. But it begs the question, What is the player doing to attain that status? The way to do that is through story. You build a narrative arc and let the player play through it."

Economic forces are driving the trend toward narrative as well. As consoles have become more powerful and more complex, the cost of creating a best-selling title has risen exponentially. No longer can a couple of programmers conjure up a game in just a few months; now a major title takes scores if not hundreds of people working full-time for as long as three years. That kind of effort requires Hollywood-level budgets, inevitably leading to a Hollywood-style fixation on sequels. You need something to keep them coming back, and you also need a way to reuse all those expensively rendered digital assets—creatures and backdrops and whatnot. As Spencer puts it, "You want to amortize the cost of development." That's why, in order to be approved, a prospective title for Microsoft must have a narrative arc that will carry it through multiple games.

THIS IS HOW MICROSOFT APPROACHED *Gears of War,* an Xbox 360 exclusive from Epic Games, a highly successful developer based in an office park on the outskirts of Raleigh, North Carolina. The *Gears* franchise—the first two installments came in 2006 and 2008, and *Gears 3* is due out in April 2011—has become the second-biggest seller for Microsoft after *Halo,* the shooter whose must-have status among hard-core gamers established the software giant as a viable competitor of Sony in the gaming arena.

To the uninitiated, *Gears of War* might not seem to have a lot more going for it storywise than *Doom*. It's a third-person shooter (you look over the shoulder of the character you're playing) rather than a first-person shooter, but otherwise the basic story dynamic is pretty much the same: *Die, suckers, die!* This time you're facing the Locust Horde, a nasty assemblage of beasts and humanoids that lurked underground until they suddenly surfaced and set about annihilating the humans. You the player are Marcus Fenix, a hard-core fighter rescued from an abandoned prison by your buddy Dominic Santiago. As the leader of Delta Squad, a four-man team fighting for the survival of the few remaining humans, your mission—the way you earn your hero status—is to plant an underground bomb that will wipe out the Locust Horde.

The game isn't easy, but it's exciting in a testosterone-fever sort of way—especially if you can get your hands on the assault rifle with the chainsaw bayonet, a nifty innovation that lets you chew up the enemy in close combat, spewing gore all the way.

If that's all there were to it, *Gears of War* would be a none-too-memorable genre title instead of a game that sold nearly 6 million copies in the two years before the release of its sequel—which in turn sold more than 2 million copies in 20 countries the weekend it came out. But neither *Gears of War* nor *Gears of War 2* is just a shooter. Running out with guns blazing is a sure way to get cut down; these are games that reward stealth, cunning, and tactical thinking. Their look is not merely a dark vista of a ruined planet; it's vivid with detail, in the way a fictional world has to be to feel convincing. And the story, while undeniably thin, nonetheless has its moments of subtlety and grace.

"*Gears of War* will never be remembered as a great work of fiction, and we're okay with that," says Cliff Bleszinski, design director at Epic. Better known as CliffyB, Bleszinski is a rock star in the gaming world, a guy who drives a red Lamborghini and once stuck a "Cliffycam" on his blog so fans could watch him work. "The story is pretty straightforward, but there are characters people love and remember"—chief among them Marcus and Dom. These two are as tough and hard as they come, but there's an undercurrent of vulnerability that seeps out at certain moments—as in the excruciating scene in *Gears 2* when Dom finally finds his long-lost wife, Maria, only to realize she's been terminally damaged by torture.

"I find that a lot of the narrative in video games exists just as a cool excuse for fun things to happen to the player," Bleszinski says. "The thing about narrative is that if you can get someone to wonder what happens next, that's very, very powerful. With

BioShock"—a game from a rival developer that transpires in an underwater metropolis that has collapsed into chaos—"I wanted to beat it because I wanted to see what would happen. But it's not just story. Often it's the premise—the setup, the context of your actions, the way it makes you feel you're in the world."

In a lengthy profile in *The New Yorker*, Tom Bissell described Bleszinski and his peers as having "established the principles of a grammar of fun." That's certainly their goal, but Bleszinski's own assessment is more modest, and probably more accurate. "My two loves have been video games and films," he says. "But movies have had 75 years to teach audiences what to feel. We're still continuing to master our craft."

However convincingly they're rendered, in-game narratives introduce a familiar tension between author and audience. As with any participatory narrative, the issue is control. The designer creates the game, but the player holds the controller—so who's telling the story?

One way of settling the issue is to disable the controller. That's what happens during cut scenes, the video interludes that run from time to time between bouts of gameplay. Players are expected to sit still and watch while the plot is advanced. Sometimes, as in the *King Kong* game, the cut scenes feature major stars like Jack Black, but as a rule the acting is woefully amateurish. Yet the main thing gamers have against these interludes is the enforced passivity: deactivate the controller for too long and their fingers start to twitch.

The master of the cut scene is Hideo Kojima, designer of the *Metal Gear* franchise, a series of games that together have sold more than 20 million copies across the planet. Building on an earlier pair of games that Kojima created for the Japanese market in the late 1980s, they spin a tale of military delirium that spans some 50 years.

In the first installment, *Metal Gear Solid*, a genetically engineered supersoldier who goes by the code name Solid Snake (Soriddo Sunēku in Japanese) is called out of retirement after a rogue US Army unit led by his twin brother, Liquid Snake (Rikiddo Sunēku), seizes a nuclear weapons facility on a remote Alaskan island. Armed with an enormous mecha called Metal Gear REX, a walking tank capable of launching a nuclear attack on any part of the planet, Liquid threatens to annihilate the White House if he isn't given the body of their father, a legendary military commander known as Big Boss (Biggu Bosu), whose genes he wants so he can transform himself and his men into ultimate fighting machines. Solid Snake's mission: infiltrate the island, free the hostages his brother has taken, and eliminate the rebel threat. By the end of the game, multiple acts of betrayal, manipulation, torture, conspiracy, and heroism have left Liquid Snake dead and Solid Snake heading off into the wilderness. Subsequent installments are even more convoluted, to the point that Kojima himself has said he has trouble keeping the story straight.

An acknowledged film fanatic, Kojima is known for his cinematic cut scenes, which in *Metal Gear Solid 4* take the action away from the player for periods approaching a half hour at a time—a total of more than eight hours. Though some gamers detest this, Kojima enjoys in the game world an auteur status to rival Godard's in cinema. I spoke with him at the 2009 Game Developers Conference in San Francisco's Moscone Center, shortly after he was presented with a lifetime achievement award in recognition of his work at Konami Corporation, the Tokyo slot machine manufacturer and video game developer where he has spent his entire career.

It was a rare public appearance. A slightly built figure in a gray shirt and black leather sport jacket, Kojima had spiky black hair falling manga-style across his eyes. Despite the hip exterior, his manner was a little stiff, with a Japanese reserve that contrasted markedly with Cliff Bleszinski's made-in-America enthusiasm. "I don't plan to retire just yet," he assured the audience in somewhat halting English. Then he ticked off the things he had yet to achieve: directing a film, writing a novel—but "most of all," he added, creating more games.

Yet for all the intricate plotting and elaborate story lines of his *Metal Gear Solid* titles, even Kojima admits there's an inherent contradiction between narrative and games. "I believe that even today we can tell only a simple story without really interfering with gameplay," he said through an interpreter as we sat at a table backstage. "But in the future I think it will almost be a requirement of all storytellers when they create games, how they can tell a more complex story without conflicting with the gameplay."

Kojima is ruefully aware of the controversy his use of cut scenes has caused among gamers; at mere mention of it, he threw his head back and laughed out loud. Still, those sequences are there for a reason—because he wants to engage the player not just in a sensory experience but in an emotional one. "It's quite a challenge for me, because making a story line so emotional that people can really get into it involves first the camera," he acknowledged. "But when I take control of the camera, that sometimes distracts the players. So I'm really conflicted about what to do about it. I'm still working on this part.

"I think in the future it's not about cut scenes in terms of playing to the emotions," he went on. "It's more about the players feeling their emotions, and then the camera switching automatically when they're scared or they're afraid or something. So I'm not thinking about making more cut scenes and trying to force people to be emotional. I believe the game should really feel what the players are feeling and change according to that." With the arrival of game systems like Microsoft's Kinect, which uses a camera mounted on the screen to "read" players' moves and interpret their facial expressions, such a game no longer seems outside the realm of possibility. Actually building one, however, is another matter.

There's another way to resolve the narrative tension between game designer and player: let the player tell the story. The triumph of this approach was signaled in 2002, when *The Sims* overtook *Myst* in popularity. Instead of the strictly linear progression of many earlier games, or the labyrinth of branching story lines of games like *Myst*, *The Sims* lets you explore an open world of myriad and unpredictable possibilities. As a player you create your own characters, proto-people who live in a world that's governed, as ours is, by certain basic rules. Out of the interaction of your choices and these rules a narrative emerges—a narrative largely of your own devising.

The Sims is hardly the only game to offer some kind of emergent storytelling. One of the most influential examples is the *Grand Theft Auto* series, which has sold some 90 million copies worldwide. Produced at a studio in Edinburgh called Rockstar North, these games can be played in a linear fashion, with cut scenes and scripted missions. As a low-level bank robber trying to impress the crime syndicate in *Grand Theft Auto III*, for example, you might be sent to off a rat at a sex club, or to rescue some guy from the Colombian cartel. When you've completed these tasks, you get money and maybe you advance in the game. But *GTA III* and the games that follow it also allow for an entirely different kind of gameplay. On your arrival in Liberty City, the game's simulacrum of New York, you might choose to knock down a little old lady, hijack a car, and take off with the police in hot pursuit. It's all up to you.

"*Grand Theft Auto III* was brilliant," said Will Wright, creator of *The Sims*, when I spoke with him in his sparsely furnished offices on a low-rise industrial street in Berkeley. "The graphics weren't that great, the physics in the game weren't that great, but the systems interacted in interesting ways. If I hit something with my car, I could flip the car over and crash. If I drove into a crowd, people would scatter out of the way and call the cops on me. And the emergent interactions between these low-level models of physics and behavior and environment and weather led to a sense of place.

"I've never felt like I was actually Mario stepping on mushrooms," he continued, referring to the exploits of Nintendo's roly-poly plumber in the Mushroom Kingdom. "I have felt like I was driving a car through the city in *Grand Theft Auto*. You really get the sense of a living, breathing city. And then you have the freedom to say, Ooh, I'm gonna go rob somebody or pick up a hooker or change my outfit or steal a car. There's a limited set of things you can do, but they naturally fall together in terms of me telling my gangster story, doing things I would never do in real life but that are kind of fun to do in this little toy city."

An earnest-looking 49-year-old with longish brown hair and a careful, deliberate manner, Wright hardly seemed the type to be picking up hookers and stealing cars, even in a video game. No great surprise that with its gleeful violence, in-your-face attitude, and occasional errant sex scene, *Grand Theft Auto* has provided an irresistible target for moralists everywhere. As a US senator from New York, Hillary Clinton accused it of "stealing the innocence of our children." Like many others, she failed to recognize it for what it is: a wicked parody of life in America as imagined by a bunch of mildly disaffected young Brits. Admittedly, *The Sims* is a much nicer environment. You could take your parents there. You could even replicate your parents there, if you had a mind to. But both series essentially serve the same function: they act as a setting for narratives that players create.

"When people tell me stories from their gaming experiences, they don't describe the cut scenes," Wright pointed out. "They have no emotional investment in those, because they didn't create them. The stories they get really passionate about are the ones about things they did that nobody else did. Like, Oh, I found this cool exploit in *Grand Theft Auto*!"

Go to YouTube and you'll find more than 800,000 videos tagged *GTA*. A large percentage of them are stories from players—screen captures uploaded by people eager to document their exploits. In a clip called "*GTA IV* Cool Death Gameplay," a 23-year-old Canadian documents what happened when he hijacked a police car on a bridge, with Liberty City PD helicopters in hot pursuit: his car caught fire and spun out of control, flinging him out the door and into the river below. (So much for the stereotype of the mild-mannered Canadian.) In "*GTA IV* - Prank Call Police Chase," another player calls for help, shoots the responding peace officers, seizes their vehicle, and lays waste to countless police cars and any number of shrieking pedestrians as he leads the cops on an epic chase—at the end of which he runs away from the wreckage and hails a cab to go bowling with his cousin. "Just another day in *GTA* life," one viewer commented cheerily.

BECAUSE THEY ARE SIMULATIONS, the stories that emerge from games like *Grand Theft Auto* are unpredictable, even to their authors. As the guy who posted "*GTA IV* Cool Death Gameplay" observed in his comments on YouTube, "For all you idiots that think this was planned . . . your [*sic*] wrong." It couldn't have been planned, because in its open-world mode, *GTA IV* is a program that predicts the interaction of careening automobiles, squishy humans, helicopter gunfire, and any number of other factors to chart what would happen if you hijacked a police car and took off down a bridge. You do what you want, and the game tells you what happens next—just as life does when you cross the street without looking, but with less dire consequences.

Stories that come out of *The Sims* tend to be a little more thoughtful than those from *Grand Theft Auto*, but they're hardly dull. "I spend a lot of time scanning the *Sims* community," said Wright, "and I've seen amazing stories that people have told because they played *The Sims* in a particular way." He mentioned Alice and Kev, two characters created by Robin Burkinshaw, a student of game design at Anglia Ruskin University in England, using *The Sims* 3, an update released in June 2009. Alice, a student, and Kev, her father, are homeless. Burkinshaw began by taking away all their money, leaving them destitute in an empty park. Then he started a blog to document how they would cope.

Homeless people often have more than their share of handicaps, and so it was with Kev; Burkinshaw made him angry, mean-spirited, and insane. Alice was sweet but unlucky and suffered, not surprisingly, from low self-esteem. What happened after that was determined largely by the game. When Burkinshaw sent Kev to look for romance in the park, he turned up without any clothes. Alice grew increasingly depressed and angry until finally she told her father off—much to his surprise, and Burkinshaw's. In the blog's comments section, readers cheered her on. "I find myself getting a little more emotionally involved after every post," one confessed. "Whoa," wrote another. "The Sims are making a story themselves. It's like you don't have to write anything."

Wright is not averse to traditional storytelling. "I love movies," he said. "There is something about having a professional storyteller with a unique vision telling you a well-crafted story. But I've never wanted to tell a story in a game. I've always wanted to support the user's story, because I think that's the value of games—that the user is telling the story. You might have some domain in which that story occurs, like in a fantasy environment with orcs, or in World War II during the Battle of the Bulge. But within that box, you really want to give the user maximum freedom. I think of traditional linear storytelling as a roller coaster and games as a dirt bike."

WRIGHT'S OWN STORY IS very much of the dirt bike variety. Raised in Atlanta and then, after the death of his father, in Baton Rouge, he decided early on he wanted to be an astronaut in order to pioneer space colonies that could relieve overcrowding on Earth. After attending three colleges—Louisiana State, Louisiana Tech, and the New School in New York—without getting a degree, he moved in with and eventually married his roommate's older sister, an artist and social activist in Oakland. Along the way he designed a video game, a shooter called *Raid on Bungeling Bay* that could be played on the Commodore 64 personal computer.

A year later, in 1985, a version was released for the Nintendo Entertainment System, a game console that was already big in Japan and had just been introduced in the rest of the world. Founded in Kyoto in 1889 to make hand-painted mulberry-bark playing cards, Nintendo had tried and failed to expand into the taxicab business, the love hotel business, and the instant-food business before venturing into the nascent video game industry in 1974. Along with the game console, Nintendo came out with *Super Mario Bros.*, the second in Shigeru Miyamoto's *Mario* series, which Wright was soon hooked on.

On the face of it, *Super Mario Bros.* hardly seemed serious: the whole point was to get Mario to save Princess Peach of the Mushroom Kingdom from Bowser, the hideous turtle monster. But what struck Wright about it, and about successors like *Super Mario World* (1990), was that they were all about emergence: from a few simple rules, a complex system arose. It was a concept he would put to good use in his next game, *SimCity*.

SimCity is a game that simulates urban life. It was inspired partly by "The Seventh Sally," a story from Stanislaw Lem's collection *The Cyberiad*. The story concerns Trurl, a godlike robot who finds a despot adrift on an asteroid and builds a tiny kingdom for him to rule. When his fellow robot Klapaucius asks in astonishment how he could have done such a thing, Trurl gets defensive:

> "You must be joking!" Trurl exclaimed. "Really, the whole kingdom fits into a box three feet by two by two and a half . . . it's only a model . . ."
>
> "A model of what?"

"What do you mean, of what? Of a civilization, obviously, except that it's a hundred million times smaller."

"And how do you know there aren't civilizations a hundred million times larger than our own? And if there were, would ours then be a model?"

Before building the modeling software that's at the heart of the game, Wright immersed himself in the work of two prominent academics. One was MIT's Jay Wright Forrester, a pioneer in a branch of cybernetics known as system dynamics, who argued that Earth could be managed more rationally by a computer simulation than by humans. The other was John Horton Conway, a Princeton mathematician who had built a simulation game that demonstrates how complex life-forms can emerge from combinations of simple cells. In his latest book, *The Grand Design*, Stephen Hawking and his coauthor, Leonard Mlodinow, use Conway's game to disprove the need for a divine creator. Wright applied the concepts of computer simulation and emergent properties to an urban environment and came up with a game that essentially put you in the role of a municipal despot.

People playing *SimCity* had several choices. If they liked, they could try to cope with real or imaginary scenarios in existing cities—the San Francisco earthquake in 1906, a Godzilla-like attack on Tokyo in 1961. Or they could create their own cities and see what would happen if they raised taxes, changed the zoning, or did other things that city governments do. But Brøderbund, the software company that had brought out Wright's shooter, failed to understand this one because it didn't follow a key rule of the game industry: there was no way to win it. So Wright and a partner started their own company, Maxis Software, and in 1989 they brought out *SimCity* themselves. Sales were slow at first, but they built steadily as the game started winning awards.

Meanwhile, Wright was spending a lot of time at home caring for his young daughter. Before long, he found his interest moving from urban systems to human needs. He read "A Theory of Human Motivation," the 1943 paper in which Abraham Maslow laid out his hierarchy of needs, which range from basic life functions (food, water, sleep, and so on) to the higher-level goals he called "self-actualization." He consulted books on patterns of architecture and theories of the mind. Melding all this into a model of human happiness, he began to develop *The Sims*.

With *The Sims*, history repeated itself. Maxis, trying to capitalize on the success of *SimCity*, was churning out spin-offs: *SimTown*, *SimFarm*, *SimIsle*, *SimEarth*, *SimLife*—some of them designed by Wright, some by other people. The company went public in 1995, putting it under pressure to generate more hits—a task that proved increasingly difficult. With sales sliding and losses piling up, the board dismissed Wright's idea as nothing more than an interactive dollhouse. It was not a smart decision.

Two years later, Electronic Arts bought the company for $125 million, netting Wright $17 million in EA stock and giving him an enthusiastic backer. When *The Sims* came out in 2000, it was an instant hit. EA has now sold more than 125 million copies of *The Sims* and its successor games in 60 countries and 22 languages. Among other things, this means that Wright can pretty much do what he wants.

IN 2009, WRIGHT DECIDED HE WANTED to leave EA and launch, with its backing, a new venture he calls Stupid Fun Club. The idea is to incubate new entertainment ventures—

games, stories, what have you. In Wright's mind, the two are almost interchangeable anyway.

"Think of *Star Wars*," he said. "You've got lightsabers and the Death Star and the Force and all this stuff that leads to a wide variety of play experiences. I can go have lightsaber battles with my friend. I can play a game about blowing up the Death Star. I can have a unique experience and come back and tell you a story about what happened. The best stories lead to the widest variety of play, and the best play leads to the most story. I think they're two sides of the same coin."

As we spoke, Wright and I were sitting at a metal-and-glass conference table in a second-floor atrium at Stupid Fun Club world headquarters in Berkeley. Wright shares a stripped-down little business complex—part eighties, part Bauhaus—with a furniture manufacturer and a high tech machine shop. Except for the table, the room was almost empty. High ceilings and concrete floors gave it an echo. Large, plate-glass windows looked out onto the small parking area below. It was a Thursday morning, but no one else was around.

"For me, the deeper aspect is model building," Wright continued. "We're always building models of the world around us to help us predict what's going to happen, and play is one of the primary ways in which we build these models. I think storytelling lives alongside play as another mechanism for building models."

What Wright was saying is that stories are as much a simulation as games are. This is not a new idea; it's implicit, for example, in Robert Louis Stevenson's response to Henry James in 1884. But it is a powerful one. Steven Pinker once described fiction as "a kind of thought experiment" in which characters "play out plausible interactions in a . . . virtual world, and an audience can take mental notes of the results." While perhaps not the most poetic assessment of literature ever penned, this view does seem to be borne out by recent experiments in neuroscience.

In a paper published in 2009, for example, four researchers at Washington University in St. Louis conducted functional MRI scans of 28 people as they were reading a series of stories. The narratives were all taken from *One Boy's Day*, a 1951 book about the life of a seven-year-old schoolkid named Raymond. The experiment demonstrated a close correlation between the actions described in a story and the parts of the brain that process those actions when a person actually performs them.

Functional magnetic resonance imaging works by showing blood flow within the brain. It can't show what a person is thinking, but it can show which parts of the brain are being activated. When Raymond picked up his workbook, blood flowed to the parts of the readers' brains that are associated with grasping motions. When he walked over to his teacher's desk, the frontal cortex and hippocampus lit up—the areas of the brain that deal with location in space. When Raymond shook his head no, the part of the brain that deals with goal-directed activity was activated. This suggests, the authors wrote, "that readers understand a story by simulating the events in the story world and updating their simulation when features of that world change."

"You've only got a limited bubble of experience in your entire life," Wright continued, "and you're going to perform better if you can build from a larger set of experiences than you could have personally. As a caveman, you know, your fellow caveman left the cave and a tiger almost ate him. So he comes back and tells you the story—This tiger almost ate me! And the next time you leave the cave, you'll look around and make sure there's not a tiger there."

With *Star Wars*, a story provides a framework for play. With *The Sims*, play gives rise to stories. Stories become games; games become stories. "So we have these toy experiences, which we call play," Wright went on. "And through storytelling, we share experiences others have had. That's why for me, play and storytelling go hand in hand as the first educational technologies that evolution tripped over."

7. The Hive Mind and the Mystery Box

ON SEPTEMBER 22, 2004, NEARLY 19 MILLION PEOPLE across the United States stopped what they were doing to watch an hour-long simulation of a plane crash. It wasn't billed that way, of course—it was billed as the premiere of a dramatic new series about a group of passengers who survive a midair breakup and find themselves on a mysterious tropical island. Fortunately for ABC, then the least-watched broadcast network in the country, the billing worked. But it was much more than just the ratings that made *Lost* important. *Lost* was television for the hive mind.

The show opened with an extreme close-up of a very dazed man in a suit. We see Jack Shephard, tie askew, body battered, coming to in a bamboo grove on some kind of tropical island. He turns out to be a survivor from Oceanic Flight 815, bound from Sydney to Los Angeles with 324 passengers on board, which broke up and crashed into an uncharted island. Stumbling to the beach where the plane's smoldering midsection has fallen,

Jack finds other survivors. Some are critical; others are just in a daze. One gets sucked into a still-roaring jet engine, showering the beach with sparks and shrapnel. Hoping to find a radio, Jack plunges into the jungle to search for the forward chunk of fuselage. He reaches the cockpit to discover everyone dead except the captain, who regains consciousness just long enough to be hurled into the sky by a shrieking, unseen force.

Clearly this is no ordinary island. But what is it, exactly? That would be up to the viewers to figure out.

"*Lost* creates the illusion of interactivity," Damon Lindelof said one afternoon. Lindelof, who created the show in partnership with the movie and television producer J. J. Abrams, is a short figure with what appears to be a three-day growth of hair and a look of barely contained enthusiasm. Other shows, Lindelof was saying, go to great lengths to avoid unanswered questions. "This show is ambiguous. We don't say what it means."

Lost debuted the month after 42 Entertainment launched *I Love Bees*, the alternate reality game that Microsoft had commissioned as a promotion for *Halo 2*. There was nothing overtly similar about the two; one was a prime-time network television series that was long on mystery and suspense, the other an Internet-enabled scavenger hunt to promote a new video game. But it wasn't long before *Lost*, too, became an Internet phenomenon, because people who started watching it needed some way to figure out what was going on—and what better way than the Net? Abrams and Lindelof didn't exactly plan this, any more than George Lucas had planned for *Star Wars* to generate a near-infinite number of other narratives. But in telling their story in nonlinear fragments and leaving it to the audience to piece them together, they created, in essence, a kind of participatory fiction.

"The show became an excuse to develop a community," said

Carlton Cuse, Lindelof's partner. The two of them were sitting side by side on a sofa in Cuse's office in the *Lost* bungalow—a one-story brick structure on the Disney lot in Burbank, designed like most of its neighbors in a faux-moderne style to complement the studio's 1939 Animation Building. "And the basis of it was that people were able to debate open-ended questions—questions that we insisted be open-ended, and that would get fans engaged in the show."

The number sequence 4 8 15 16 23 42, for example. "The Numbers," as they came to be known, were first featured late in the show's debut season, when another survivor, the very large Hurley, discovers them in the notes of a shipwrecked Frenchwoman who had been marooned on the island for years. Hurley, who suffers from an eating disorder and occasional bouts of mental instability, looks very perturbed when he sees the Numbers. In a series of flashbacks, we see why.

First he's watching TV when the winning Mega Lotto numbers are called out: 4, 8, 15, 16, 23, and the meganumber—42. On realizing he's won, Hurley faints and smashes through the coffee table. Later, at a press conference outside the house, he announces that he's going to send his grandfather on a cruise; within moments, grandpa collapses and dies of a heart attack. He drives up in a brand-new Hummer to show his mother her new mansion, but she trips on the curb and breaks her ankle. He looks up to see the house on fire. Before he can call for help, the police pull up, guns drawn, and arrest him for dealing drugs.

Another flashback shows him visiting a man named Leonard in a mental hospital. "What do the Numbers mean?" Hurley asks, but Leonard just keeps muttering them, over and over—until Hurley says he used them to win the Lotto. That sends Leonard around the bend. "You've opened the box!" he screams.

"You shouldn't have used those numbers! It doesn't stop! *You've got to get away from those numbers!*" As he's being dragged away by the attendants, Leonard blurts out how he got them—from a man in Australia who used them, Hurley later finds out, to win a contest at a local fair. The man survived a head-on collision on the way home from the fair. Later he blew his head off with a shotgun.

Back on the island, Hurley asks the Frenchwoman what the Numbers mean. She doesn't know. She was on a ship that picked up a radio transmission of a voice repeating those numbers; when the ship changed course to investigate, it ran aground, and since then she has lost everything and everyone that mattered to her. At the end of the episode, on another part of the island, the camera slowly zooms in on the hatch of a compartment the crash survivors found buried in the earth several episodes before. The steel hatch, viewers were beginning to realize, was the portal to an even bigger mystery. Or maybe the same mystery—for as the camera pulls in closer, you can make out a sequence of numbers etched into the rim: 4 8 15 16 23 42.

LIKE MOST GROUNDBREAKING TELEVISION, *Lost* almost didn't get made. The show was conceived in the summer of 2003 at an ABC management retreat at the Grand Californian Hotel in Disneyland. The network had been in decline for years, even before its 1996 purchase by Disney. Prime time was dominated by shows from its rivals—*Survivor, CSI, Law & Order, ER*. Everyone at the retreat, from Disney COO (and former network chief) Robert Iger on down, was expected to pitch an idea. Lloyd Braun, then the head of ABC Entertainment, laid out a series based on the *Robinson Crusoe* saga. He described it as a cross between *Survivor*, the Swedish import that had helped start the reality TV trend, and *Cast Away*, a recent Bob Zemeckis movie starring Tom Hanks as a FedEx systems analyst whose plane goes down on a Pacific island. He called it "Lost."

Along with maybe three dozen other ideas from the meeting, Braun's was sent out to Hollywood agents and producers to see who might be interested in developing it. Aaron Spelling, who had produced a long string of network hits ranging from *Beverly Hills, 90210* to *Dynasty*, had had a similar idea, so the project went to him. Spelling assigned it to a writer who saw it as a realistic, *Lord of the Flies*–style social drama. When Braun saw the pilot script, he hated it. So he took the idea to J. J. Abrams, who at the time was best known as the creator of ABC's *Alias*, a cult hit that was part science fiction, part CIA thriller.

Abrams wasn't really interested, but he grudgingly agreed to think about it. Then the network paired him with Lindelof, a promising young writer whose biggest credit to date was the NBC crime drama *Crossing Jordan*. The two clicked. They came back with an audacious concept: Make the island supernatural—a place where strange, unexplained things happen. And play with time by introducing lots of flashbacks that could get the characters off the island and show them back in the real world.

Braun loved the idea. His bosses at Disney did not. Years earlier, as a young ABC executive, Robert Iger had championed David Lynch's *Twin Peaks*, another surreal mystery series, only to see its ratings nose-dive once the mystery was revealed. Never an Abrams fan, despite the modest success of *Alias*, Iger found this project uncomfortably reminiscent of Lynch's. Michael Eisner, Disney's CEO, was even more underwhelmed. But they had given Braun the authority to greenlight pilots, and this was the pilot he wanted.

By now it was February 2004, too late in the normal network development process for Abrams and Lindelof to write a script—so Braun greenlit the project without one. No matter that they would have to stage a plane crash and shoot on location in Hawaii at a cost of $12 million, making the *Lost* pilot among the priciest two hours of television ever made. No matter that Abrams and Lindelof had less than three months to write, cast, crew, shoot, and cut it. No matter that Iger called it "a waste of time," or that Eisner gave it a 2 on a scale of 10. Braun pushed ahead. "If we're pregnant enough," he said, "they won't shut us down."

Braun had been shown the door by the time the show premiered in September. Abrams had moved on to direct *Mission: Impossible III*, his first feature film. Lindelof, left alone in charge of 71 plane crash survivors on a bizarre Pacific island, was on the verge of quitting too, until they brought in Cuse. Fourteen years his senior, Cuse had given Lindelof his first writing gig, on the Don Johnson cop drama *Nash Bridges*. That was in 1999. Now the two had to finish the story that Abrams and Lindelof had begun.

There was a risk that they wouldn't *have* a story—that the series would dissolve into incoherence because not even the producers knew what was supposed to happen. They had a basic story arc but little else. A small cadre of writers had been scrambling to hone a narrative, develop backstories for the characters, and figure out what would happen after the pilot episode. "J. J. likes to deal with big ideas," says Javier Grillo-Marxuach, who was a member of the writing team. "But there's ideas and then there's execution. The job of the writers was to turn those big ideas into 22 hours of television."

One of Abrams's biggest and most problematic ideas was the hatch—the steel door with the Numbers engraved on its side.

The hatch was a rabbit hole into who knew what. Abrams had wanted to introduce it from the start—no great surprise to those who knew him, since it was essentially a closed box, and boxes have always held a strange fascination for him.

In his first TV series, the teen drama *Felicity*, the title character's Wiccan roommate had a mysterious wooden box that kept viewers guessing for years. Nearly a decade later, in a 2007 talk at TED, the Technology-Entertainment-Design conference in California, Abrams described his lifelong infatuation with Tannen's Magic Mystery Box, a $15 cardboard box he had bought at a New York magic shop as a kid. He has never opened it, though it sits even now on a shelf in his office.

"I realized I haven't opened it because it represents something important to me," he explained at TED. "It represents infinite potential. It represents hope. It represents possibility. And what I love about this box, and what I realize I sort of do in whatever it is that I do, is I find myself drawn to infinite possibility and that sense of potential."

Mystery, he went on to say, is the catalyst for imagination. What are stories if not mystery boxes? What is *Lost* if not a mystery box? *Star Wars*? What creates mystery if not the deliberate withholding of information? And what is mystery, really, if not character? "I mean, look inside yourself and figure out what is inside you," Abrams said, "because ultimately, you know, the mystery box is all of us."

This was the biggest of big ideas. But it did not, in itself, add up to a compelling story. Lindelof and Cuse were not going to put the hatch—that is, the mystery box—into *Lost* until they knew what was inside. It took them months to figure out what that would be—which is why the survivors discover it in episode 11 instead of episode 2.

"J. J. understands that nothing is more exciting than a locked box," said Lindelof. "But the longer you have people trying to open that box, the better the contents need to be." And that $15 magic box Abrams bought as a kid? "I think the reason he hasn't opened it is because he knows it can never measure up."

IN SEPTEMBER 2005, A 29-YEAR-OLD computer consultant named Kevin Croy opened a DVD from Netflix, put it in his player, and settled in with his girlfriend in their townhouse in Anchorage, Alaska, to watch the first few episodes of *Lost*. Season 2 was about to begin, and neither Croy nor his girlfriend had ever seen the show. They got so hooked that they plowed through the entire first season, even finagling some episodes on videocassette from friends—right up to the final scene, the one with the hatch.

Season 1 ends, in classic cliff-hanger fashion, with Jack and a couple other survivors blowing off the hatch—just as Hurley notices the Numbers engraved on its side and tries desperately to stop them. Then, with the start of season 2, the entire show was "flipped on its head," as Croy puts it. Early in the opening episode, a flashback shows Jack having a brief exchange three years before with a guy who says, "See you in another life, yeah?" as they part. Then, back on the island, a few of the survivors descend into the hatch—where they find this same man living in the underground compartment that lies at the bottom of it. *Huh?*

That night, Croy started googling. "See you in another life"—what was that supposed to mean? He was expecting to find a wiki, a fan-built encyclopedia that would tell him anything he wanted to know about *Lost*—something like Wookieepedia, which *Star Wars* fanatics had launched a few months earlier. But all he found was a few online message boards about the show and a handful of blog posts. So he took the obvious next step. He decided to start a wiki himself.

It wasn't hard. Croy had dropped out of junior college, but a friend of a friend had hired him to work as a computer consultant for the likes of IBM and 3Com. That was a decade earlier, when he was living in the Bay Area. Now he was proficient enough that he could download MediaWiki, the free-to-anyone software that was created to run Wikipedia, and have it up and functioning in 20 minutes. After doing that, he started working on the main page and putting in entries. He created entries for the Numbers and for Oceanic Airlines. He wrote one for Desmond Hume, the mystery man the survivors found at the bottom of the hatch, and another for Jack Shephard. The date was September 22, 2005—exactly a year since the premiere of the show.

As it turned out, Croy launched Lostpedia at the perfect time. Shows in their first season generally haven't attracted a large enough and fervent enough fan base to support a group effort. But a hit show going into its second season is different. Particularly a hit show like *Lost*, which succeeded by getting you hooked on the characters and then launching unanswered questions.

"*Lost* may not be interactive directly," says Croy, unconsciously echoing Carlton Cuse, "but it creates an environment where people need to talk to each other to get the whole story." Lostpedia became the place where they gathered to do that. A paper written by a researcher at Xerox PARC describes the site as "a community engaged in social information foraging and sensemaking." "Foraging," because that's what looking for information is like. And "sensemaking," because the need to make sense of the show is why you need to go foraging in the first place.

This was not exactly what Jimmy Wales had in mind when

he cofounded Wikipedia. Wales, a Web entrepreneur whose earlier online encyclopedia had foundered because its rigorous review process scared off volunteers, enthusiastically embraced the much more open type of collaboration that wiki software enabled. Still, his idea of a wiki-based encyclopedia relied on a detached, neutral point of view. As Wikipedia grew in popularity, however, other people using its open-source software began to explore different possibilities. There was Kamelopedia, a German-language parody that's all about camels. Then came fan wikis like Wookieepedia. "I still think there has to be some sort of underlying principle," Wales says, "but what's obviously more necessary is a shared vision of what you're trying to accomplish."

At Lostpedia, that shared vision is the idea that *Lost* is a show worth watching and discussing, perhaps endlessly. But as fan wikis like Lostpedia developed, Wales came to realize that they operate very differently from fan forums and message boards, the more common way for fans to interact with one another. Outgrowths of the dial-in bulletin board systems that flourished in the eighties and early nineties, before Internet access was widespread and the Web made it easy for anyone to go online, message boards often have tens of thousands of members. The Ultimate Guitar Archive, a forum for guitar players that's one of the biggest, claims more than a million members. But with their lengthy and often barely coherent conversation threads, message boards are daunting to all but the most committed fans. The people they attract are those who want to flaunt their knowledge in all its esoteric glory.

These are the same people, it turns out, who write and edit wikis. But unlike message boards, wikis are set up in a way that allows information to be filed, categorized, and easily retrieved.

As a result, they draw a much broader audience. "Wikis are a mechanism to allow superfans to write to fans," says Wales. "So instead of just talking about the most arcane points of *Lost*, they understand that they're there to explain things to other people."

As the show developed, the communal foraging gained momentum. In 2006, a grad student started a page called "economics" to describe the survivors' approach to allocating their resources. As Jason Mittell of Middlebury College observed in another scholarly essay, that entry was fast transformed by dozens of editors from a middling term paper to an exhaustive economic analysis of life on the island. An entry called "leadership" sprang up to evaluate the executive qualities, good and bad, of Jack and two other main characters. Soon it expanded to include dozens of others. A user in Pennsylvania, seeking to document the crash that had landed everyone on the island, created an entry labeled "mid-air break-up." Eventually it not only described in minute detail the calamity that befell Oceanic Flight 815 but provided historical details of actual in-flight disintegrations dating back to 1954. After tallying the results—16 cases over a 50-year period, 2,406 people dead, 6 survivors—the entry concluded that the chances of 71 people living through such a crash in real life are "fairly astronomical."

Not surprisingly, a few of the information foragers have turned up some very silly mushrooms. One of the most intriguing entries in Lostpedia is the "apophenia" page, which is given over to "the perception of patterns, or connections, where in fact none exist." What follows is a compendium of baseless theories, imagined connections, unintended similarities, and simple continuity errors that have led viewers even deeper into woo-woo land than Lindelof and Cuse meant to take them. Because the same gold-colored stunt car was used to stage several different accident scenes, for example, many viewers concluded that the crashes were somehow linked. Others discovered portentous cloud formations in the sky. Not that anyone is terribly surprised that *Lost* would spawn this kind of thing. "They created a show that encourages people to pay attention to everything," observes Danny Horn, an executive at Wikia, the San Francisco company (also cofounded by Wales) that hosts Lostpedia on the Web. "And unfortunately, people pay attention to everything."

Meanwhile, the site just kept growing. Less than two years after its inception, Lostpedia had 19,000 registered users and 3,250 articles, not only in English but in Dutch, French, German, Italian, Polish, Portuguese, and Spanish. Already it was such an important knowledge base that even writers for the show turned to it when their script coordinator wasn't available. By the time the series reached its conclusion in May 2010, Lostpedia had 6,900 articles in 17 different languages. The English-language article on Jack alone ran to more than 10,000 words and included information gleaned from multiple episodes about his childhood, his education, his career as a surgeon, his father, his marriage, his divorce, his actions on the plane, his actions after the crash, his tattoos, and even the possible import of his surname: "Jack's last name may reflect his position as a leader because a shepherd leads a flock."

ADAM HOROWITZ BLAMES THE WHOLE THING on *Star Wars*. Horowitz and his writing partner, Eddy Kitsis, were executive producers on *Lost*, along with Lindelof and Cuse and a handful of others. Horowitz remembers seeing *Star Wars* at a theater in Times Square with his mom—he was five when it came out—and wanting to go right back in as soon as it was over. "But there's no bigger *Star Wars* geek than Damon Lindelof," he pointed out, taking a seat at the enormous conference table at the center of the writers' room in the *Lost* bungalow. This is where they once spent an entire morning arguing about whether Endor, introduced in *Return of the Jedi*, was a planet or a moon. "It turned out to be a moon," Kitsis recalled. "Or was it a planet?"

Lindelof was only four when he saw *Star Wars*. Years later, when Lloyd Braun paired him with Abrams as they were trying to develop *Lost*, Lindelof showed up for their first meeting wearing an original *Star Wars* T-shirt he'd gotten when he and his dad joined the *Star Wars* Fan Club. Abrams was wowed. Lindelof, Abrams, Joss Whedon (the creator of *Buffy the Vampire Slayer*, *Angel*, and *Firefly*)—for a whole generation of Hollywood writers in their thirties and forties, Horowitz quipped, "*Star Wars* was a gateway drug."

"*Star Wars* wasn't just science fiction," Kitsis put in. "What was cool about it was, it was a whole world. And it was about a kid in a small town"—Luke Skywalker, on the podunk planet Tatooine—"who longs for adventure."

"It tells you anybody can do anything," Horowitz added. "It doesn't matter what your circumstances are. That's a very powerful message for a kid. Luke lives on a desert planet in the far reaches of the galaxy, and he becomes a hero of the universe. It's like in Hollywood—if you believe in yourself, you can do it."

Horowitz and Kitsis met in film class at the University of Wisconsin, where they discovered a shared sensibility in each other's student oeuvre. Heading west together to conquer Hollywood, they found work as assistants to A-list producers. Eventually they got hired as a writing team, including a stint working with Abrams on *Felicity* and another with Cuse on a short-lived series for the WB. Midway through the first season of *Lost*, Cuse offered them a job writing for it.

Star Wars references were rife in the show. Near the end of the first season, when two of the survivors—Michael, an American, and Jin, from Korea—are trying to fix the raft they've built to escape the island, there are close parallels to a crucial scene in *The Empire Strikes Back* when Han Solo and Chewbacca are trying to repair the hot-rod starship *Millennium Falcon*. "No, no! No! This one goes there, that one goes there," Michael tells Jin, echoing Solo's line in the movie. Even though Michael doesn't speak Korean and Jin doesn't speak English, they are somehow able to communicate; Solo and Chewbacca had the same problem, yet they were able to understand one another as well.

But it wasn't just homages. There are also similarities in the way *Lost* and *Star Wars* are structured. Both provide overwhelming amounts of information, but in a time-release fashion that creates maximum anticipation. Kitsis calls this the Boba Fett effect, after the bounty hunter who has a passionate following among *Star Wars* fanatics, even though he had only a minor role in the movies. "You'd see these glimpses," he said. Boba Fett didn't even appear in the original movie, but not long after his initial TV appearance he was made available as a toy. "You had to send in four proofs of purchase. Then, in *The Empire Strikes Back*, he had four lines. But he made you think about bounty hunters. *Lost* owes a lot to that."

Geronimo Jackson, for instance. A fictional band from the seventies, the group was first mentioned in season 2, when Hurley and Charlie, the show's heroin-addicted rock star, discover a Geronimo Jackson album in the underground compartment at the bottom of the hatch. Neither of them has ever heard of the group. But little references keep popping up. On the season 2 DVD, Kitsis and Horowitz talk about the band's history. In season 3, in a flashback that occurs off-island, someone is wearing a

Geronimo Jackson T-shirt. In season 4, we see a Geronimo Jackson poster in one episode and an album cover in another. Yet not until season 5—much of which involves time travel to the seventies—do we actually hear a Geronimo Jackson song. Before long the song appeared on iTunes. One guy wrote on a *Lost* bulletin board that he remembered seeing them at Cobo Hall in Detroit in the early seventies. "That's the guy I did it for," said Kitsis.

On a deeper level, *Lost* echoed *Star Wars* in its balance of outward complexity and essential simplicity. For all Lucas's obsessive accretion of detail, his story boils down to a handful of timeless archetypes, the struggle between good and evil chief among them. So it was with *Lost*.

"The surface mysteries are all very complicated," said Horowitz, "but what the characters are going through are these basic crises that we're all going through." He mentioned Hurley, who spent time in a mental hospital before he encountered the Numbers. "What does Hurley want? He wants people to believe him. He wants people to tell him he's not crazy." Who wouldn't?

In its focus on character, *Lost* far surpasses *Star Wars*. In the end, Lucas's space opera feels like just that—a vast Wagnerian spectacle, with too much bombast and too little authentic emotion. For all their technical wizardry, the three prequels in particular lack the one detail that matters most—the depth of character that would make the cosmic struggle of good versus evil feel real. "Damon and Carlton have a philosophy of character first," said Kitsis. "Writers would come in and say, wouldn't it be cool if the alligator turned into a dragon? And they were like, we're much more interested in what if Jack were married."

Jack's troubled relationship with his father, Charlie's emergence from rock 'n' roll solipsism, Hurley's quest for acceptance—this is the kind of detail that gets people hooked. "Whatever power the show has had, it's just been the characters," said Horowitz. "The reason audiences reacted so strongly to the Numbers was because they were attached to Hurley, and he was a character people wanted to know. And as much as they talk about wanting to know the answers, what they really want is to be engaged."

OKAY, SURE. BUT DUDE—*What do the numbers mean?* That's what one fan demanded to know in July 2005 at Comic-Con, the annual comics and fantasy convention in San Diego. Comic-Con is the closest America has to the sprawling manga marts at Tokyo Big Sight, the massive convention center on Tokyo Bay. Sitting on a panel with Carlton Cuse and Javier Grillo-Marxuach, Lindelof took the question and rashly replied, "We may never know what the Numbers mean."

What he meant was that the Numbers were one of the show's essential mysteries—the box that should not be opened, as Leonard would have put it in the mental hospital if he'd been able to say anything before the guards dragged him off. But Comic-Con draws the superfans, the otaku, and this was not what they wanted to hear. Unwittingly, Lindelof set off an uproar.

That fall, as the show was entering its second season, the question came up again as Lindelof and Cuse were having lunch with ABC's heads of marketing, Mike Benson and Marla Provencio. "So we told them," Lindelof recalled. "And they asked, When are you going to put that on the show? And we said, We're not. Jack and Kate"—an attractive young survivor who was being escorted back by a US marshal to face murder charges—"don't care about any of that." Jack and Kate were busy trying to stay alive.

Lindelof and Cuse thought of the show as an iceberg. Only 10 percent of it was visible—that is, broadcast on TV. Everything else was backstory, implied but not revealed. But by this time, it was obvious that the show had a huge following online. Maybe they could give the Internet fans something special—something about the Numbers, perhaps? After *I Love Bees*, alternate reality games were hot. So that's what they suggested.

"Mike was very receptive," said Lindelof. "But he was looking at the Internet as a marketing tool. We were looking at it as a way to tell the story—to share the other 90 percent of the iceberg. It was the idea of going deeper—speaking to the fans who wanted to have an experience beyond the show." In theory, that shouldn't have created a conflict.

The Lost Experience began in May 2006, late in the second season, with ads that ran during the show's commercial breaks in the US, the UK, and Australia. The ads were for the Hanso Foundation, a fictional organization that had been briefly mentioned early in the season. In that episode, Desmond, the man they had discovered living at the bottom of the hatch, tells Jack he's been entering the Numbers in a computer every 108 minutes (4 + 8 + 15 + 16 + 23 + 42 = 108) because if he fails to do so, the world will end. Desmond then shows them an orientation film for something called the DHARMA Initiative, a utopian project funded by Alvar Hanso, a Danish industrialist and arms trader, and his Hanso Foundation. The underground chamber Desmond has been living in turns out to be a DHARMA Initiative station built to study the strange electromagnetic fluctuations emanating from this part of the island.

The alternate reality game was supposed to explain all this—the Hanso Foundation, the DHARMA Initiative, the Numbers themselves. Yet already there were problems. If you wanted to know what the Numbers meant, you had to play *The Lost Experience*. But you also had to be able to enjoy the upcoming season of the show whether you had played it or not. "The story couldn't be so revelatory you had to watch it," said Lindelof, "but if it wasn't revelatory enough, it would be boring. It was a very difficult catch-22."

The Hanso ads were followed by a novel, *Bad Twin*. Published by Hyperion (like ABC, a subsidiary of Disney), it was supposedly written by Gary Troup, the passenger on Oceanic Flight 815 who was sucked into one of the plane's jet engines shortly after the crash. Then it emerged that the fictional Troup had also written a nonfiction book, *The Valenzetti Equation*, that was "out of print" because Alvar Hanso had bought up all known copies of it, as well as the reprint rights. Nonetheless, a Web site for the book soon turned up, with promo copy that asked, "What if a mathematical equation could predict the apocalypse?"

That summer, at the 2006 Comic-Con, an angry young woman challenged Lindelof and Cuse during a panel discussion about the show. Many in the audience immediately recognized her as Rachel Blake, a hacker who had claimed in a video blog to have found evidence of sinister doings by the Hanso Foundation. "Have you no shame?" she cried.

"What?"

"Have . . . you . . . no . . . shame?!"

"Well, I have a little shame," Cuse replied sarcastically. "Do you have shame, Damon?"

"I have no shame."

"Don't be cute! Tell us what you know about the Hanso Foundation."

At that the crowd burst into applause. In the bizarre exchange that followed, Blake accused Lindelof and Cuse of promoting a dangerous international organization that was responsible for organ harvesting in Africa and any number of other crimes. Turning to the audience, she showed off a Web address on her T-shirt—www.hansoexposed.com—before being dragged off by security.

On the Web site were codes leading to snippets of video—a nod to William Gibson's 2003 novel *Pattern Recognition*, which involved mysterious video segments that inspired a Web cult. When fans finished assembling the *Lost* snippets in early September, they turned out to include a 1975 orientation film in which Alvar Hanso explains the Valenzetti Equation, and with it the Numbers. Hanso puts it with admirable concision:

> In 1962, only 13 years ago, the world came to the brink of nuclear war. The United States and the Soviet Union almost fulfilled the promise of mutual assured destruction. . . . After the Cuban Missile Crisis, both nations decided to find a solution. The result was the Valenzetti Equation. . . . It predicts the exact number of years and months before humanity extinguishes itself, whether through nuclear fire, chemical and biological warfare, conventional warfare, pandemic, over-population. The results are chilling, and attention must be paid. Valenzetti gave numerical values to the core environmental and human factors in his equation: 4, 8, 15, 16, 23 and 42. Only by manipulating the environment, by finding scientific solutions to all of our problems, will we be able to change those core factors and give humanity a chance to survive.

So they were toying around with the doomsday equation. No wonder things kept blowing up.

Unfortunately, *The Lost Experience* seemed about to blow up as well. On television, Lindelof, Cuse, and ABC knew what they were doing. As soon as they ventured beyond TV, all these new questions came up. How to extend the narrative without leaving everyone else in the dark was just the start of it. Who, after all, was *The Lost Experience* really for? As far as Lindelof and Cuse were concerned, it was for the fans. But ABC's marketing people wanted it to bring in additional viewers. They also wanted something cutting-edge, to demonstrate how innovative they were.

Three goals—making the fans happy, bringing in new fans, and making everybody involved look cool—would have been more than enough. But then it came out that they were also expected to work the show's advertisers into the game. Jeep, Verizon, Sprite, the jobs site Monster.com—each had its own *Lost Experience* Web site to be built. One measure of the game's success, the producers discovered, would be how much traffic it sent to the sites.

As the summer progressed, another issue became apparent: despite the anticipated payoff at the end, the game was beginning to seem tedious. Playing it required solving an endless number of puzzles, most of which yielded something like a 90-second reward. No wonder the number of players kept dropping. "The big thing we learned," said Lindelof, "is that there's a direct ratio between time invested and reward expected."

But the lesson of *The Lost Experience* was in fact bigger than that. As successful as *Lost*'s producers had been in creating a television show that felt like a game and generated an online community, they had a much harder time when creating a game and building a community were actually the goals. While juggling conflicting agendas and wrestling with internal conflicts—was it part of the narrative, or was it a marketing effort?—they failed to implement the kind of reward pattern that would have drawn people in. Along the way, they stumbled across the difference between a mystery and a puzzle. The show was all about mystery; but in the game, the mystery of the Numbers got downgraded to a series of puzzles. "We felt it was a noble experiment," Cuse concluded, "but one that was not particularly successful."

IF IT WASN'T THE NUMBERS that fans were obsessing about, it was the four-toed statue. In the last episode of season 2, three of the survivors are sailing around the island in a boat that belongs to Desmond when they discover an enormous stone foot—a foot that on closer inspection turns out to have only four toes. That was it; for the next three years, from May 2006 to March 2009, the statue was never seen and rarely, if ever, mentioned. In the meantime, Lostpedia users published theories about its origins (ancient Egypt? Greece or Rome? Atlantis?), its identity (Anubis, Egyptian god of the underworld? Narasimha, an incarnation of the Hindu god Vishnu? John Locke, a central character in the show? some pharaoh?), the cause of its destruction (earthquake? volcano? tsunami? nuclear explosion?), and its significance in the show.

"Sometimes the audience surprises you with its infatuations," said Cuse. "We wanted to tell the audience that there were people on the island a long time ago. We did not expect the fans to become obsessed with what the statue represented."

Then, at the end of season 5, in a flashback that took viewers back to the nineteenth century, the statue was shown in its entirety. And shortly afterward, through a puzzle in a special issue of *Wired* that was guest-edited by Abrams, it was revealed to be Tawaret, the Egyptian goddess of fertility. "This show is an exercise in delayed gratification," Lindelof noted dryly.

Which is another way of saying it's an exercise in extremely controlled storytelling. Like *Mad Men*, which on the surface it didn't seem to resemble at all, *Lost* relied for its effect on the hoarding and selective release of information. Occasionally the show's creators would part the curtain, giving the fans a tantalizing glimpse of something that would keep them occupied for months, if not years. This deliberate withholding of information is what created the "illusion of interactivity," as Lindelof put it. Far from giving the audience a role in the storytelling, the participatory aspect of *Lost* was actually a result of its creators' strict control.

Viewers were ambivalent about the role they wanted to take. One of the most persistent questions the producers got was, how much of this has been plotted out in advance? "The fans want the story to be completely planned out by us," said Lindelof, "and they also want to have a say. Those two are mutually exclusive."

Well, sort of. Like Dickens, whom they've several times cited as an inspiration, the producers of *Lost* had an overarching framework for their story, but in completing it they did take note of their fans' responses. "There are two different endings for *Great Expectations*," Lindelof observed—an unhappy one, in which Pip and Estella part forever, and the published one, urged upon Dickens by the famously wretched novelist Edward Bulwer-Lytton, which suggests that they will find happiness together. "That tells you a lot."

In *Lost*, the same "sense of immediate audience participation" that guided Dickens can be seen in the fate of Nikki and Paulo, two of the 71 survivors of the flight. Nikki Fernandez, an actress, and Paulo, a chef, were LA lowlifes who had been flying back from Sydney after having murdered her older lover and made off with an $8 million cache of diamonds. They didn't turn up until season 3, and as soon as they did, fans started complaining. Where did these two come from? And why were they so annoying?

Eleven episodes later, in March 2007, Nikki and Paulo made a sudden exit from the show. Improbably—but who's to say what's improbable in the context of *Lost*?—both are bitten within minutes of each other by Medusa spiders. The spider bites induce paralysis, leading the other survivors to think the two are dead. Nikki's eyes open as she and Paulo are being buried, but nobody notices except the audience.

For Lindelof and Cuse, the scene was a tacit acknowledgment of their mistake. "Okay, you want us to kill them?" said Cuse. "We will not only fucking kill them, we will bury them alive."

"It was a mea culpa," Lindelof added. "A love letter to the fans, apologizing for having wasted their time."

In May 2007, shortly after this happened onscreen, Lindelof and Cuse were able to convince ABC to agree to set an end date for the series. Now that the show was a hit, Disney execs were as loath to see it end as they'd once been to put it on the air. This is a familiar dynamic of bad television—a once-brilliant show lives long after the spark is gone because the network wants to milk the ratings cow dry. Bad enough with an episodic series like *ER*, which endured 15 seasons before NBC pulled the plug. For *Lost*, a lack of closure would be fatal. Lindelof and Cuse, whose contracts were expiring shortly, made setting an end date a condition of their staying with the show.

Lindelof compared the show's journey to a road trip from LA to New York. "We knew the beginning, and we knew the end," he said, "but the middle was tricky. We didn't know how much gas we had, or whether the car would make it. Not until halfway through the third season were we able to prevail upon them. Ending the show was the only way to save the show—but we had to drive around in circles a lot before we were able to get to that point."

But what if the show didn't have to end? What if, like a truly open world, it could go on indefinitely? As we sat in their bungalow, Lindelof started to speculate about a marriage between a television show and a massively multiplayer game. "In *World of Warcraft*, there is no end to the game," he said. "You want to create a world people can stay in, as opposed to creating a world people can visit. We've only been about creating portals."

Or maybe a different kind of marriage. "*World of Warcraft* seems nerdy," Lindelof continued. "But Facebook doesn't seem nerdy. Twitter doesn't seem nerdy. I feel that the essential medium of the Internet is social networking. But how do you marry social networking to storytelling?"

"To me, it's about immersion," said Cuse. "That was the thing that struck me about *Avatar*—the immersive quality of it. I'm seeing that 24 frames-per-second, 2-D storytelling is antiquated. If you could take that immersive quality of *Avatar*, the 3-D quality, and combine that with worlds you can immerse yourself in and get narrative content in as well—they're different experiences. If we knew how to do that, we would do it. But we haven't figured it out."

8.

Television: The Game

Anybody want to work for the Dunder Mifflin Paper Company? Great opportunity here: Dunder Mifflin is the outfit featured in *The Office*, one of the funniest and most innovative comedies on television. Be part of the exciting technology changes sweeping the office supply industry! Rub virtual shoulders with Steve Carell! Get paid in Schrute bucks! Commute through cyberspace and never have to actually go to Scranton, Pennsylvania!

Dunder Mifflin Infinity, the online arm of the fictional Dunder Mifflin Inc., was launched with an October 2007 episode of *The Office* in which Ryan Howard, one of the show's more obnoxious characters, shows up after a stint at corporate headquarters with a scheme to reinvigorate the company. Ryan wants to give everyone BlackBerrys and put the sales operation online. He's young and hip and going places. He wears a lot of black, and he hasn't shaved in a while. Dunder Mifflin Infinity is his plan for bringing the hapless paper company into the twenty-first century.

Game shows have been part of television since the 1940s, when programs like *Kay Kyser's Kollege of Musical Knowledge* tested contestants' (and viewers') command of popular music. Dunder Mifflin Infinity—rebooted in September 2010 as Dunder Mifflin Sabre to reflect the company's acquisition by Sabre Corp, a printer company whose products have an unfortunate tendency to catch fire—was something different: a game about a show. Like the new Dunder Mifflin Sabre, DMI was an online contest designed to deepen the audience's connection with *The Office*, which has been one of the very few bright spots in NBC's recent prime-time lineup. It also functioned as a social networking site—a Web destination that encouraged fans to get involved not just with the show but with each other. In a very limited way, it offered them the kind of immersion Lindelof and Cuse were describing.

At Dundermifflininfinity.com, people with a "consummate passion for all things paper" could sign up to become a virtual employee. All employees were given a weekly task for which they were paid in Schrute bucks (named after Dwight Schrute, a leading character in the show). Once they had earned at least Sb $2,000, they could apply to be hired by one of DMI's 100 branches, which as an expression of the company's "small-cities ideals" tended to be located in places like Ypsilanti, Michigan, and Woonsocket, Rhode Island.

By the time of the Sabre merger, DMI had some 260,000 virtual employees, of whom maybe 20,000 were what NBC.com called "power users." These were people who did the tasks every week, communicated via message board, used DMI as a social networking site, watched episodes while messaging each other, got together in person to watch the show, staged theme parties, and posted their party videos on the site. "I have no idea if they have real jobs," said Nate Federman, one of two "digital writers" NBC.com hired for the site.

For more casual users, the weekly tasks were at the heart of the experience. To accompany the October 2009 "Niagara" episode, for example, the show's Web writers came up with a task called "Niagara Do's and Don'ts." The episode focuses on Jim and Pam, the winsome young couple whose budding romance was long one of the show's signature elements, going to Niagara Falls to get married. Jim, fearing with good reason that his coworkers might not behave in an entirely appropriate manner, presents them with a list of do's and don'ts. Topping the list is his admonition not to re-create the "JK Wedding Entrance Dance" video from YouTube—a strut down the aisle to Chris Brown's "Forever," equal parts touching and hilarious, that had been uploaded by a pair of Minnesota newlyweds. The YouTube clip was a pop culture sensation, racking up 3 million views in the first 48 hours after it appeared and landing the happy couple on *Good Morning America* and *The Today Show*. Inevitably, the guests at Jim and Pam's wedding do re-create the dance. So Dunder Mifflin Infinity employees were asked to make their own list of do's and don'ts for weddings or other occasions—funerals, birthday parties, what have you. Branch winners would receive Sb $250; the corporate winner would be awarded Sb $350.

There was a wonderfully twisted symmetry to this particular task: a user-posted video on the Web inspires a TV show to challenge its viewers to post their own commentary on the Web. But that sort of give-and-take is key to the appeal of *The Office*: a half-hour comedy in mock-documentary format, it presents in microcosm a fun-house version of the world we already know. Dunder Mifflin Infinity and the new Dunder Mifflin Sabre go a step further by inviting you to step inside the fun house. "It's based on the feeling of being taken away to another world," said Greg Daniels, the show's writer-producer, sounding not unlike James Cameron discussing *Avatar*. "And you like that world so much you want to get involved in it."

Daniels is a television veteran. Lanky, with a mild, almost self-effacing manner, he could pass for a television character himself. He first made a name for himself as a writer on *Saturday Night Live*, sharing an Emmy in 1989. After that he spent several years on *The Simpsons* and then helped create Fox's other long-running animated series, *King of the Hill*. He adapted *The Office* from the UK original, which had been a hit for the BBC, and then created NBC's *Parks and Recreation* with Michael Schur, a member of his writing team.

Both *The Office* and *Parks and Recreation* depart from the strict and increasingly moribund tradition of network sitcoms, which ever since the 1950s have been shot on film with three cameras in a single take and then augmented with a laugh track so the audience will know what's funny. As "mockumentaries," Daniels's shows have their own rules: single camera, no close-ups, no sound track, limited production values, nothing to indicate we aren't really watching an audiovisual presentation about Dunder Mifflin Inc. or the Pawnee, Indiana, Department of Parks and Recreation. It's comedy with a knowing wink, TV for the media-saturated: instead of taking their cue from the laugh track, viewers are in on the joke.

Daniels is as earnest and droll as his preferred format. When I met him at the *Parks and Recreation* offices, near the intersection of Gunsmoke Avenue and Gilligan's Island Road on a storied back lot in LA's San Fernando Valley, he warned Schur not to monopolize the interview: "I want to get in the book too!" Then he explained that he had first heard about the Internet in the mid-nineties. "I was a writer on *The Simpsons*," he recalled, "and someone said, There's this thing called the Internet—it connects all these academics and government workers, and it's a place where they discuss *Simpsons* episodes." He went for a look and found scholarly papers on such topics as the uses of fable and allegory in the "Lisa's Wedding" episode, which he himself had written. "It was incredibly erudite," he recalled.

"Lisa's Wedding" aired in March 1995, five months before the Netscape IPO triggered the first wave of enthusiasm for all things Internet. By the time Daniels got *The Office* on the air in March 2005, the Net had become a place where people discussed anything imaginable—including, soon enough, *The Office*. Web sites dedicated to the show started popping up soon after it debuted. Fans were trying to interact with the show—ranking their favorite episodes, selling each other T-shirts and coffee mugs. Daniels and his team, monitoring what people were saying and doing online, could hardly help but register the demand. "For a long time it felt like we were one step behind the viewers," said Paul Lieberstein, the actor-writer-producer who's been running the show since Daniels and Schur started *Parks and Recreation* in 2008.

"There just seems to be a desire for extra stuff," said Schur. "Webisodes. Things to find on the Internet. They want *stuff*."

"I think it's a great way to judge the quality of a show," said Daniels. "If you're a fan, it's a guarantee the show is going to be rich and interesting. If it's not there, then they haven't put a lot of work into dreaming up something original."

"EXTRA STUFF" FROM *THE OFFICE* began to appear after Daniels got a visit from Stephen Andrade, the head of NBC.com, and some other execs from the network. Andrade has an infectious enthusiasm. He's a big guy, a little on the burly side, with a florid complexion and short, strawberry blond hair. "I loved the show," he told me one afternoon in his office, which is in one of several buildings clustered by the main entrance to the Universal lot, NBC's West Coast headquarters. "Internally there were questions about how successful it would be. But we said, We could do a lot with this."

So in September 2005, as Damon Lindelof and Carlton Cuse were beginning to think about *The Lost Experience* a couple miles away at Disney, and Kevin Croy was launching Lostpedia in Anchorage, Dwight Schrute started blogging. Dwight, played by Rainn Wilson, is the terminally awkward, staggeringly puerile, wildly egomaniacal sidekick to Steve Carell's Michael, the regional manager in charge of Dunder Mifflin's Scranton office. If Daniels found the Internet to be about *The Simpsons*, Dwight found the Internet to be about . . . Dwight:

> Hello America. Dwight Schrute here. Assistant Regional Manager of Dunder-Mifflin Paper Products.
>
> This is my web log. Or "blog". I call it "Schrute-Space". Because my last name is "Schrute". And it is a space. For me to write in.
>
> I am excited to have the BILLIONS of people who rely on the internet every day (whether it be to look up weather and traffic, to research academic papers and/or to download pornography) turn to SCHRUTE-SPACE to get their daily fill of what Dwight has to say.
>
> First Entry:
>
> I hate Salmon. It's so pink. And it smells like fish. Salmon sucks!

One user responded, "Dwight, I think you're kinda gay. But Im [*sic*] not a homophobe, so that's cool." Another said, "I don't know if you realize this, but you're a real dork." Another said simply, "Yeah, salmon sucks." "What's cool," Andrade remarked, "is that people would comment as if it were a real person." And in a way it was, since the early posts were composed by Wilson himself, writing in character.

Dwight turned out to be a big fan of *Lost*. In one blog post, he even offered his own theories about the show. "Who has ever heard of Oceanic Airlines!" he wrote. "I think it was a fake airline that purposefully crashes and does experiments on its passengers." Here, too, the fandom crossed over into the real world. At the 2006 Writers Guild Awards, where *Lost* won for best dramatic series, Damon Lindelof and Eddy Kitsis ran over to the *Office* table and invited everybody to their afterparty. The *Office* crew later sent over reams of Dunder Mifflin stationery as a thank you. "We're huge, huge, *huge* fans of *The Office*," says Kitsis. "It's a demographic thing—the demographic that grew up with the Internet."

By this time, Daniels had started posting deleted scenes online. Like every half-hour show on US network TV, *The Office* has to be cut to precisely 22 minutes in order to accommodate 8 minutes of ads. But the shows are shot long—about 37 or 38 minutes. The hardest part for the producers is when they have to shave off the final four minutes or so to make the fit. But there was no reason they couldn't put the deleted scenes on the Web site. For that matter, there was no reason the show on the Web had to come in at 22 minutes—which is why they eventually started posting "producer's cuts" online as well.

It was Dunder Mifflin Infinity that turned *The Office* into a game. Although developed in-house, the experience was refined for NBC.com by Bunchball, a tiny startup in Silicon Valley. Bunchball uses game mechanics—fundamental tenets of game design, such as taking turns and awarding points—to keep users coming back to the Web sites it builds. "It's all about giving people goals," explained Rajat Paharia, Bunchball's founder, "and rewarding them for doing something."

We were sitting in the lobby of the W Seattle. Paharia had just given a talk titled "Driving User Behavior" at a conference held by the Casual Games Association, the trade group for companies that make simple, easy-to-play video games that are more like solitaire than like *Grand Theft Auto*. "People love having goals," Paharia continued. They love other things too: getting points, moving up to a new level, collecting things. Especially collecting things. "But people hate having holes in sets," he added. "They'll do *anything* to complete them."

Dunder Mifflin Infinity was designed to engage people, using mechanisms that are common to every game from *World of Warcraft* to golf. Paharia described it as an "incentive system." When users do something on the site—perform a task, make a comment, rate somebody else's comment—the system awards them points in the form of Schrute bucks. "And once you have a point system," Paharia explained, "there's a bunch of things you can do."

One thing you can do is satisfy people's thirst for status by putting up leader boards—which in this case means posting a list of top-performing employees and top branches. You can sate the lust for acquisition by placing a virtual desk on users' computer screens and selling things they can pay for with Schrute bucks. That way they get to flaunt their wealth by displaying stuff on their screens—er, desks—and express their creativity in the way they arrange it all. ("People have spent amazing amounts of time on their desks," Paharia observed.) You can also offer opportunities for advancement by giving people a chance to "level up"—move to the next level, or in this case, earn a promotion. Some items they can buy for their desks only if they've risen to a management level.

Dunder Mifflin Infinity and Dunder Mifflin Sabre not only give fans a way to participate in the show; they also enable NBC to outsource the expensive and time-consuming process of creating extra stuff for fans to find on the Internet. They're designed to get the users to do most of the work, and to be happy doing it. Advertisers are happy too, because it gives fans of the show a way to interact with them as well. Toyota started selling model cars that users could display on their desks. MasterCard gave every "employee" an Sb $200 "gift card" that could be used to buy other things. Paharia seemed undone by the circularity of it all. "NBC is paying people fake money to do real work," he marveled, "and MasterCard paid NBC real money to give away fake money." Who knows where this could go?

WHEN ANDRADE FIRST STARTED WORKING on *The Office*, NBC.com consisted of about six people. Andrade himself had joined the operation as an attorney in 1996. One of his first assignments was to handle the legal work for the partnership with Microsoft that led to the creation of the Web/cable hybrid known as MSNBC. Since then the network has tried, as he put it, "every conceivable approach" to the Web.

One of the most promising early experiments involved *Homicide: Life on the Street*, an ensemble police drama that ran for seven seasons in the nineties. Based on a book by David Simon, the former *Baltimore Sun* reporter who later went on to create *The Wire* and *Treme* for HBO, the series had a dark and gritty feel that stemmed in part from its being shot with handheld cameras on location in inner-city Baltimore. Though never a ratings champ, it won four Emmys and any number of other awards and attracted guest stars on the order of Steve Buscemi, Marcia Gay Harden, Neil Patrick Harris, and James Earl Jones.

Even then, television was losing viewers to the Web. NBC was worried, and not without reason. In 1996 I interviewed a number of people at 30 Rockefeller Plaza—NBC headquarters since Rockefeller Center went up during the Depression—for *Fortune*. The people at 30 Rock knew the game was changing. "The idea that ten years from now, people are going to be comfortable sitting in front of a television set—my instinct and our focus groups tell me they're not," said Bob Meyers, one of the NBC execs in charge of the effort. "My little focus group at home sure isn't—they expect a TV to act like a PC."

This had huge implications for broadcasting. For decades, network programmers had labored not just to attract eyeballs but to funnel them from one day part to the next. The arrival of the remote control complicated this task considerably but did not render it impossible. Now network execs had to deal with the Internet and a proliferation of cable channels as well. That meant they had to replicate the programmer's art on a far grander scale, across not only time slots and day parts but a panoply of different media, from broadcast to cable to Internet and back again. The quest for control was growing dizzying in its complexity.

To augment *Homicide*, NBC.com sent a team of Web producers to the Baltimore pier where it was shot and had them interview everyone from the stars to the set decorator. Eventually the series even spawned its own Web serial, *Homicide: Second Shift*, which followed another set of cops who went to work after the shift on TV went home. Sometimes characters from the TV show crossed over to the Web series, and vice versa; on one occasion, even the story line crossed over. It was a pioneering effort. But Web video in the nineties was expensive to produce, unappealing to advertisers, and painful to watch, given that almost no one had broadband. The whole effort was about a decade ahead of its time.

"Only in the last two or three years have we gotten to where I thought we were going to get in 1996," Andrade told me when I saw him in Universal City. *The Office* was his breakthrough show. "Comedies work really well," he continued, "because there are ideas in the jokes that you can expand online. But I think we can make almost any show work." Which is good, because that's what his task has become.

TEN YEARS AFTER ITS INITIAL experiments with *Homicide,* the idea of extending television shows online suddenly became part of NBC's core strategy. The announcement came in May 2006 from Jeff Zucker, then chief of television operations at NBC Universal, the entertainment combine created by the merger of General Electric's NBC with Vivendi's Universal Studios. Zucker spoke during the spring upfront, the annual razzle-dazzle at which the US broadcast networks introduce their fall lineups to advertisers. The upfronts are a storied ritual of broadcasting, a week of lavish parties and elaborately staged presentations culminating—hopefully—in a fevered auction during which Madison Avenue hurls money at the networks. Year after year, even as their audience kept drifting away to cable and video games and the Internet, the networks had managed to command more and more money for their airtime because advertisers in search of a mass audience had nowhere else to go. But this year, for the first time, it wasn't working.

It particularly wasn't working for NBC, which in 10 years had slipped from number one among the nation's four major television networks to number four. From the mid-eighties on, NBC had seemed unbeatable in prime time. *The Cosby Show, Cheers, Seinfeld, ER*—between 1985 and 1999, NBC had the top-ranked show in the country for 11 out of 14 seasons. But first *Seinfeld* and then *Friends* and *Frasier* had run their course, and the network seemed unable to replace them. Now CBS was on top, riding high on the success of Anthony Zuiker's *CSI* franchise, which was so popular it had managed to turn forensics into a fad, and *Survivor.* NBC was beginning to look not just dated but sad.

NBC's upfront presentation was at Radio City Music Hall, the 1930s song-and-dance palace just down the street from 30 Rock, its glamorously streamlined form a reminder of the era when the National Broadcasting Company was America's premier radio network. The afternoon got off to a fairly promising start. Steve Carell came onstage to say some very funny things. There were not one but two self-referential comedies inspired by *Saturday Night Live*: Tina Fey's *30 Rock*, which looked kind of cool; and Aaron Sorkin's *Studio 60 on the Sunset Strip*, which seemed oddly self-important. There was a strange new series called *Heroes*, about ordinary people with superpowers. And then Zucker took the stage.

Zucker's big news was "TV 360," an initiative that would offer advertisers more than just television. TV 360 meant taking what NBC.com had done with *The Office* and extending it across the prime-time lineup and beyond. There would be all kinds of extra stuff—Webisodes from the high school football drama *Friday*

Night Lights; a new home page for *The Tonight Show* and *Saturday Night Live*; a "show behind the show" from *30 Rock*; an online comic from *Heroes*; a Web-only version of *The Biggest Loser*, the weight loss reality program, featuring would-be contestants who didn't make it onto the actual show; even online beauty makeovers from iVillage, the Web site that NBC Universal had just bought. It was all about using "the power of the Web," Zucker declared, to "extend the television experience and build communities and a level of engagement like nothing else out there"—communities that advertisers could tap into. Now NBC would not only seek to channel viewers across multiple platforms, across broadcast and cable and the Internet; now it would be channeling advertisers as well.

If NBC was going to go 360, the obvious place to start was *Heroes*. The new series had *Lost* written all over it. It was created by Tim Kring, the writer-producer behind NBC's Boston crime series *Crossing Jordan*—the show where Damon Lindelof had first been noticed. Jeph Loeb, a co–executive producer, had been a writer on the second season of *Lost*. Jesse Alexander, another co–executive producer, had worked with Lindelof and J. J. Abrams at the inception of *Lost* and with Abrams before that on *Alias*. Best of all was the concept: with the success of *Lost*, NBC was all too eager to have a serial drama with an ensemble cast and a story that would go over big at Comic-Con.

In the case of *Heroes*, that meant characters out of the comics: a high school cheerleader whose body spontaneously regenerates; a New York artist who can see into the future, but only after shooting up; a Tokyo office worker who can travel through time; an online stripper with dual personalities, one of which has superhuman strength; an LA policeman who can read minds; a politician who can fly; a male nurse with the power to mimic other people's powers; a serial killer who steals other people's brains so he can make their powers his own. There's also a conspiracy involved, and all kinds of fancy genetics, and a threat to destroy New York City.

The pilot was screened at Comic-Con in July 2006, the same week that Lindelof and Cuse were accused during the *Lost* panel of orchestrating a Hanso Foundation cover-up, and it went over big. When it aired on television that fall, the series premiere drew 14 million viewers—nearly 5 million fewer than *Lost*'s opening episode that season, but still more than any new drama NBC had premiered in the previous five years.

Jesse Alexander took charge of the 360 aspect of the show—everything beyond the TV screen. It was a good fit. Like Abrams and Lindelof, Alexander was a child of *Star Wars*. He was 10 years old when it came out. He had bought all the comics and all the action figures, and soon he was using his Darth Vader and Luke Skywalker figures to make little *Star Wars* films with the Super 8 camera his dad had bought him. He understood fan participation and deep media storytelling instinctively, because that's how he had grown up.

At *Alias*, he had taken a cue from Neil Young's *Majestic* and Jordan Weisman's alternate reality game for *AI*. A character would mention a Web site on the show, and when fans went there they would discover not only the site Alexander had built but audio files he had hidden there. He'd gone online in character as a spy and handed off information to another spy while fans watched. *Heroes* was a chance to do this in a way that was much more integrated into the story. Alexander and his team did online comics that appeared after every episode and were later published as graphic novels. They interviewed members of the cast and crew for online video commentaries for NBC.com. They produced the *Heroes 360 Experience*, a small-scale alternate reality game that fans could play by visiting Web sites and MySpace pages, calling a toll-free number, and sending text messages.

As Zucker had hoped, all this proved enticing to major sponsors like Nissan. Ads for its spiffy new Versa four-cylinder subcompact, recently introduced in the US and Canada, appeared constantly during commercial breaks. And just in case anybody skipped the ads, the Versa was also written into the plot. In episode 3, when Hiro flies to LA and rents a car to drive to New York, he doesn't pick up just any car; he insists on a Versa. "Nissan Versa. Nissan Versa," he chants at the rental counter. "That's a popular choice," the rental agent replies. "Let me check to see if we still have any left." Surprise! They do. Hiro keeps the car through seven more episodes. The Versa also showed up on the first page of every *Heroes* comic. Similar tie-ins were done for Sprint and Cisco.

Even so, *Heroes*' second season was a disaster. Fans were complaining that the pace was too slow. They didn't like it that Hiro spent the first six episodes time-traveling in seventeenth-century Japan, or that new characters kept turning up on the show willy-nilly. Ratings dropped. Kring apologized in *Entertainment Weekly*: "We've heard the complaints," he said in an interview, "and we're doing something about it." But there were few signs of improvement. The plot twists got even more confusing. Ratings fell further. Loeb and Alexander were fired two months into season 3. A lot of people concluded that the production had lost its way.

"At the start of *Heroes*, NBC was very, very excited about trying to have a successful genre franchise along the lines of *Lost*," Alexander recalled over lunch one day at the Universal commissary, which occupies a one-story building surrounded by golf carts—the vehicle of choice for navigating the studio's 415-acre back lot. At $4 million per episode plus cost overruns, the show was never cheap to produce. But it had other advantages. "That kind of genre programming really does build a very devoted fan base," Alexander continued. "And it travels internationally in a way that is incredibly important to the television business these days." Would that be enough to sustain NBC? Would anything?

In November 2007, as NBC and the other networks were struggling to redefine their business, the screenwriters brought everything to a halt. The main issue was compensation for new media. The networks were making money selling ad tie-ins on comics and other material, but the people who wrote them weren't being properly compensated. At first they weren't being compensated at all; writers on prime-time network series typically got $30,000 per episode, but if they wrote "Web content," they were expected to churn it out in their spare time. When they did start getting paid, there was no mention of residuals—additional payments when the material was repurposed. Internet work wasn't covered under existing Hollywood labor agreements. More than a decade after the Netscape IPO set off the first Internet boom, the relationship between television and online was still ad hoc and undefined.

A strange interlude ensued. For a brief few months, Hollywood was transformed from an industry to a lab. Guild rules forbade writers from working in film or television, but there was no injunction against Web productions—even Web productions funded by a film studio or a television network. For writers and producers, it was a nice setup. They could get instant feedback from viewers, crack jokes that would never fly on network TV, own their shows, maybe even make a little money. It was almost as if they were reinventing television online.

Hollywood had been dabbling in the Web already. Everyone in town took notice when two 27-year-olds in Beverly Hills—Mesh Flinders and Miles Beckett, a wannabe screenwriter and a plastic-surgeon trainee—emerged as the creators of *lonelygirl15*, the YouTube sensation of 2006. Presented as the real-life video blog of a sweet yet troubled Christian teen named Bree, *lonelygirl15* was outed three months later as a fictional series whose star was in fact an actress straight out of film school. At first there was an uproar: Bree was not who she said she was, and a lot of people got upset. But most of them kept watching anyway. And like the fans who commented on Dwight Schrute's blog, they wrote to her as if she were a real person. They told her their secrets; they offered her advice. After a few weeks, Flinders and Beckett realized they needed to get someone to write back.

Michael Eisner, having resigned under fire as CEO of Disney, financed a slickly produced Web series called *Prom Queen* that came out in April 2007. Then, a couple months before the writers strike began, Marshall Herskovitz and Ed Zwick announced that they, too, were making a Web serial. Herskovitz and Zwick were longtime fixtures in Hollywood—the duo behind *The Last Samurai* and *Legends of the Fall*, as well as such hit TV series as *Once and Again* and *thirtysomething*. When they made a deal with NBC to air their new Web series, *Quarterlife*, in prime time, a lot of people in the business began to think of online video as a farm club for television.

On the surface, this seemed to make sense. Instead of spending $2 million to make a half-hour pilot, why not shoot some high-quality Web episodes at $10,000–$30,000 a pop, post them online to build buzz, string them together to make a television series, and then port the whole thing back to the medium where the money is? *Quarterlife* seemed the perfect prototype: its episodes just happened to be 7–10 minutes long, roughly the interval between commercial breaks on TV. But while it did okay online, its premiere on NBC drew just 3.9 million viewers—an all-time low for the network in that slot. It was canceled almost instantaneously.

By the time that happened, the strike had come and gone, leaving behind a boomlet of professionally produced Web series. *Dr. Horrible's Sing-Along Blog*, Joss Whedon's three-part video with Neil Patrick Harris, was viewed 2.25 million times in five days before the volume of traffic brought the site down. *Childrens Hospital*, a twisted parody of TV hospital shows from Rob Corddry of *The Daily Show*, became a hit for the Web site of the WB. *Gemini Division*, starring Rosario Dawson of *Sin City* and produced by former CBS Entertainment chief Jeff Sagansky, cut product integration deals with Acura, Cisco, Intel, Microsoft, and UPS.

"You feel you're in the vanguard of something that can explode," Sagansky told me one afternoon as we sat in his exquisitely appointed townhouse on the Upper East Side of Manhattan. "You know TV—it's been around in its present form since *Hill Street Blues*," the eighties ensemble show whose extended story arcs paved the way for every episodic series from *ER* to *24* to *Lost*. "But this is all new."

What was most obviously new was that Web shows were short. *Dr. Horrible*'s three acts clocked in at 14 minutes each; episodes of *Prom Queen* were only 90 seconds long. Hulu, a joint venture of Fox and NBC Universal to show movies and TV shows online, would later demonstrate that people would happily watch long-form programming online. But at the time, most people assumed the Web was short-attention-span theater.

In fact, what was more interesting about these shows—*Prom Queen*, *Quarterlife*, *Gemini Division*—was how much they were influenced by video games. With Activision, one of the world's biggest game publishers, headquartered in Santa Monica and Electronic Arts establishing a major studio in Playa Vista, crossover between games and television was inevitable. Brent Friedman, the *Gemini Division* screenwriter, was typical. After years as a television writer, he had started writing games at EA, only to realize he had to relearn his craft because the conventions of film and television don't work in an interactive world. Now he and others like him were creating TV/game mashups.

At one level, the resemblance was purely a matter of narrative structure. In a one-hour drama, he explained one day as we stood on the *Gemini Division* set, "you put the characters together over some beers and allow them to bring out the plot. It's exposition disguised as dialogue." But games dispense with the entire first act, the part that sets the plot in motion. "When the story begins, you're in-world—you have a gun, all hell is breaking loose, and your job as a player is to stay alive and figure out where you are." Web video is subjected to that same compression algorithm.

At the same time, blurring the line between television and video games offered a new way to engage the audience, both with the narrative and with each other. All the main characters on *Prom Queen* had MySpace profiles with their own text and video blogs. When fans friended them and sent them messages, the producers scratched their heads: were people just playing along, or did they somehow think these characters were real? After that, social networking features became standard equipment for Web serials. Even as Rosario Dawson was dodging simulated life-forms and agents from the mysterioso Gemini Division, viewers on the show's Web site were being recruited as Gemini agents, enabling them to talk with other agents—er, viewers—by Webcam. "I think this is where entertainment is heading," Friedman said. "It's where I want entertainment to head, because that's what I want to experience."

The strike ended in February 2008, three months after it began. The guild won most of its demands, including jurisdiction over Internet-based media and residuals for online shows, as well as for movies and television programs distributed online. Now that there were rules in place, shows like *Heroes* and *The Office* were able to hire full-time writers for digital. And so most writers returned to movies and TV—but they brought with them a new appetite for experimentation, as well as a nascent sense of what video entertainment might become in a fully interactive world.

It would take more than a 360 approach to help NBC. Gone were the days when a hit series like *Friends* could command $450,000 for a 30-second spot. Fox could still get top dollar for *American Idol*, but the average price for a prime-time ":30" in the 2008–09 season was more like $120,000. The financial import was dire. In early 2008, JP Morgan had estimated the worth of NBC Universal at $55 billion. Yet when GE sold a controlling interest to Comcast in December 2009, the deal valued the company at only $30 billion. Comcast wanted NBC Universal's cable channels, which included Syfy and USA; so inconsequential was the broadcast network that it wasn't even mentioned until nine-tenths of the way through the official, 2,700-word announcement.

But it wasn't just NBC. The audience for all four of the major US broadcast networks was dwindling fast. In the 2008–09 season alone, ABC lost 10 percent of its viewers, NBC lost 14 percent, and Fox lost nearly 18 percent. Most of television's signature shows—*Mad Men, Battlestar Galactica, Curb Your Enthusiasm*—were now on cable, where they drew a level of attention that was increasingly disproportionate to their actual number of viewers. As the mass audience scattered, network programmers started moving away from niche shows in a last, desperate scramble for the evaporating middle. CBS's success was built on none-too-challenging series like *The Mentalist*, a Sherlock Holmes retread that proved just as popular in Britain and France as in the United States. Other networks were turning to similar fare.

Yet even at CBS, producers were no longer satisfied with the old formula. "It's not just about an hour on Thursday and an hour next Thursday," said Anthony Zuiker, creator of the *CSI* franchise, when I saw him at his bungalow on the same Studio City lot where Greg Daniels was working. "Television is not going to make a miraculous rebound without the assistance of other platforms. The one-hour broadcast will be a launching point for a continued narrative on different devices."

The setting was only-in-LA—a two-story shingled bungalow on a small-town street, surrounded by hulking beige soundstages and inaccessible without a drive-on pass. Zuiker, with his round face and his Vandyke beard, seemed like a larger version of David Suchet in his Hercule Poirot role: slightly pudgy, extremely precise, and well aware of his own talents. Less than fifteen years ago, he was driving a tourist tram in Las Vegas; now he's one of the most successful producers in television. His *CSI: Crime Scene Investigation*—a hit from the moment the first episode was aired in September 2000—was the most-watched drama series on the planet in 2009, with nearly 74 million viewers worldwide.

In its obsessive and graphic focus on forensics, *CSI* breached a taboo. Detective shows had long been a staple, but never before had the science of the freshly dead been featured on network television. By setting *CSI* in Vegas, Zuiker spiced up his necro fetish with a soupçon of sleaze. The result was an occasion for global rubbernecking. Somewhere in the car wreck of life, viewers seem to be hoping for a shard of reassurance. In mortality is proof that we exist. We want gore, preferably in 1080p.

But not in 1080p alone. For Zuiker, that insight came in 2002, when he got his first BlackBerry and found himself checking email and taking phone calls as he watched TV. "Eighty percent of the people watching television have a phone in their pocket," he said. "How do we incorporate that device into the storytelling without interrupting the broadcast?"

Like everyone else in Hollywood, Zuiker had time on his hands during the writers strike. He took long walks and thought about what he didn't consider back when he was starting *CSI*—"the opportunity for immersion," as he put it. What made it possible was not just the Internet but the proliferation of devices for accessing it—computers, game consoles, smart phones. "Technology services a need we have behaviorally. There's a need to go deeper. There's a need to get involved."

A year after the strike ended, in early 2009, Zuiker applied his storytelling philosophy to the oldest device around—the book. The result was something he called the "digi-novel"—a paper/video hybrid that uses the Web to deliver two-to-four-minute "cyber-bridges" between chapters. The debut title was *Level 26: Dark Origins*, a crime thriller that aimed to do for serial killers what *CSI* did for forensics. Admittedly, it was awkward to keep switching from printed book to Web video—but less than a year later, Apple introduced the iPad, and suddenly the idea of combining text and video didn't seem awkward at all.

To complement the videos, Zuiker partnered with Miles Beckett, the co-creator of *lonelygirl15*, to create a *Level 26* Web site with the now-requisite social networking features—user forums, personal profile pages where you can upload photos and fan fiction, a "community" function that puts you in touch with real-world crime-scene investigators and with Zuiker himself. "I hope to take the digi-novel philosophy to other platforms," Zuiker noted, and in October 2010, when Sqweegel—the serial killer from *Level 26*—appeared on an episode of *CSI*, he did that too. The same month, CBS announced a *CSI* game for Facebook.

By then the BBC had outdone them all by releasing four episodes of *Doctor Who* as free-to-download video games written by the same people who write the show. Players assume the role of the Doctor, the civilization-saving humanoid who travels through time and space in a police box. "A lot of people who fall into the geek category are quite obsessive about *Doctor Who*," says Dan Taylor, the senior Internet executive at the BBC's Television Centre in London. "People really do want to wallow in the brand."

WHILE ANTHONY ZUIKER WAS TAKING immersion mainstream, the Nielsen Company was touting it as a new measure of success. Nielsen's IAG subsidiary has been promoting not ratings but engagement as a metric for gauging a show's worth to advertisers. According to IAG, cult hits like *Lost*, *Heroes*, and ABC's *Desperate Housewives* command viewers' attention more effectively than do such shows as *American Idol* and *Dancing with the Stars*, which far more pcople watch. "Viewers who pay attention," *Advertising Age* reported, "are more likely to follow a program more closely—and, the theory goes, the commercials that support it."

Would network television ever abandon the ratings chase for viewers who care? People scoffed—but in fact, NBC already had a good example of the IAG theory on its own schedule. The show was *Chuck*, which in early 2009 became the focus of intense attention online. But this time, the network had nothing to do with it. It happened spontaneously, in a way that showed just how possessive audiences could become.

Chuck is a comedy/action hybrid about a hapless computer geek who accidentally gets the entire database of the US national security apparatus downloaded into his brain. Highly unlikely, it's true, and yet funny in an updated *Get Smart* kind of way. Complicating matters is the fact that Chuck—that's Chuck Bartowski, a member of the Nerd Herd, the tech support team at the Burbank outlet of the fictional Buy More home electronics chain—turns out to harbor the government's only copy. The suddenly data-rich Chuck is intercepted by American intelligence agents whose mission is to put him to use thwarting terrorists until the government can reconstruct the database. At that point, unbeknownst to Chuck, he will unfortunately have to be terminated.

As played by Zachary Levi, the previously unknown actor who landed the title role, Chuck Bartowski is sweet, endearing, and somehow oddly believable. He doesn't talk into his shoe as Maxwell Smart did in the sixties Mel Brooks/Buck Henry sitcom, but his bumbling performance as an undercover agent does suggest that tech support may be his true calling. He wears a pocket protector the size of Rhode Island; and though he's tall and good-looking, his voice is high-pitched and breathless and usually on the verge of going out of control. He is Everynerd, charged (quite literally) with every secret in the US government's collection.

Created by Josh Schwartz, the writer-producer behind Fox's hit teen drama *The O.C.*, and his college buddy Chris Fedak, *Chuck* made its debut in September 2007, two months before the writers strike began, and won instant praise for its wit, warmth, wackiness, and intelligence. But while it was shown in scores of countries across the planet, NBC had it in a tough time slot in the US—8:00 p.m. Monday, as a lead-in to the now-flailing *Heroes*. That put it up against ABC's *Dancing with the Stars* and Fox's popular medical drama *House*, which routinely drew twice as many viewers. Not surprisingly, audiences were slow to find *Chuck*, though those who did tended to like it very, very much. So much that when NBC threatened to cancel it after its second season, they organized in protest.

This in itself is nothing radical. There have been fan protests—some successful, most not—over all kinds of borderline shows. One of the most concerted efforts involved *Jericho*, a postapocalyptic tale whose fans inundated CBS with more than 20 tons of peanuts when it was canceled after its first season. Twenty tons of peanuts is one way to get attention, but it was clear from the ratings that the protest organizers weren't representative of the broad, general public—and that's who broadcasters want to reach. As *Time*'s James Poniewozik later observed in his blog, "Four million people who watch a show *really hard* are still just four million people to an ad buyer." No one had ever focused on the networks' other, even more critical constituency: advertisers.

By early April 2009, near the end of its second season and a month before NBC was due to unveil its fall lineup at the upfronts, it was obvious *Chuck* was in danger. Prominent fans rallied to its cause. Television critics promoted the show in print, on their blogs, and on Twitter. Kath Skerry declared "*Chuck* Week" on Give Me My Remote, her popular TV blog, even changing its Web address temporarily to www.givememychuck.com.

Thousands of people took note of all this. One of them was Wendy Farrington, a 30-year-old sales associate in the New Jersey offices of a multinational pharmaceutical company. An attractive woman with dark, flowing hair and an engaging manner, Farrington lives in a small town in Pennsylvania. She liked several shows—including at one point *Heroes*, though like many other people, she had dropped it during the second season—but she considered herself a super *Chuck* fan. "The premise is kind of silly," she told me. "But it doesn't take itself too seriously. I like the action, and I love all the pop culture references. It's like *The Princess Bride*," the now-classic 1987 Rob Reiner comedy, "but with spies. Mondays suck, but that was one hour that always made me smile."

THE DAY THAT SAVED *CHUCK* BEGAN like many others, with Wendy Farrington visiting the bulletin boards for one or two of her favorite shows. But this day something special happened. She was on the user forum at Television Without Pity—a site owned by the NBC Universal cable channel Bravo, coincidentally—when somebody commented that they'd be better off writing to advertisers than trying to pressure the network. She laughed. Then the idea clicked: why not?

One of *Chuck*'s major sponsors is Subway, the sandwich chain, which uses the show to tout its $5 footlong subs. In 2008, according to the research firm TNS Media Intelligence, Subway spent more than $34 million advertising on NBC, much of it on *Chuck*. The show's season finale was coming up in three weeks, on April 27. What if every *Chuck* fan went to a Subway that day, ordered a $5 footlong, and left a note about *Chuck* in the comment box?

Later that morning, in the midst of a long conference call, Farrington scribbled the phrase "Finale & Footlong" on a Post-it. During her lunch break, she went online to find someone to contact at Subway. She wrote letters to the Subway exec (not the right one, as it turned out, but no matter) and to executives at NBC. Before the end of the day she went back on Television Without Pity, started a thread called "Keep *Chuck* Alive," and announced her "Finale & Footlong" campaign to do just that.

The idea picked up momentum fast. Poniewozik announced that he would be buying a footlong. Farrington became co-moderator of the "Save Chuck!" Facebook group, which attracted nearly 5,500 members from around the world. Zachary Levi, the star of the show, declared on a fan site that the "Finale & Footlong" campaign was "an absolutely spot-on idea" and announced that he would be ordering a turkey breast on wheat— "that is of course until they offer the Bartowski special." By late April, "Save Chuck" was the fifth-highest-trending topic on Twitter.

Months earlier, before any of this happened, Farrington had booked a vacation in England for the second half of April. Now she discovered that Levi was going to be there too, at the T1 Starfury fan convention in Birmingham. She decided to go. It was a pretty small affair, so when she got there, she was able to find him and introduce herself. Levi was fascinated: "You started that? We never get to meet the people who start that."

"Well," she replied, "we never get to meet you either."

Two days later, as the convention was wrapping up, Levi led a couple hundred people on a march to the nearest Subway shop. When they got there, he gave Farrington a hug, told the counter man they would all need separate checks, and got behind the counter himself to help out. He spent the next two hours making sandwiches.

The next day, April 27, Subway experienced a major spike in sales. It was not the first time *Chuck* had given the brand a boost. For the episode that aired two weeks earlier, Subway had paid NBC to write a product placement into the script: Chuck's best friend delivers a Subway chicken teriyaki sandwich to their boss at Buy More, talks about how delicious it is, and even repeats the catchphrase "five-dollar footlong." The placement was so brazen that *Ad Age* reported it as emblematic of how far marketers were willing to go to "amp up" their presence in shows. Now *TVWeek* was reporting that it was the most effective placement Subway had done in years—and that Tony Pace, the head of marketing for Subway's franchisee organization, had called a senior executive at NBC's ad sales department to tell him Subway hoped the network would renew the show.

Even so, the *Chuck* vigil dragged on for weeks. The show wasn't mentioned when NBC announced its fall schedule just before the upfronts. It remained in limbo until May 19, when Ben Silverman, the head of NBC Entertainment, announced that the network had worked out a deal with Subway to save the show. At the same time, the comedy series *My Name Is Earl* and the psychic drama *Medium* were both canceled, even though *Medium* had almost as many viewers as *Chuck*. "The demand for *Chuck* that came out of the online community, the critical press, and our advertiser base made us have to pick up that show," Silverman said in a conference call with reporters. "For these other shows, there was not any of that kind of attention or energy."

All spring, as the "Save Chuck" campaign built, NBC.com was watching from the sidelines. Now, with the show renewed,

Andrade wanted to build on the momentum the fans had started. To the fans, however, NBC was a distant, almost forbidding presence. "There was no communication path to the network," said Farrington. Still, she was a sales rep; she was used to cold-calling strangers. She picked up the phone and dialed 30 Rock.

A few weeks later, on a conference call with several NBC execs, she learned about NBC.com's plan for keeping the energy alive: a new *Chuck* site built to house an online contest called "Mission: Chuck Me Out." You could earn points by sharing the greatness of *Chuck* with people through Twitter and Facebook and the like. You could compare yourself to other players on a leader board. Farrington suggested they have fans send in photos of themselves to appear in the show, during one of the brain flashes Chuck gets when something triggers an information surge from the wealth of spy data that's stored in his head. It turned out they were already planning that as the grand prize. "It was freaky," she told me.

But the real *Chuck* game was still being played. Fans like Wendy Farrington had created it themselves on message boards, on blogs, on Facebook, on YouTube, on fan sites. With "Finale & Footlong," they had spent real money to keep watching a fake nerd on TV. By the time the show came back for its third season in January 2010, a YouTube video of Levi's march through Birmingham had been viewed more than 60,000 times. A different YouTube clip of the same event had been viewed more than 20,000 times. Yet a third had racked up some 40,000 views. Farrington's "Save Chuck!" group on Facebook had swelled to more than 22,000 members. As the countdown began for the season premiere, the Facebook page filled up with messages: "Can't wait for Chuck!" "5 more hours!!!!!!!!" "20 mins!!!!!!!!!!" "CHUCK!!!!!!"

That was the prize for this game, and it was one each of these fans could share, Andrew and Kemal and Mohammod and Josh and Chiara and Gianluca and many thousands of others across the planet—they got to see a show that made them smile. And even more important, perhaps, they got to help make that happen. As one of them had remarked in a message board comment to Farrington the previous spring, when it was still far from clear whether *Chuck* would be renewed, "Anyway, this is kind of fun!"

9. Twitter and Nothingness

Meet Noah Brier. It's not hard to do, because in addition to his physical presence, Noah has a blog, a couple Web sites, a Facebook profile, a LinkedIn profile, a Flickr account for his photos, a YouTube channel for his videos, a SlideShare account for his business presentations, a Last.fm profile for the music he's listening to, a Delicious account for the Web pages he wants to bookmark, a Twitter account for random observations and comments, and a Dopplr account so he and his friends can track one another's whereabouts and maybe meet up if they find themselves in the same city. "I'm big on connecting with people," he explained as we sat in a lower Manhattan Starbucks. This is an understatement. At 28, Brier has made himself ubiquitous, in the way that the Web now enables people to be: present, even when he's not.

He's not alone in this. In July 2010, Facebook announced that it had over 500 million users worldwide—more than a quarter of the two billion people online, according to the latest estimate from the International Telecommunication Union. "Half a billion is a nice number," Mark Zuckerberg, the site's cofounder and CEO, declared in a video on the Facebook blog, "but . . . what matters are all of the stories we hear from all of you about the impact your connections have had on your lives."

Meanwhile, a Nielsen survey found that Spanish Web users were averaging five and a half hours per month on social networking sites (primarily Facebook), Brits and Americans and Italians six hours, Australians almost seven. This is how a salesperson in a New Jersey pharmaceutical office can organize, almost overnight, a global movement capable of influencing a US broadcasting network's programming decisions. Jeffrey Cole, director of the Center for the Digital Future at USC, observes that people now simply assume they'll be able to find someone on Facebook. "You know a technology has made it," he adds, recalling an earlier transition, "when the question goes from 'Do you have a fax?' to 'What's your fax number?'"

Brier doesn't spend much time on Facebook, because he finds it too full of pointless distractions. But on Flickr, the photo-sharing site, he uploaded a snapshot of himself every day, more or less, between May 2006 and October 2007. There are pictures of him at the airport, in a taxi, in a green shirt, in a pink shirt, in Florida, in Ireland, in midsentence, clean shaven, unshaven, wearing a fake mustache, looking sleepy, looking hungover, looking—as the caption describes it—"slightly goofy." SlideShare offers a more professional view; it's where he keeps presentations like the one he did on social media and branding at a 2007 ad conference in Chicago. But the center of his online existence is his blog, which he started shortly after graduating from New York University in 2004. It's where he comments on everything from politics to movies to marketing. It's also how he made two of his most important connections to date: his first big job as a marketing strategist, and his girlfriend.

These days Brier works as head of planning and strategy at the Barbarian Group, a highly regarded interactive marketing firm in New York City. In the bio that appears on the company's online "barbaripedia," he observes that the most important thing the Internet has given us is "an understanding of links and networks (two things we thought we understood before the web, but actually didn't)." *BusinessWeek* wrote him up not long ago as one of the top four innovators in social media. One evening in 2008, the story explained, he started thinking about how brands are really defined—not by marketers, but by consumers. He woke up in the middle of the night and started building a Web site where people could register their impressions of different brands. The site is called Brand Tags, and it displays logos, one at a time, along with a space where people can type the first thing that comes to mind. It also shows the results, with the most frequent tags biggest. Among the top 10 results for NBC: peacock, news, 30 rock, friends, the office. For the BBC: news, quality, smart, reliable, english. Alternatively, you can search by tag. Among the top 10 brands labeled "stupid": *American Idol*, MTV, Hummer, and Facebook. It's not exactly scientific, but that doesn't make it any less revealing.

Then there was the time he asked readers of his blog if they'd like to meet in person, maybe over coffee. Another New York marketing blogger, Piers Fawkes, sent him an email suggesting they discuss it. When they did, Fawkes asked what sort of gathering he envisioned. Like-minded individuals getting together to talk, Brier said. Fawkes did a quick search and discovered that the Web domain likemind.us was available. They registered the domain name and posted notices about the upcoming event on their respective blogs.

About 15 people showed up for the first likemind, which was held in a Greenwich Village coffee shop. There was no agenda, but the discussion was lively and spontaneous. "I sat there and I couldn't understand how this group had formed," Brier recalled. "Especially when it happened again the next month." The idea spread to San Francisco when Brier suggested it to two friends there. Next came Seattle. By mid-2010 there were likemind gatherings in some 70 cities across the planet—Amsterdam, Ankara, Atlanta . . . Worldwide, a thousand people were showing up—many of them in marketing, and most only a degree or two removed from Brier or Fawkes. "There's no topic," Brier said. "There's no moderator. Just a desire to meet other people and have a conversation about whatever people have a conversation about. That's the amazing thing."

"MAN IS BY NATURE A SOCIAL ANIMAL," Baruch de Spinoza famously wrote in *Ethics*, his 1677 magnum opus, echoing Aristotle. We are embedded from birth in a network of fellow humans—some we know, many we don't, but we rely on them all. Because the Internet has made the network such a central metaphor, we are conscious of this in a way that the average seventeenth-century European perhaps was not. But social networks not only far predate "social networking"; they are as fundamental as storytelling, in ways that are closely related.

The currency of social networks is connections—links, if you will—which are as crucial in life as they are on the Web. Links determine whether you have a lot of friends or just a few, whether you're central or marginal, whether you're off on your own or in the thick of things. The power and ubiquity of links was demonstrated in the late 1960s in a now-famous experiment by Stanley Milgram, a Harvard psychologist who was looking into the question of how tightly we're connected. The "small world problem," as it's called, had been formulated by the Hungarian writer Frigyes Karinthy in 1929. In the 1950s and '60s, Ithiel de Sola Pool of MIT and Manfred Kochen of IBM constructed a theoretical model and concluded that the odds were 50-50 that anybody in the United States could reach anybody else in the US through two intermediaries. But it was Milgram who put it to the test.

Living in Boston, the self-styled Hub of the Universe, Milgram decided to find out how many steps it would take for a letter to reach a person there from someplace impossibly remote. He picked Wichita, Kansas, and Omaha, Nebraska—cities that "seem vaguely 'out there,' on the Great Plains or somewhere," as he later wrote. Randomly chosen individuals in those cities were sent an envelope addressed to someone in Boston, along with instructions to forward it to the friend or relative they thought most likely to know that person. Of the letters that got through to their intended recipients, the number of intermediaries ranged from 2 to 10, with 5 as the median. The implication was that any person in the US was only about six steps away from any other person. Hence the phrase "six degrees of separation," which John Guare coined as the title of his 1990 Broadway play.

In 1967, when Milgram's research results were published, they ran counter to the, as he put it, "many studies in social science [that] show how the individual is alienated and cut off from the rest of society." Mass media were at their peak. Social atomization was rampant. "Alienated from society" was code for "youth in revolt." Now, nearly 45 years later, mass media are in decline. The Internet has us focused not on alienation but on connections. If anything, people worry that they're too connected for their own good. And Milgram's study seems timely in an entirely different way. "Each of us is part of the giant network that we call society," writes Albert-László Barabási, a network theorist at Northeastern University in Boston. "Our world is small because society is a very dense web."

THE MOST DEPENDABLE WAY TO FORGE A LINK, whether to a colleague in a new job or to strangers on Twitter, is by relating information—a process that often involves telling a story. Stripped of all the apparatus of advanced civilization and pecuniary gain—stripped of Hollywood and television and publishing—storytelling is a simple act of sharing. We share information. We share experience. Sometimes we overshare. But why do we share at all?

Because life is a constantly functioning information exchange. "We attend to one another compulsively, with lightning-fast emotional radar," writes Brian Boyd of the University of Auckland in *On the Origin of Stories*, an investigation into the evolutionary basis for storytelling. This radar is most notable in its absence. The reason *The Office* is so fascinating—the British original has been adapted for numerous other countries, including France, Germany, and Russia in addition to the US—is that the show is a radar-malfunction train wreck. Almost every character is so completely lacking in emotional connectedness as to be unaware that it's even missing. The exceptions are a single young man and woman—Tim and Dawn in the UK template, Jim and Pam in the US version, Paul and Laetitia in the French adaptation, Ulf and Tanja in the German. They're the ones we can identify with, the normal human specimens consigned to spend their workdays in a mockumentary loony bin.

Both Boyd and *The Office* make clear that the function of this emotional radar is to keep us from running aground. Being social animals, we need social feedback to keep our bearings. Fortunately, we seem to derive as much benefit from providing this kind of information as we do from receiving it.

The most obvious thing we get is status: telling a story, (almost) any story, gives us an opportunity to claim the attention of people around us. So we compete to tell stories, to fill in the details of other people's stories, to offer our own comment. And we get a payoff in the form of an ego boost.

There are other advantages to providing social information. When we share stories, we strengthen our links to other people. Within a group—any group, from family to office to cult—stories establish norms and articulate a defining myth. Gossip is useful because it sets the bounds of acceptable behavior, but that's not why we love it—we love it because it gives us the thrill of sharing pseudointimate details of other people's lives while subtly (or not so subtly) expressing our disapproval. Both as tellers and as listeners, we use stories strategically and selectively to advance our goals. Sometimes we lie. And yet, as Boyd observes, "In the long run we serve our own interests best by earning reputations as tactful tellers of reliable, relevant, and, we hope, sometimes riveting reports."

For most of the twentieth century, there were two quite distinct modes of storytelling: the personal and the professional. The stories we told informally—on the phone, at home, at work—existed in an entirely different realm from the professionally produced narratives on TV and at the movies. But where once there was a divide, now there's a blur. Blogger, Flickr, YouTube, Twitter—each of them encourages us to express ourselves in a way that's neither slickly professional nor purely off-the-cuff.

Half a billion people have taken to Facebook because it lets them tell their stories, with all that that entails—the ego boost, the status bump, the strategic positioning. But it also connects them to a different side of storytelling, one that's focused not on any direct advantages it might offer but on the link it forges with the audience.

"Social media is powered by empathy," remarked a panelist during a discussion at the Futures of Entertainment conference at MIT. It was November 2009; Henry Jenkins had gathered a couple hundred academics and practitioners in a classroom on the school's blandly functional campus for his annual conference on transmedia storytelling. Empathy? Really? It seemed a startling assertion. Had this guy—David Bausola, a London entrepreneur—somehow not heard about the coarsening of social discourse, the rampant flaming and general Web-induced civilizational decline engendered by anonymous online commentary, ubiquitous piracy, and assorted other Net-native ills?

Apparently not.

Empathy is a hotly debated topic these days. In May 2010, six months after the MIT conference, a paper presented in Boston at the annual meeting of the Association for Psychological Science made the case that empathy among college students was on the wane—dramatically so, in fact. Sara Konrath, of the University of Michigan's Institute for Social Research, analyzed the results of 72 studies conducted from 1979 on and found an empathy drop, so to speak, of approximately 40 percent—most of it occurring after 2000. She arrived at this figure by plotting students' responses over the years to a standard battery of statements: "I am often quite touched by things that I see happen." "I would describe myself as a pretty softhearted person." That sort of thing. Though she speculated about the reasons—media saturation, violence in video games, a tune-out factor encouraged by social media, fame fantasies fed by reality TV—it was clear that no one could provide a real explanation at this point. Konrath hopes to address the issue in future research.

Until then, it will be difficult to know what to make of her results, but the idea that social media is responsible for an empathy deficit seems suspect. Citing actual examples instead of number-crunching surveys, one could at least as readily argue that mass media—radio and television in particular—stoke fear and anger while social media *promote* empathy. Consider the case of MadV, who in 2006 posted a 41-second video on YouTube in which he wrote "One World" on his palm and invited people to respond. It quickly became the most responded-to video ever posted on YouTube. Michael Wesch, the anthropologist at Kansas State, cites examples like this when he depicts YouTube as a global forum that enables people to sit alone in a room and commune with strangers from across the planet. "It comes down to your horizon," he says. "Who do you include in your in-group? I would guess there are more people who consider the whole planet in their in-group than ever before."

Obviously there's abusive behavior online. But to blame rudeness on the Internet is like blaming highways for road rage. It's an easy cop-out, a way to dodge responsibility for what seems to be a much more general decline in impulse control. It was not, for example, the cloak of online anonymity that induced a congressman to shout "You lie!" during a 2009 speech by the president in the Capitol. But more than that, to say such behavior is omnipresent online is to distort the picture. Despite some very well-documented examples to the contrary, the general tone in social media is overwhelmingly, well . . . social.

There may be a reason for that—a biological basis for empathy. In 1991, brain researchers at the University of Parma made a startling discovery. The scientists had been sticking electrodes into the heads of macaque monkeys in an attempt to map the premotor cortex of the monkeys' brains—an area of the frontal lobe that's involved in rehearsing actions. As Daniel Goleman explains in his book *Social Intelligence*, the electrodes were so thin they could be implanted in individual neurons, enabling the scientists to see which neurons were firing whenever the monkeys did something.

They found the brain cells to be extremely specialized: some fired only when the monkey was holding something in its hand, others only when the monkey was tearing it apart. Then one afternoon, a research assistant returned from a lunch break with an ice cream cone. As he lifted the cone to his lips, one of the researchers noticed a neuron lighting up in a monkey that was watching. The scientists tried putting a piece of food on a table, taking it off the table, taking it from another researcher's hand, each time with the identical result: the same neurons that fired when a monkey did something itself also fired when the monkey watched a person doing it.

Subsequent research revealed the same phenomenon at work in humans. A 1999 study at UCLA used functional MRI, which is far less precise, to show that the same area of the brain is activated when participants watch someone else move a finger as when they move their own finger. The 2009 study of people reading stories from *One Boy's Day* had a similar result. Watch someone bite an apple or kick a football, scientists say, and the motor system of your brain is activated almost as if you had done it yourself. Brain researchers see such results as evidence of "mirror neurons" in the premotor cortex—cells that mirror the experience of cells in other brains, as if the observer and the observed were one. As Vittorio Gallese, one of the researchers at the University of Parma, put it, these mirror neurons "enable social connectedness by reducing the gap between Self and others."

Other neuroscientists have discovered similar mirroring mechanisms in different regions of the brain. In an fMRI study at University College London, researchers looking into pain—obviously something humans empathize with—attached electrodes to the hands of 16 couples. They found that with each couple, much of the same brain circuitry was activated regardless of which partner actually got a shock. The same team had another group of volunteers play a game with the researchers, some of whom played fairly and some of whom did not. When shocks were administered to the researchers afterward, the test subjects' pain centers lit up when those who had played fairly were hit. But they lit up less—much less in the case of men—when the unfair opponents got a jolt.

Because fMRI works by measuring changes in blood flow within the brain, it can't show the workings of the brain at anything close to the cellular level. For obvious reasons, neural probes like those performed on the monkeys in Parma cannot ordinarily be done on living humans. In 1999, however, a team at the University of Toronto was able to use the same technique on a group of human subjects who were undergoing a form of brain surgery known as cingulotomy—a treatment of last resort for chronic depression and for obsessive-compulsive disorder. While the patients were under a local anesthetic, scientists inserted superthin electrodes into their brains. As with the monkeys, the scientists found that the same neuron that responded when the subject was expecting a pinprick also fired when the subject saw another person being pricked.

The discovery of these mirroring mechanisms is considered a milestone in neuroscience. The theory is still controversial, the target of would-be debunkers at NYU and elsewhere, but it's solid enough to have gained widespread acceptance as a general explanation for empathy. It's not the whole picture; if it were, we'd be too freaked by what happens to other people to function ourselves. It doesn't tell us why some people do not feel empathy. It doesn't explain autism or psychopathy or schadenfreude. But it says a great deal to think our brains are structured to make us feel the emotions of others by inducing that state in ourselves. Good stories convey emotion. If all we cared about was how we could profit from telling them, life would get boring pretty quickly. Empathy gives us a deeper reason to connect.

IT'S PROBABLY NOT AN ACCIDENT that the man behind Blogger and Twitter, two of the most important social media services of the past dozen years, came from a farm in the middle of Nebraska. Evan Williams grew up near Clarks (population 316, more or less), which boasts a grain elevator or two and lies alongside a two-lane federal highway in a county that's pool-table flat and averages 16 people per square mile, or one every 40 acres. Clarks is not entirely isolated—Central City, the county seat, is 12 miles down the road, and you can drive to Omaha in about two hours—but it's still pretty lonely: Stanley Milgram's definition of nowhere was Williams's distant metropolis.

Williams, whose family raises soybeans, corn, and cattle, was one of 14 kids in his class in the only public school in town. After high school he went to Lincoln to attend the University of Nebraska, but he dropped out after a year or so and wandered around the country—Key West, Dallas, Austin, Lincoln again. Then he ended up back in Clarks, contemplating the horizon.

That was in 1996. He might have stayed there if it hadn't been for the World Wide Web, which had emerged from CERN five years earlier. Williams had set up a little company in Lincoln to build Web sites for people, but he barely knew what he was doing and hardly anybody there wanted a Web site anyway. So he decided to move to California, where the Web was really happening.

He landed in Sebastopol, a quaint little town in the hills north of San Francisco, working for Tim O'Reilly, a publisher of books and programming manuals and an early Web proponent. Before long, Williams went freelance, developing Web sites for the likes of Hewlett-Packard and Intel. He and a partner, Meg Hourihan, created an advanced project-management program that had an interesting feature—an easy-to-use note-taking function that kept everything written on it in chronological order. In his spare time, Williams and another colleague expanded this feature into a program that made it easy to post their thoughts online.

A handful of computer savants had been keeping Web diaries for years, but you needed some knowledge of programming to do it, and at this point people hadn't even agreed on what to call them. At the end of 1997, however, someone had decided to call his journal a "weblog." A little over a year later, another weblog owner, Peter Merholz, announced he was going to pronounce it "'wee'-blog. Or 'blog' for short." Williams and Merholz were friends, so when Williams released the new program in the summer of 1999, he called it Blogger. You still needed to know a little basic HTML to set up your "blog," but once that was done the only thing you had to do was type in what you wanted to say, click a button, and wait for people to find you. Suddenly, self-publication online became cheap and almost effortless.

Williams had limited expectations for his little program. There were only about 50 blogs in existence at the time, and the most common reaction he got when he told people they could start one was, Why would I want to do that? The feeling was intensified by the bursting of the tech bubble, which convinced many observers that the Internet was as much a fad as CB radio, which peaked in the late seventies before collapsing into oblivion. Yet by the end of 2000, the blog population had reached a few thousand. By the middle of 2002, Blogger alone had 600,000 users.

Most bloggers, Hourihan and Williams among them, used their blogs the way people had always used diaries, as a chronological record of their personal lives. These unfolding narratives could be startlingly revealing. They could also have political consequences. In 2002, bloggers seized on a comment by Mississippi Senator Trent Lott praising the long-ago presidential ambitions of South Carolina Senator Strom Thurmond, who had run on a segregationist platform in 1948. The established media barely deemed Lott's comments newsworthy—he had said similar things before, after all. But because bloggers tend to link to one another freely, and because Google search results are ranked largely on the number of incoming links a site has, their voice was amplified beyond their actual readership. Soon the media had no choice but to cover what had happened. In the ensuing hubbub, Lott was forced to resign as the Republicans' Senate majority leader.

In early 2003, Williams sold Blogger to Google in an all-stock deal, just as the blogosphere, as it came to be called, was developing into a key component of what Tim O'Reilly called "Web 2.0"—the second generation of Web services, the ones that didn't just deliver information or goods or entertainment but invited people to participate. Along with Blogger came a host of others: Wikipedia in January 2001. The social networking site Friendster in March 2003. Its rival MySpace in August 2003. Facebook—at that point only for Harvard students—and Flickr in February 2004. Digg, where people share and rate stories, in December 2004. YouTube in May 2005. Google launched its own online video-streaming service the same year—"a platform for the world's video to live on the Web," its product manager told me at the time. But as ambitious—one might say hubristic—as Google Video was, YouTube turned out to be the service people used. In October 2006, Google announced a deal to buy its scrappy little Web video competitor for $1.65 billion. A couple months later, "user-generated content" was so big that *Time* mag azine made "You" its person of the year.

THE QUESTION FOR WILLIAMS WAS, what next? He had announced his departure from Google in an October 2004 blog post, shortly after Google's IPO made him an instant multimillionaire. He started a podcasting service, but when Apple began offering podcasts on iTunes, it quickly overshadowed anything he could provide. Without a definable business strategy, Williams's company floundered. Then one of his employees, a software engineer named Jack Dorsey, came up with an idea for a service that would work like SMS, the Short Message Service on mobile networks, yet enable people to broadcast messages to groups of people rather than send them out individually. Williams was intrigued. Dorsey built a prototype in two weeks. He called it Status, though eventually the name was changed to Twitter.

Jack Dorsey was 29 years old at the time, a soft-spoken guy who wore faded jeans and had a shock of black hair falling across his forehead. As a teenager in St. Louis, he had developed an odd obsession with dispatch routing—ambulances, couriers, fire trucks, messengers, police cars, taxicabs, all the things that tell you what's going on in a city *right now*. He'd written dispatch routing computer programs, and after a spell at NYU he'd moved to the Bay Area and started a dispatch software company. One day he saw Williams—at this point a celebrity in California tech circles—on the street in San Francisco. He asked Williams for a job on the spot, and Williams took him on.

By this time, Dorsey was as wrapped up in SMS and instant messaging as he was in routing systems, and he realized that what was missing in his urban updates was ordinary people. That was essentially the idea behind Twitter: to give people a simple way to broadcast status updates on themselves. You can say anything you want, as long as you can say it in 140 characters or less. (Because of bandwidth constraints, the number of characters in an SMS message is limited to 160 characters, so 140 would leave enough room to add the user's name.) That's the only rule, and it has enabled Twitter to achieve a significant paradox: maximum freedom through ultimate constraint.

The initial assumption was that the status updates people sent out would be fairly mundane stuff—microstories about where they were and what they were having for breakfast. That happens all too often, though even the minutiae of daily life can be fascinating when it comes in the form of a Twitter feed from your best friend, or from a NASA astronaut in space who's responding to questions from the planet below. But it wasn't long before Twitter evolved into a channel for instant news and communication. Though Twitter provides endless opportunities to be frivolous, it also provides a strong impetus to convey information of real value—because that's how you gain followers. And in the game of social networking, friends and followers are even more enticing to collect than the virtual desk ornaments in Dunder Mifflin Infinity.

But all this became apparent only gradually, as major events took place and people turned to Twitter because it was the cheapest, easiest, fastest way to report them. In May 2008, when a devastating earthquake struck China's Szechuan Province, the first word out was on Twitter. In January 2009, when an Airbus A320 ditched in the icy waters of the Hudson River after its jet engines ingested a flock of geese on takeoff, the first photo was sent out via Twitter by a witness on his cell phone. In June 2009, when Iranians took to the streets in protest after the presidential election, Twitter was used to get word to the outside world. As Jonathan Zittrain, a cofounder of Harvard's Berkman Center for Internet & Society, observed in the *New York Times*, "The qualities that make Twitter seem inane and half-baked are what make it so powerful."

On Twitter, the personal and the global become conflated. One person tweets about going out for coffee. Another person tweets that a private plane has just flown into an office building in Austin. Or the same person does both within the same few minutes. Word spreads in serendipitous and seemingly random ways because, as a system for broadcasting information, Twitter works by collapsing degrees of separation. Because I follow somebody who follows somebody, one day I see a stream of tweets from John Moe, a humorist who's the host of the public radio show *Weekend America* and author of *Conservatize Me*, a send-up of right-wing politics. These comments come immediately after news of the suicide of Andrew Koenig, the 41-year-old actor who played Boner on the eighties sitcom *Growing Pains*. Though Koenig and Moe were a few degrees removed from one another, they had shared the same real-world social network. And there was nothing funny about Moe's tweets that evening:

- *19:34:* Horrible news about Andrew Koenig. Sorry for all who loved him. His pain is over but for those left behind, it's just starting.

- *19:38:* If you're suffering from depression, please get help. Your family & your friends need you to do so. It doesn't have to be this way forever.

- *19:55:* I didn't know Koenig, a few mutual friends, but I can't stop crying tonight.

- *19:57:* Here's what the person who dies never gets to know: the death reverberates forever, it damages survivors forever. Nothing's ever the same.

- *19:59:* People in that pit often write that loved ones would be better off without them. But it's not true. I wish I could get them to hear that.

- *20:05:* Twitter's a great platform for jokes but it's a place to share important information too.

- *20:08:* My brother Rick shot himself in 07. I think about it constantly. I share this not for pity but to pull this issue into sunlight. Thanks.

• • •

THE NEW BUZZWORD IS "HYPERCONNECTED." A magazine writer profiling Williams described him as "not just a practitioner of hyperconnectedness" but the person who more or less invented the concept. This isn't quite true, of course; the idea was in the air he breathed, left there by Tim Berners-Lee and Ted Nelson and Vannevar Bush and Nikola Tesla and Alexander Graham Bell, who invented that first great social networking device, the telephone. Twitter, Facebook, YouTube—each offers a way to link. Each link represents a story, an event, an ego boost, a microburst of hatred, an act of empathy, a sharing. Together they form a dense web of connections. And the more links there are, the more connected everyone becomes.

In January 2010, traffic on Twitter was clocked at 35 million messages per day, up from 300,000 per day at the beginning of 2008. In February, it hit 50 million. Meanwhile, Twitter has insinuated itself into many other social networking services, including Facebook, and Facebook has opened itself to nearly every Web service imaginable. So your tweets pop up on your friends' Facebook pages when they log in. Your tweets are embedded in your blog and who knows how many other places. Your blog and your Facebook profile and your Flickr photo stream all point to one another. And they all link to countless other people's blogs, YouTube channels, Flickr streams, and so forth.

This is where network theory kicks in. The growing profusion of links makes the brain analogy not only fashionable but inevitable. Neurons and synapses, nodes and links—figuratively speaking, the electrochemical jelly within the skull is being replicated on a far vaster scale by billions of brains connecting electronically. If each node on a network has only one connection, the distance from one node to another can be great, Barabási points out. "But as we add more links, the distance between the nodes suddenly collapses." Evan Williams is helping to collapse the world.

In this newly collapsing world, each of us is a node. Being a node can be awkward, even painful at times, as Williams himself found out in March 2010, when he showed up to give a keynote interview at South by Southwest Interactive, the tech culture spin-off of the venerable music festival in Austin. The event got a tremendous buildup, fueled not only by Williams's celebrity within the geekiverse but by speculation that he would finally announce a strategy for selling ads on Twitter, which for 2009 had estimated revenues of only $25 million.

Instead of addressing what the standing-room-only crowd wanted to hear, however, Williams briefly described a new and less than earth-shattering program to link Twitter with other sites. The interviewer—Umair Haque, an economist and Web wonk who blogs for the *Harvard Business Review*—failed to press him for details, and the two quickly moved on to generalities, some interesting, most not. Williams talked about wanting to make it easier for people to help each other by sharing information. Haque offered some vague and rambling queries and went on about how he had once booked a lousy hotel and how Twitter had salvaged his vacation by generating so much attention that his travel agency refunded his money.

This was a dangerous route to take. Two years earlier, Twitter had experienced its breakout moment when it facilitated an audience revolt against another keynote interview at SXSW—this one involving Mark Zuckerberg, the CEO of Facebook, and a young *BusinessWeek* reporter named Sarah Lacy. The audience had quickly taken offense at Lacy's interviewing technique, which was alternately flirty and aggressive. With Lacy interrupting her subject and talking over his answers, the mood turned ugly. "Talk about something interesting!" yelled a voice from the back of the room. Clearly taken aback, Lacy made a comment about "mob rule." Wrong move. In short order the audience took over and started questioning Zuckerberg directly. "Someone, like, send me a message later of why exactly it was that I sucked so bad," Lacy cried out petulantly. "Check Twitter!" came the retort.

The response to Haque's mode of questioning was equally swift and almost as merciless. Making the most of Williams's tool for sharing, people in the audience silently shared their dismay. This time, instead of taking over the discussion, they just headed for the exits. Meanwhile, Haque and Williams chatted away, seemingly oblivious, as the tweets piled up online:

- Why isn't Umair Haque asking the Twitter CEO any difficult questions? Lots of softballs and love fest.

- Where's people already sleeping at #evwilliams keynote/ interview #sxsw. Umair Haque's observations, questions take boredom to a new level.

- Enough with the pompous self-promotion, @umairh. Seriously, I don't want to hear you talk about your blog posts.

- Things only slightly drier than #evwilliams keynote: Lubbuck [sic] County, TX; Death Valley; P.G. Wodehouse.

In one sense, it was a case of empathy being turned against its enabler—or more precisely, against the interview its enabler was doing. (Many tweets explicitly spared Williams from blame for the fiasco.) But more directly, it was a case of empathy spontaneously deployed by a group of people who were frustrated at the situation they found themselves in. People in the crowd experienced a shared dismay, and through Twitter they acted on it. Whether Twitter served as a force for good in this instance depended on your point of view. But Williams had no problem with it; on the contrary, he saw it as a useful source of feedback. No sooner was the discussion over than he tweeted,

> ■ I heard on the backchannel that people want me to answer tougher questions. What'ya want to know? Will answer 10. Go.

Inevitably, because this is the way networks work, Williams-style hyperconnectedness will assume a life of its own, unpredictable and emergent. Right now we're experiencing the first rush of excitement, experimentation, and fear. Through Twitter and Facebook and Blogger and Flickr and YouTube, we're becoming increasingly engaged—engaged with TV shows, with the brands that advertise on TV shows, with one another. Which is why, when NBC.com was trying to maintain the momentum Wendy Farrington and the other fans had built up with the "Save Chuck" campaign, Facebook was so obviously the way to go. "It's kind of a marketer's dream," Stephen Andrade told me, a note of wonder in his voice. "But it's not marketing the way you normally think of it. People are seeking it out!"

10.

This Is Your Brand on YouTube

Andy Puzder had a problem. It was early 2009, and as chief executive of CKE Restaurants, the fast-food company that owns Carl's Jr., he was about to introduce a new burger—the Carl's Jr. Portobello Mushroom Six Dollar Burger, a gooey combination of burger, mushrooms, Swiss cheese, and mayonnaise layered with lettuce, tomato, and onion. But after 12 years in fast food, Puzder was no longer sure he knew how to introduce a product. He felt a little lost.

Carl's Jr. likes to say its burgers are for "young, hungry guys," but young, hungry guys weren't watching all that much TV anymore, and they probably didn't register the ads when they did watch. Besides, the recession had just taken a serious chunk out of his ad budget. At 58, Puzder wasn't so young himself, and he realized the people around him weren't either. At a meeting in Los Angeles with the boutique agency that created most of the chain's advertising, he went around the room dropping bombs:

"You're too old! You're too old! You're too old!" It was early 2009. He wanted new ideas, and he didn't think he was getting them.

The people in the LA office of Initiative, CKE's media agency—the agency that buys the airtime and print space the ads appear in—did not want Puzder telling them they were too old. So they arranged for him to visit a facility in Los Angeles called the IPG Emerging Media Lab. Owned by Initiative's parent company, the global agency conglomerate Interpublic Group, the Emerging Media Lab mainly conducts trend research for IPG agencies and their clients. But its offices, in a glitzy, low-rise complex on Wilshire Boulevard just down from the Los Angeles County Museum of Art, also feature one of those homes-of-the-future setups that are so big in consumer electronics centers like LA and Tokyo. That's what the Initiative folks wanted him to see.

Four years earlier, in 2005, Puzder had paid Paris Hilton a small fortune to shoot a television spot. The ad showed her crawling suggestively across the outside of a sudsed-up Bentley while wearing a skintight unitard and chomping on a burger. The spot made waves, particularly after the Parents Television Council and other self-styled watchdog groups condemned it as soft-core porn. "Get a life," Puzder retorted, relishing the controversy. But then, after its initial run on shows like *Desperate Housewives*, *The O.C.*, and *The Apprentice*, an extended version of the ad racked up more than 1 million views online—and this was when YouTube was still in beta. Now the lab people were telling him that as far as young hungry guys were concerned (in ad industry parlance, that would be males 18–34), there was effectively no difference between YouTube and TV. For Puzder, it was an "aha" moment.

A few weeks later, the lab got a visit from the Carl's Jr. franchisee organization for the Middle East, in from Kuwait. Next, the board of directors, all the top executives, and the team from the creative agency came trooping through. Meanwhile, the Initiative group was plotting out how to create not television spots, but something else. A stream of "engagement content," Robert Holtkamp, the account director, told me. "Compelling content that people would find for themselves and want to consume."

Advertising has always been about compelling content. It has almost never been about letting people find it for themselves. Of course, how they would find it wouldn't be entirely left to chance. The idea was to put it where young hungry guys live online, which is to say, on Facebook and YouTube. Once the "engagement content" made it to that point, it would find them. Or at least, that was the theory.

To test it, Initiative contacted nine top YouTube stars—regular video uploaders whose subscribers number in the hundreds of thousands—and offered them $5,000 each to shoot a video featuring the new Carl's Jr. Portobello Mushroom Six Dollar Burger and run it on their channels. They were told they should speak in their own voice. Other than that, the only request was that the videos all address a single question: How would you eat the new Carl's Jr. Portobello Mushroom Six Dollar Burger?

Judging from the results, the short answer seemed to be, with your mouth open. But there were endless variations, none of them remotely resembling anything you'd see on television. Dave Days ate his after singing to it. HotForWords—Marina Orlova, a Moscow-schoolteacher-turned-world's-sexiest philologist—ate hers after smuggling it into the library. Smosh—the duo of Anthony Padilla and Ian Hecox—ate theirs after Ian threw it in the air, hopscotched down the street, taught his dog to sit, taught his mom to sit, knitted a sweater, fell down on the grass, did some break dancing, and caught it in midair with his mouth. Nigahiga—Ryan Higa, a Japanese American in Hawaii with more than 1 million YouTube subscribers—ate his after wiping his armpit with the box. iJustine—Justine Ezarik, a witty blonde with nearly 100,000 subscribers—ate hers with a knife and fork and lots and lots of ketchup. Phil DeFranco, known to his YouTube viewers as sxephil, tried to eat his with a knife and fork too—but iJustine punched him in the face, knocked him off his chair, and started eating it herself. Alphacat—Iman Crosson, a comic whose Barack Obama impersonations had just won him an invitation to perform at Aretha Franklin's birthday party—ate his instead of the healthy bowl of steamed vegetables his girlfriend had prepared for him. Cory Williams, a.k.a. "Mr. Safety," ate his while ignoring cries for help from a buddy he had sent wobbling down the highway on a skateboard. WasteTime-ChasingCars, the nom de video of a Denver high school student named Mac, declared, "I eat my Carl's Jr. Portobello Mushroom Six Dollar Burger while jumping over cars"—right before a car sped past and he jumped over it. "How do you eat your burger?"

All nine videos went up on Friday, June 3. Initiative had set up a partnership with YouTube to make sure the videos would be heavily featured. But the illusion of control that accompanies a television campaign was impossible to maintain. No one really knew what would happen. Would the users like the videos and pass them along? Or would they see this as a big company trying to play in their space? Would the campaign go viral, or was Carl's Jr. setting itself up for ridicule? "The client was nervous," Holtkamp admitted. "When they throw up a commercial on TV, there aren't thousands of comments they can read immediately. But the sheer volume of viewing ended up telling the tale."

Initiative had been hoping for 3 million views, tops, and

assumed the whole thing would fade away after a week or so. Instead, people watched the videos well over 3 million times in the first week, and then they kept on watching them. Rather than getting an alert about a video on one channel, people got alerts about several, and then they found out there were still more. "We didn't really realize the degree to which followers of one were followers of another," Holtkamp said. "There was a massive amount of overlap." If they saw one or two, they had to see them all. Then they would copy the little patch of embed code on the onscreen video viewer and paste the videos into their own blogs for more people to see.

After a few days, people started making spoof videos. Shane Dawson, a YouTube regular with close to 1 million subscribers, spoke for many when he donned a blond wig, a blue do-rag, red lipstick, and fake pearls and stood before his camera to demand, "Why didn't they come to *this* bitch to ever taste they burger? Like, do I not look like a bitch that would go to Smarls Jr. to eat a damn burger?" At one point, counting the Shane Dawson spoof, Carl's Jr. had 8 of the 20 most popular videos on YouTube.

But the Portobello Mushroom Burger explosion wasn't happening only on YouTube. iJustine had more than six times as many Twitter followers as she had YouTube subscribers, and every time one of them tweeted about it, more people went to watch. People sent each other links by email. The videos started popping up on Facebook. Comments poured in relentlessly. "It started this unbelievable chatter," said Holtkamp. "It just kind of caught fire. And given the nature of YouTube, we could actually just watch it happen."

As *Adweek* observed in an article about the campaign, "These networks"—YouTube, Twitter, Facebook—"comprise a new kind of media buy." There was just one catch: for the most part, no media were actually bought. Great for the client—but the agency got virtually no commission, even though it had set the whole thing up. Lori Schwartz, director of the Emerging Media Lab, admitted that this is a bit of a problem. "If we're not making money off the media buy," she said, "where are we making money? That is the current struggle."

ADVERTISING USED TO BE SUCH a simple business. A company had a product to sell. An ad agency came up with a way to sell it and bought print space or airtime to get the message out. Consumers saw the ads and rushed out to buy the product. Or not, in which case the company selected a new agency and the process started all over again.

There were endless permutations on this scenario. In the 1950s, Rosser Reeves's "unique selling proposition" held sway—the theory that to be successful, an ad had to make a claim that was both unique and of interest to the consumer. In practice, the unique selling proposition was a blunt instrument, effective but unsubtle. In his 1961 book, *Reality in Advertising*, Reeves shows us what he means by taking a potshot at a Coke campaign that at that point had been running for 30 years:

> Let us pick up a magazine, and leaf through it, if only to sharpen our definition. As we lift it from the table we glimpse the back cover, in full, glorious color. It shows Santa Claus taking a soft drink out of the icebox and smiling at the consumer. There is no copy.
>
> Where is the proposition to the consumer? Where is the uniqueness? And where the sell?

Sadly he continues his perusal, encountering a ham that claims to make mouths water (don't they all?), an insurance company that salutes motherhood, a beer that promises good living, a gasoline that extols the joy of driving—all this in a chapter titled "The Tired Art of Puffery." And then he writes,

> In the midst of all this, drop a real U.S.P.:
>
> "STOPS HALITOSIS!"
>
> The U.S.P. almost lifts itself out of the ruck and wings its way to some corner of the mind.

Ted Bates & Company, Reeves's New York ad agency, produced countless campaigns of the anti-halitosis variety. "M&M's—melts in your mouth, not in your hands." "Anacin, for fast! fast! fast! relief." Again and again, the product's big selling point was hammered relentlessly into the victim's head. This was the hard sell.

At Ogilvy & Mather, Reeves's brother-in-law, David Ogilvy, countered with his "brand personality" theory. According to Ogilvy, the trick was not to tout some "trivial product difference," as he somewhat rudely put it, but to associate the brand with a consistent set of images chosen for their cachet and allure. (Ogilvy and Reeves spent years not talking to one another.) Thus Hathaway, a middling shirt company in Maine, became the epitome of urbane sophistication by virtue of being worn by "the Hathaway man," a middle-aged gent with a mysterious eye patch. This was the soft sell.

Like Reeves, Ogilvy focused primarily on an ad's content—what it said. But the early 1960s—the period captured in *Mad Men*—saw the triumph of an entirely different approach. Bill Bernbach of Doyle Dane Bernbach maintained that what really mattered was the execution. DDB's "creative revolution" broke all the rules with a series of wildly successful ads for the Volkswagen Beetle that carried taglines like "Think Small" and "Lemon." In a time-bending *Mad Men* edition of *Advertising Age* dated June 23, 1960, the fictional Don Draper dismisses "the Tinkerbells" [*sic*] of the industry and says, "We're not going to be bankrupted by the next fad." But like traditional shops on the real Madison Avenue, Draper's firm was up against the clever sell; and in the sixties, the clever sell prevailed.

For all these sectarian debates, the business kept motoring along, generating healthy profits for all concerned. But by the nineties, it was apparent to anybody who looked that the wheels were starting to come off. For decades, the scarcity and expense of physical resources (printing presses, radio spectrum) had put a cap on the number of newspapers, magazines, and television networks people could choose from. With the proliferation of cable and satellite channels, however, that scarcity began to give way to an electronic infinitude of choice.

As viewers started to drift away from the broadcast networks, the cost of reaching them grew ever higher—from less than $2 per 1,000 viewers on prime-time US network television in 1972, according to the Television Bureau of Advertising, to nearly $17 in 2002. The DVR sent television networks into a panic by giving viewers the option of fast-forwarding through the ads. And then, in late 2003, Nielsen put the industry on orange alert by announcing that in the United States, men 18–34—the demographic most prized by advertisers, largely because it was the hardest to reach—were watching 12 percent less prime-time network TV than in the year before. Never mind that the falloff was only 26 minutes a week. On television, minutes are worth millions.

When a subsequent Nielsen report suggested that young

men might be coming back, the networks crowed in triumph. But a season-by-season look at the ratings during those years reveals a continuing falloff in the measure that was actually at issue. According to Nielsen's figures, the amount of time males 18–34 spent watching the broadcast networks during prime time started dropping during the 2001–02 season and just kept going down. The only thing young men consistently spent more time doing in front of their TV sets was playing video games. And even when they were watching TV, they didn't seem inclined to watch the ads. This was true even for those in the advertising business. "People don't have to listen to you anymore, and they won't," I was told by Tim Harris, the then 30-year-old co-chief of video game advertising at Starcom MediaVest, a major media-buying agency. "I mean, I resent commercials—they make me push three buttons on my TiVo."

Major brand advertisers were already beginning to think it was time to move beyond "the :30," as the 30-second spot is known in industry parlance. Time to stop paying more and more for fewer and fewer viewers on network television. "Where are we going?" Coca-Cola's then president, Steven Heyer, asked in a speech at an *Ad Age* conference in 2003, a few months before the initial, eye-opening Nielsen report came out. "Away from broadcast TV as the anchor medium." Yes, he acknowledged, people were afraid—but so what? "Fear will subside, or the fearful will lose their jobs. And if a new model isn't developed, the old one will simply collapse."

For 50 years, Coke and television had been conjoined. Decade after decade, television had taken up more and more of Coca-Cola's ever-expanding US ad budget, from just 40 percent in 1960 to more than 80 percent in 1980 to a whopping 94 percent in 2000. The partnership had yielded some memorable moments, from the groovy "Things Go Better with Coke" spots of the sixties to the carefree "Can't Beat the Feeling" campaign of the eighties. But in 2002, Coca-Cola shaved 10 percent off its network ad spending. By 2006, television's share of the company's US ad budget was down to 70 percent—adjusted for inflation, a drop of more than $100 million in six years.

Coca-Cola was not the only company that had devoted more and more of its ad dollars to television. Anheuser-Busch, Johnson & Johnson, General Mills, General Motors—major advertisers had been committing an ever-larger chunk of their ever-growing ad budgets to the tube for decades. Television's share of their spending topped 50 percent in 1959 and averaged about two-thirds from 1970 on. As television became the default medium for advertisers, the television industry ballooned accordingly. In 1986, Fox became the first commercial broadcasting network to challenge the big three since the demise of the pioneering DuMont Television Network 30 years before. Cable and satellite channels proliferated. By 1992, cable magnate John Malone was heralding the imminent arrival of a "500-channel universe."

Then, in the late nineties, the big brands began tentatively pulling back. Before long, Steven Heyer's declaration for Coca-Cola became a chorus. "There must be—and is—life beyond the 30-second TV spot," declared Jim Stengel, the chief marketing officer of Procter & Gamble, the world's largest advertiser, at an industry gathering in 2004. "Used to be, TV was the answer," proclaimed Gary Cowger, the president of GM North America, the same year. "The only problem is that it stopped working sometime around 1987."

But if television wasn't working, then what? Nobody really seemed to know. In the ensuing vacuum, wackiness abounded. "A terror has gripped corporate America," I was told by Joseph

Plummer, then chief research officer at the Advertising Research Foundation. "The simple model they all grew up with is no longer working. And there are two types of people out there: a small group that's experimenting thoughtfully, and a large group that's trying the next thing to come through the door."

Many advertisers stumbled into the brand-new field of "experiential" marketing, said to be effective at bypassing the storied ad-filtering mechanism of young males. This approach came into vogue after trend detectives noted a preference for life over stuff. When The Intelligence Group, a consulting firm owned by Hollywood's Creative Artists Agency, polled teens and young adults on whether they would rather spend $500 on a cool experience or a cool product, three out of five chose the experience. Manufacturers of stuff responded by trying to create experiences around it.

In an effort to promote the Altima, Nissan ran ads in movie theaters showing *The Matrix Revolutions*, the last in the Wachowski brothers' trilogy of cosmic infobabble shoot-'em-ups, and augmented the ads by hiring actors to shout slogans at the screen as they were playing. Toyota, not to be outdone, introduced its youth-oriented Scion line by paying college students to roam Times Square with temporary tattoos on their foreheads touting the boxy new vehicle. "This is the first time we've used foreheads," Scion's manager confided to *Ad Age*. "We'll see how it works and take it from there."

If not experiential, then virtual. Second Life enjoyed a brief vogue after *BusinessWeek* put it on the cover in 2006 and its founder gave a presentation at the annual Sun Valley mogulfest hosted by Herbert Allen, the New York investment banker. Adidas, Coca-Cola, IBM, Nissan, Sears—dozens of companies, *Wired* among them, rushed to set up a presence there. They found a vast, echoing emptiness. A new-media consultancy within Publicis Groupe, another of the global ad agency holding companies, concluded after a study that the average population density in Second Life was less than that of the most deserted regions of Idaho. And those who did go there tended to be more interested in virtual sex and free virtual money than in, say, the delights of Coke's elaborately built-out "Virtual Thirst" pavilion.

The Second Life phenomenon was predictably short-lived. By June 2010, Linden Lab, its parent company, was in retrenchment mode, laying off 30 percent of its workforce. The spotlight was shifting to popular new games like *FarmVille* that are played on Facebook or the iPhone.

Created by a San Francisco startup called Zynga Game Network, *FarmVille* was released in June 2009. By the end of the year it could claim some 65 million regular users, 40 percent of whom were tending their virtual farms every day. There's no charge to play, but virtual farmers do pay real money to buy fake products. In July 2010, *FarmVille* took things a step further by introducing its first product integration (or "in-game crop integration," as a Zynga executive put it)—organic blueberry bushes from Cascadian Farm, a 15,000-acre operation owned by General Mills. It remains to be seen whether *FarmVille* will become a viable ad medium. But in raw numbers at least, the new game's 30-million-plus daily players do compare favorably with the 18 million adults 18–49 that the major US broadcast networks averaged in prime time during the 2009–10 season.

Bob Garfield, an influential writer for *Ad Age*, refers to the current situation in media and advertising as "the chaos scenario." Cable channels superseding the broadcast networks, video games elbowing their way onto the TV set, iPods replacing radios—as individuals we're more connected than ever, and yet as a market we're atomized. As goes the mass market, so go mass media, spelling chaos for the media industry itself and for the advertisers that rely on it to reach consumers. Looking around him, Garfield detects an ever-intensifying downward spiral:

> Fragmentation has decimated audiences, viewers who do watch are skipping commercials, advertisers are therefore fleeing, the revenue for underwriting new content is therefore flat-lining, program quality is therefore suffering (*The Biggest Loser*, Q.E.D.), which will lead to ever more viewer defection, which will lead to ever more advertiser defection, and so on.

It's easy to get carried away with this stuff, and Garfield does. Take those ad-skipping DVRs, a source of panic among television people from the moment TiVo hit the market in 1999. Is the panic justified? Perhaps not. Millward Brown, an international research firm, found in a recent study of 1,000 US households that the people with DVRs actually remembered ads as well as those without them. When the firm played sped-up ads to test audiences in South Africa, those people, too, had recall scores above the norm. In fact, the chairman of Millward Brown South Africa concluded in a peer-reviewed paper, fast-forwarding through television commercials makes little difference in what viewers remember, because they have to pay close attention to the ads in order not to miss the start of the show.

Garfield dismissed this argument as "idiotic" and "absurd" when it was proffered by Jeffrey Bewkes, who's now CEO of Time Warner, at the 2007 Bear Stearns Media Conference. And

Millward Brown is no more a neutral party than Bewkes is; the firm is owned by WPP, yet another of the global advertising conglomerates. But the idea is supported by common sense—ever try to fast-forward through the ad block with the sound off and your eyes shut?—as well as by other research. When Patrick Barwise of the London Business School and Sarah Pearson of the consultancy Actual Consumer Behaviour conducted an in-depth study of eight UK homes, they found that the inhabitants used their DVRs only 30 percent of the time, and even then they received "significant ad exposure."

The real threat to ad viewing on television remains those old standbys, the refrigerator and the bathroom. The DVR merely highlights the obvious: that a significant number of viewers will avoid TV spots any way they can—even if they have to study them for three seconds in order to avoid watching them for 30.

This is the real message of the DVR: a lot of people don't like the ads they see on TV. They especially don't like the ads interrupting their favorite shows. It doesn't matter if there's a unique selling proposition or a brand personality or even a creative revolution. And with that secret out, the $600 billion global advertising industry becomes unsupportable in its current form. If people don't like your ads, how are you supposed to sell them something?

That's what the chief marketing officers at big advertisers are trying to figure out. These are people who make, on average, $1.5 million a year—in some cases, much more—in a job with an average turnover rate of two years. They're under pressure—big pressure. And the answers they're getting are leading them away from media in general and television in particular. No more "broadcast TV as the anchor medium," as Heyer put it. So, yes, technology has unleashed chaos on the media industry. The question for ad people is, How can their business reinvent itself?

ADVERTISERS HAVE BEEN FINDING the same thing other people with a story to tell are finding: that to tell it, they need not only to entertain their audience but to involve them, invite them in, let them immerse themselves. There's a place for television in this scenario, but it tends to be as a support medium. The actual involvement happens not on TV but online.

This first became clear with Burger King's 2004 "Subservient Chicken" campaign, created by the Barbarian Group for the ad agency Crispin Porter + Bogusky to promote the chain's "Have it your way" theme. Like Carl's Jr., Burger King is a fast-food operation that appeals largely to young guys. The idea behind "Subservient Chicken" was off-the-wall but clever: if you can order a chicken sandwich your way at Burger King, what could you do with an actual chicken—or better yet, some dude wearing a chicken outfit?

The television spot showed the chicken man performing embarrassing tasks at the command of some Abercrombie & Fitch types. At a companion Web site, you could type in your own commands—sit, squat, do a cartwheel, play air guitar, pee in the corner—and watch the chicken perform them. (Ask for anything racier and the chicken would waddle toward the camera and wag its finger disapprovingly.) The grainy video made it look like a live Webcam performance, but that was just an illusion; in fact, the chicken man's reactions were prerecorded. The site was intended to be an add-on to the TV campaign, a little something extra. But according to Crispin Porter, it got a million hits in its first 12 hours—and that was before the TV spot even aired.

"Subservient Chicken" took a lot of flak within the ad business for not making an overt attempt to sell chicken sandwiches. But to Crispin Porter, that was the point: don't shout the message. It was the same subdural approach Jordan Weisman took to introduce his alternate reality game for *AI*. From the anthropologist's point of view, there's a reason why this works: it has to do with the difference between competitive behavior and cooperative behavior. As Brian Boyd writes,

> Signals that evolve through competition tend to be costly, as arms races develop between insistent senders and resistant receivers. Messages become louder, longer, more repetitive, massively redundant, like the roars of red deer stags or Superbowl advertisers. Signals used for cooperative purposes, by contrast—"conspiratorial whispers"—will be energetically cheap and informationally rich.

It's not enough just to break through the clutter, in other words. And rarely is it worth the effort required to smash through the filter. You need to disarm the filter—and the best way to do that, the most economical and efficient way, is to signal that your signal is nonthreatening. "The days of putting some stupid message up and forcing everyone to see it—that's so over," Alex Bogusky, Crispin Porter's then creative director, told me. "With this generation it's, 'I know you're marketing something to me, and you know I know, so if you want me to try a new chicken sandwich, that's cool—just give me some crazy chicken to boss around.'"

• • •

Two years later came another landmark in the marriage of television and online: a contest to see who could create the best TV spot for the newly redesigned Chevy Tahoe. "The 'Subservient Chicken' campaign was a trailhead," the creative director of the Campbell-Ewald agency, Stefan Kogler, told me when I flew to Detroit to check it out. "Or maybe a rabbit hole. It empowered people, and this was sort of the same thing."

The MBAs who populate ad agencies and corporate marketing departments spend years learning the art of control—what their cleverly calibrated messages should and shouldn't say, where they should appear, how often they should appear there, and what should appear nearby. Empowering people has never been on their agenda. But Internet advertising promises abilities that marketers have long lusted after, like the capacity to target people who might actually be interested in what they're selling and to engage those people in conversation. And when consumers are enlisted to tell the story, it's seen less as advertising than as peer recommendation. So Chevy decided to have an online contest to see who could create the best TV ad for the new Tahoe. It was the wikification of the 30-second spot.

Consumer research showed a high correlation between potential Tahoe purchasers and viewers of NBC's *The Apprentice*, the Donald Trump reality show. So in March 2006, Chevy bought an episode—not just commercial time but the entire show, which that night featured a cutthroat team of Donald Trump wannabes plotting ways to sell auto dealers on the many virtues of the new Tahoe. During the commercial breaks, viewers were asked to go to a special "microsite" where they found some video clips, a little music, and a few simple editing tools to mix and match any way they liked.

The contest ran for four weeks and drew more than 30,000 entries, the vast majority of which faithfully touted the vehicle's many selling points—its fully retractable seats, its power-lift gates, its (relative) fuel economy. But then there were the rogue entries, the ones that subverted the Tahoe message with references to global warming, social irresponsibility, war in Iraq, and the psychosexual connotations of extremely large cars. One contestant, a 27-year-old Web strategist from Washington, D.C., posted an offering called "Enjoy the Longer Summers!" that blamed the Tahoe for heat-trapping gases and melting polar ice caps. An entry called "How Big Is Yours" declared, "Ours is really big! Watch us fuck America with it." The same contestant (hey, no rules against multiple entries, right?) created an ad that asked the timeless question, "What Would Jesus Drive?" On its own Web site, the Tahoe stood accused of everything but running down the Pillsbury Doughboy.

For Chevrolet, this was a moment of truth. With attack ads piling up on its site, spilling over onto YouTube, and spinning out into the blogosphere, what would Chevy do? Nothing, as it turned out. "When you do a consumer-generated campaign, you're going to have some negative reaction," said Ed Dilworth, a top Campbell-Ewald executive. "But what's the option—to stay closed? That's not the future. And besides, do you think the consumer wasn't talking about the Tahoe before?" Of course consumers were talking; the difference was, now they could be heard.

By any objective measure, the "Tahoe Apprentice" campaign had to be judged a success. In four weeks the microsite attracted almost 630,000 visitors, nearly two-thirds of whom went on to Chevy.com. Apparently they liked what they saw, because sales took off, even though it was spring and SUV purchases generally peak in late fall. That April, according to the automobile information service Edmunds, the average Tahoe was selling in only 46 days; the year before, models had languished on dealers' lots for close to four months.

The lesson for marketers was that the story of Tahoe—of any brand—was no longer theirs to control. Yet the vehicle's fans (forget its critics) were eager to tell its story—as eager as *Harry Potter* fans are to help spread their gospel, as *Star Trek* fans, as the fans of any product. Just in case anyone failed to get the point, Scott Donaton, then editor of *Advertising Age*, took up the issue in his column. A show of hands, Donaton asked, from all those who thought the campaign proved the dangers of user-created content. "Ah, yes," he wrote, "there's quite a few arms raised—you're all free to go, actually; the marketing business doesn't need your services anymore. We have a toy railroad set as your lovely parting gift."

In retrospect, "Tahoe Apprentice" was naïve only in assuming people would need to be given stock video and editing tools to assemble something resembling a TV spot. Even in 2006, users were more resourceful than that. Unsolicited Chevy videos were already turning up on YouTube that were far more sophisticated than anything "Tahoe Apprentice" yielded, pro or con. There was "Chevy Lowrider Commercial," which shows vintage Chevys hopping down the street; and "Chevy Ridin'," a slide show of custom Chevys set to the gangsta rap hit "Chevy Ridin High." There was even "Chevy Tahoe Memorial," an elegiac video in black and white that shows a young man jumping, drifting, and ultimately wrecking his much-loved SUV.

It wasn't long before these YouTube tribute videos morphed into "ads" people made for their favorite products. In September 2007, an 18-year-old in England made one for his iPod Touch. Nick Haley, a political science student at the University of Leeds, had been listening to "Music Is My Hot, Hot Sex" by the São Paulo group Cansei de Ser Sexy (Portuguese for "tired of being sexy"). Somehow the line "My music is where I'd like you to touch" got lodged in his brain. "I was like, This song is too perfect," he explained later. "It's punchy, loud, fast and naughty." So he went to his MacBook and made a "commercial" for the new iPod Touch, combining "Music Is My Hot, Hot Sex" with video from Apple's Web site and using production tools that are available to anyone with a laptop. Then he uploaded it to YouTube.

Within days, Haley's video was discovered by someone in marketing at Apple's Silicon Valley headquarters. The Apple people alerted their ad agency, TBWA/Chiat/Day, in Los Angeles. Haley was on a city bus in Leeds when he got an email from the agency. At first he thought it was a joke. But within days he was on a plane to LA to work with the creative team on a professional version. They had it on the air by the end of October. As for CSS (as the band is known), sales of its music in the US increased exponentially after the ad appeared on MTV; within weeks, the song was on *Billboard*'s Hot 100.

Nick Haley's story suggests several things. First, the nature of online distribution—serendipitous discovery on a global scale, from Brazil to England to California to the entire US. Second, an extremely media-savvy view of advertising. It's like Bogusky said: this generation knows you're trying to sell them something, and you know they know, so let's just drop the pretense and make the whole exercise as much fun as possible. Why the hypocrisy?

The conventional 30-second television spot, reviled as it may be, served a purpose. It compartmentalized the ad function, tucked it away in its own separate box, allowed us the illusion that our entertainment was somehow unsullied by it—even if it swallowed up 8 minutes out of 30. Other types of advertising—the in-your-face product placements for Subway on *Chuck*, for instance—break the bounds. Even *Ad Age* bemoaned the arrival of "shockingly intrusive" placements such as Subway's. Yet *Chuck* fans not only didn't object, they used the brand as a rallying point.

As for music, the idea that a rock group would license its songs for a commercial used to be unthinkable. In 1995, when Microsoft asked to use an R.E.M. song to promote the latest version of Windows, the response from the band was, "Our music is not for sale." It's a long way from that to a college student using a sexy tune to create his own "commercial" for a product he loves.

This leads us to the third development that Nick Haley's "Music Is My Hot, Hot Sex" video embodies: the growing role of ordinary people—consumers, civilians, call them what you will—in creating a brand identity. The insight that led Noah Brier to create Brand Tags in 2008 has become common knowledge. Brands that once yelled at us—"fast! fast! fast! relief"—now want to hear what we have to say. Brands that once sought to define our identity—Gap Kids, the Marlboro Man—now look to us to define theirs.

Billee Howard, global strategy chief at the public relations firm Weber Shandwick, sees in this the future of marketing. So what if brands can't talk at the consumer anymore, if they can get the consumer to speak for them? So what if the brand has to surrender control, when in fact it can attain a kind of control that could never be attempted before? "You appear to let go," Howard said one day as we sat in her midtown Manhattan office, the late afternoon sun slanting through the East Side canyons. "But in fact you have more control than ever."

By subtly directing brand perceptions while encouraging the consumer to help create those perceptions, Howard maintained, the marketer can help the brand and the consumer to, in effect, become one. "You can't rely on ads," she said. "A brand becomes relevant by infusing itself directly into the culture"—through music, through YouTube, through public events that are reported in the media. "Advertising used to interrupt life's programming. Now advertising *is* the programming. And if you're actually being marketed to successfully, you have no idea."

Decades from now, when historians try to identify the pivot point between advertising that interrupts life's programming and advertising that *is* the programming, one artifact they're likely to seize upon is Coca-Cola's "Happiness Factory." Simultaneously a last hurrah for television and a harbinger of the future, "The Happiness Factory" was the *Star Wars* of television spots—an animated fantasy so fully imagined and entertainingly produced it could almost have become an immersive world all its own. It spawned not just a series of TV ads but an expanded universe, from online contests to a pop song that hit the top 40.

Conceived by the Amsterdam office of Wieden+Kennedy, an independent agency headquartered in Portland, Oregon, "The Happiness Factory" dramatized a delightful conceit: that inside every Coke machine is a snowy mountain wonderland where furry little creatures toil with unabashed joy at the task of providing liquid refreshment to the humans waiting outside. As the spot begins, a slightly built young guy with a scraggly beard walks up to a Coke machine on a busy city street and drops a euro coin into the slot. We follow the coin as it falls into a fantastical landscape of mountains and waterfalls—a panorama that suddenly comes alive with industry. A trio of helicopter-like Chinoinks carry an empty bottle into position. An enormous mechanical arm drops out of the sky and fills the bottle with Coke. A gaggle of kissy puppies leap onto the bottle and smother it with love. A gap-toothed capper is catapulted onto its top to seal in its fizzy goodness. A sacrificial snowman is fed into a snowblower to make it icy cold. Fireworks light up the sky as it's paraded toward the chute. Finally, as the bottle tumbles down into the outside world, we see the guy reach in to grab it. Walking away with the bottle in his hand, he turns back with a quizzical look on his face, then shrugs and moves on.

First aired in 2006, the spot was developed as part of an enormous rebranding campaign designed to lift Coke out of the doldrums. Coca-Cola at the time had become a tarnished brand. Obesity was pandemic, and consumption of bottled sugar water was frequently cited as a reason. The Oscar-nominated documentary *Super Size Me* had recently shown just how devastating a steady diet of Big Macs, french fries, and 42-ounce Cokes could be. Mega-scaled, two-liter bottles of soda pop had become symbols of bloat. Bottled waters and energy drinks were the hot category now. Could Coke ever again become an iconic brand?

To fix their problem, Coke's marketing chiefs arranged a competition among a half dozen of the world's top agencies. The theme they specified was "happiness in a bottle." Unfortunately, says John Norman, who at the time was an executive creative director at W+K Amsterdam, "Coke had been promoting happiness for years. It had become too sweet." Dan Wieden, one of the agency's cofounders, gave them his own directive:

the tone of their work should be "refreshingly honest." Not sweet—optimistic.

Posted on a wall in the "war room" of the Amsterdam office, on one of the seventeenth-century canals that ring the old city, was a piece of paper on which someone had written, "Always Look on the Bright Side of Life"—the title of the iconic song from *Monty Python's Life of Brian*. What about "the Coke side of life," Norman asked—the sunny side, as opposed to the shady side? And so "The Coke Side of Life" became the theme of their campaign—an invitation to say yes to the idea of happiness in a bottle.

The factory idea was an outgrowth of that. At first the factory was to be a place where various happiness clichés—bunny rabbits, clowns—would be chopped up and fed into a bottle. They were talking with Spike Jonze about directing a live-action spot when he asked, Are they really gonna let you chop up a clown? Shortly afterward, Coca-Cola's chief creative officer flew out from corporate headquarters in Atlanta with the answer: no, they weren't. They weren't going near the ingredients, period. No clowns; no secret formula. Just happiness.

From there the Happiness Factory evolved into the animated fantasy world—"*The Lord of the Rings* meets *Harry Potter* meets *Monsters, Inc.*," as Norman describes it—that ended up onscreen. As imagined by Psyop, the animation studio on the Lower East Side of Manhattan that produced the spot, it wasn't just happy; it was thrillingly, ludicrously, over-the-top happy. The result—aired on television networks and in movie theaters in more than 200 countries, a viral phenomenon on YouTube when YouTube was only beginning to become a phenomenon itself—quickly emerged as one of the most loved Coke ads ever.

"Nobody could have predicted it," says Sylvain Lierre, a Coca-Cola account director at W+K Amsterdam. "It just happened."

That's when Coca-Cola executives began to wonder what else they could do with the idea. They brought in Jeff Gomez, who heads a New York–based consultancy called Starlight Runner Entertainment. Gomez works with major corporations—Disney, Hasbro, Microsoft—to develop entertainment properties into immersive worlds. He had become enamored of this kind of deep, multilayered storytelling as a kid. "My escape was fairytales, dinosaurs, and *Godzilla*," he said one afternoon as we sat in his office, in a century-old building on Union Square. In the mid-seventies, at age 12, he moved from the Lower East Side to Honolulu, "6,000 miles closer to *Godzilla*," and stumbled across the media mix strategy then being developed by Japanese publishers. "I discovered that in post–World War II Japan, manga could quickly become television series, a line of toys, even a feature film. I had just come from *Yogi Bear*"—reruns of the early sixties cartoon show. "My mind was blown."

Eventually Gomez made a career out of helping US companies develop their own media mix franchises. He was instrumental in the evolution of *Pirates of the Caribbean*, which began as a Disney theme park attraction in the sixties and has now mutated into a series of novels and video games in addition to the blockbuster films starring Johnny Depp. He was brought in to consult on *Halo* after Universal pulled out of the movie project and Bungie announced it was splitting off from Microsoft. More recently, he was a key figure behind the 2010 decision by the Producers Guild to establish a credit for transmedia producer.

Gomez is big on myth. "We see ourselves as stewards," he said. In too many cases—*Star Wars* being an obvious exception—the producers of a movie or a television show or a video game haven't plumbed their story deeply enough even to identify its message, much less whatever underlying myth it may embody. "So the message changes and the audience becomes frustrated," he went on. "It's our job to figure that out. And to do that you have to crack the IP"—the intellectual property, the core of the story. "That means immersing ourselves in it and figuring out what makes it timeless and relevant. There's an aha! moment that's very specific to each property. It's the moment when I've found the true emotional connection."

As they sought to crack the Happiness Factory, Gomez and his team interviewed people in Amsterdam, in Atlanta, on the Lower East Side. After four months they produced a lavishly illustrated 150-page book, somewhat like the "show bibles" television producers routinely create for their series, but far more extensive. "We develop entire story worlds," he said, "from a platform-neutral perspective. We're not worried about whether it's a TV show or a game. We're taking the intellectual property and making it so robust as to furnish dozens, hundreds of hours of content. And we have to allow for audience interaction on a large scale. You can't just have five characters. You have to build out a community and be contactable by audience members."

When Gomez was putting together his Happiness Factory mythology, W+K and Psyop were already at work on "Happiness Factory—The Movie," a three-and-a-half minute minifilm showing what happens when the factory runs out of Coke; and "Inside the Happiness Factory," a mockumentary in which actual employees give voice to the characters inside the factory. After these came all sorts of iterations, from the "Now Hiring" Web site, where people were invited to apply for a job in the Happiness Factory, to the "Open Happiness" single sung by the hip-hop/R&B singer Cee Lo, which made the pop charts in Australia, New Zealand, the US, and several other countries. (In China it hit number one.) "Every iteration moved through Starlight Runner so we could maintain the integrity of the fictional world," said Gomez. "We served as the clearinghouse."

At one point, they were even plotting ways to take the Happiness Factory beyond marketing. In a 2008 speech at a media conference in Wales, Jonathan Mildenhall, Coca-Cola's global ad chief, hailed the Happiness Factory as a new kind of advertising platform and raised the possibility that it could give rise to a series of movies or comics. Plans were devised for spinning off Happiness Factory narratives years into the future. At this point, however, they seem unlikely ever to materialize.

"There was a lot of exploration," said Gomez. "The difficulty is that the main thrust of the narrative is centered on a factory that produces Coca-Cola." That would seem to be a good thing, except that a Saturday-morning TV cartoon show, say, could be attacked on the basis of the very health concerns that the "Coke Side of Life" campaign was devised to overcome in the first place. "It's knotty," Gomez said.

MEANWHILE, W+K HAS BEEN PURSUING a different kind of thinking, one that combines the narrative flair of the Happiness Factory—the sort of thing the agency has always excelled at—with an approach that involves the audience directly. Out of this came one of the most talked-about campaigns of 2010: "The Man Your Man Could Smell Like," for Old Spice.

A 71-year-old brand owned since 1990 by Procter & Gamble, Old Spice was up against Unilever's Axe, an upstart product whose message was, as W+K digital strategies director Renny

Gleeson describes it, "put on our stuff and get laid"—a unique selling proposition if ever there was one. The strategy behind the Old Spice campaign was more reality-based: most of the people who buy men's grooming products are women, and they want their guys to smell nice—but not from using their L'Oréal. The ad itself was as over the top in its way as the Happiness Factory. It featured the strikingly handsome Isaiah Mustafa, a one-time player in the National Football League, wearing nothing but a towel as he stood in front of the shower—no, on a boat—his hand now dripping diamonds—wait, on a horse?

This initial ad came out in February, allowing Old Spice to leverage the online fascination with Super Bowl ads without actually spending the $2.5 million or so it cost to buy 30 seconds of airtime during the game. Instead of the Super Bowl, the spot debuted on the Old Spice Facebook page and quickly went viral on YouTube. By early April, it had racked up nearly six million views and the previously unknown Mustafa had become a pop culture sensation, making appearances on NBC's *Today*, ABC's *Good Morning America*, *The Early Show* on CBS, and *Oprah*.

As Mustafa's fame grew, it became apparent to the team at W+K that they needed a way to let viewers connect with him. So they started to wonder: what if people asked him questions on Twitter and he responded with videos on YouTube—in real time, and with television production values? The result was "Subservient Chicken" for real—not canned responses, but an actual dialogue with viewers.

It began with an announcement on Facebook and an alert sent to a handful of bloggers. Then, early on the morning of Tuesday, July 13, Mustafa joined an agency team—art directors, creative directors, technology geeks, social media strategists—for two very intense days in a video studio in Portland. Tweets came in; 20 or 30 minutes later, clever response videos popped up on YouTube—186 in all, each one addressed to the person who had provoked it. Kevin Rose, the founder of Digg. George Stephanopoulos, the *Good Morning America* host. Orli, a blogger in Israel. Demi Moore. PingChat, a messaging app for mobile devices. Perez Hilton, the controversial gossip blogger. "As soon as people realized that this was not a one-off, that he was actively responding to them, it became a game," said Gleeson. "A lot of folks were crafting their tweets specifically with the idea of getting a response." Eliciting a reply video from Mustafa became a jackpot-like reward—"and reward-based systems," Gleeson added, "are the things that motivate human beings."

One last thing about the Old Spice campaign: not long after the initial spot appeared, it was accompanied on YouTube by pop-up text ads for Axe that slyly referred to a video campaign of its own—one that purported to be about soccer balls. "Embarrassing Dirty Balls? Let Axe Show You How the Detailer and Shower Gel Clean Your Balls."

It's a tough world out there.

FROM "SUBSERVIENT CHICKEN" to "the Happiness Factory" to "The Man Your Man Could Smell Like," most interactive advertising efforts have meant getting people involved with a brand and its story. But what if you didn't try to tell a story, or even try to enlist other people to tell it for you? What if you just went straight into the life-programming business? That's the way they think at R/GA, the advertising firm that routinely picks up Digital Agency of the Year honors from *Ad Age* and *Adweek*.

"Do people like storytelling?" asked Nick Law, R/GA's chief creative officer for North America, when I saw him at the agency's New York headquarters. "Of course people like storytelling. But given the choice, they're probably going to go to HBO."

A 44-year-old Australian with a scruffy beard and unruly shock of reddish-blond hair, Law has the raffish look of a vintage rock 'n' roller. But the appearance belies his background, which includes two decades in corporate identity and advertising firms in London and New York. Since 2001 he has worked at R/GA, which was started in the late seventies as a graphic design and video production shop by two brothers, Richard and Robert Greenberg. Then known as R/Greenberg Associates, the company gradually morphed into a digital-effects studio working on TV spots and feature films. By the time Law arrived, Richard Greenberg had left and his brother Bob had reinvented the firm yet again, this time as an interactive advertising agency.

What distinguishes R/GA from other ad shops, even innovative agencies like Crispin Porter and Wieden+Kennedy, is its willingness to rethink absolutely everything. If marketing were being invented today, what form would it take?

Law sees the ad industry in its current incarnation as the legacy of William Bernbach and the creative revolution of the sixties. "Bernbach said you could make it entertaining," he said. "That approach proved to work particularly well in TV—if you're going to interrupt the entertainment, you'd better make it entertaining. And in the format of TV advertising you never have to ask, Why would people watch this? They watch it because they're watching *I Love Lucy*. But when you start to ask this question, you realize people don't want to watch toilet paper give them a 30-second narrative—not when they could be watching real entertainment from real entertainment producers."

R/GA's offices occupy an unadorned white building on the gritty fringes of the garment district, a few blocks from Times

Square. Set back from the street behind a white-walled courtyard where a few cars are parked, the structure has a stark, Bauhaus-like simplicity. Inside, white walls and white shelves provide a home to Greenberg's extensive collection of outsider art.

"For me, if you look at television advertising now," Law continued, "it's a ballooning of entertainment at the expense of information. It's a poor man's Hollywood." But what civilians actually want, he argued, is information. "That's why they're starting out more and more with Google search.

"What I'm suggesting is that there's not just one way to look at advertising, through the lens of entertainment. There are all these other things. So it resets the answer to the question, What should we be making? Twenty years ago I'd be thinking, how do I turn this idea into a 30-second spot? Now I make a decision: Should we be doing something to encourage a community? Should we be giving information? Should we be nesting entertainment in there? Because if advertising is just going to be about entertainment, we're all going to be making viral videos."

THE FULLEST CURRENT REALIZATION for this way of thinking is Nike+, an R/GA–assisted partnership between Nike and Apple that turns running—generally a fairly solitary activity—into a social experience. When Law says people get information from their community and community from their information, he is not in fact offering a Zen kōan. Nike+ is what he has in mind.

Introduced in the summer of 2006 and refined multiple times since, Nike+ bears no resemblance to conventional advertising. It consists of a sensor that goes into your shoe, a wireless connection so the sensor can broadcast data to an iPod or iPhone strapped to your arm, and a software interface that lets you easily upload this data from your iPod to the Internet. The sensor calculates your speed by measuring the length of time your foot is on the ground and transmits that data to your arm. After your run, you sync the data with your computer through iTunes, which automatically sends it to Nikeplus.com. There you have access to your entire running history, complete with graphs and goals. You can record your progress and match yourself against other people. You can form a club and challenge other people on the site, anywhere they happen to be on the globe. Nike+ turns running into a game, one you can play by yourself or with others.

Nike already had one of the longest-running and most memorable ad campaigns around: "Just Do It," built around a slogan that's become so closely identified with the brand that the word "Nike" no longer even has to be mentioned. Introduced in 1988 and in use ever since, "Just Do It" is credited with enabling Nike to zoom past Reebok, the dominant sport shoe brand of the eighties, growing its worldwide sales from under $900 million to $9.2 billion in 10 years. As powerful as it is, however, "Just Do It" is ultimately just a slogan. Nike+ is a tool—an application that provides very personal, user-specific information while ushering you into a global community of runners.

"Just Do It" emerged from a meeting between Nike, headquartered in suburban Beaverton, Oregon, and its Portland-based ad agency, Wieden+Kennedy. Nike+ came out of an entirely different process. It's the product of a three-way development effort involving engineers at Nike, Apple, and R/GA. The team at Nike's Techlab did the initial prototyping; the Apple group perfected the sensor; designers and programmers at R/GA, under Law's supervision, developed the software and the interface that made it work.

Law drew a diagram on a whiteboard to explain R/GA's approach. He was sketching out a four-part talent map divided up according to way of thinking:

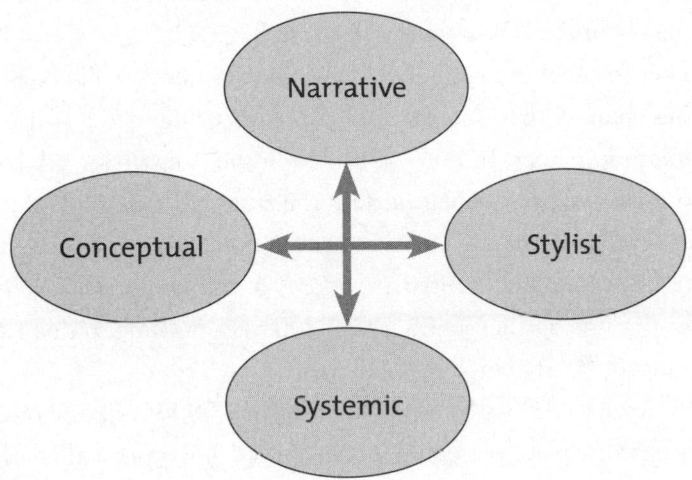

At the top are the storytellers; on the left are the idea people; on the right are the people who make everything look good. These are the familiar components of any ad agency team. At the bottom are the newcomers, the systems thinkers. The ones who are there because 60-odd years ago, Norbert Wiener introduced cybernetics, and with it a way of thinking that combines an engineering sensibility with a view of the whole.

Law pointed to the systems node. "In the old world"—meaning the world before the Internet—"the bottom half of this diagram didn't exist. But you don't get from 'Just Do It' to putting a monitor on your arm. Nike+ was conceived down here"—where the systems thinkers live.

Law referred to Nike+ not as a campaign but as a platform—as in a software platform, a structure on which individual applications can be built. He also described it as "a media channel," in the same way that television and radio are media channels, or that YouTube has become a media channel for brands like Carl's Jr. But he noted an important distinction between this and other media channels: "We own it. We're not buying it."

There's another distinction Law didn't mention. This is a media channel that doesn't read like advertising; it reads like a popular movement. In 2007, Nike+ won the Advertising Club of New York's international award for the most brilliant work of the year. Yet *Wired* ran a 4,200-word cover story about it that didn't mention R/GA's role or its function as a marketing tool. Nike+ blurs the line so thoroughly that its marketing function can go unnoticed.

In August 2008 and again in October 2009, Nike showed what such a platform could do. It staged an event called the Human Race, a 10-kilometer race held in some two dozen cities across the planet on a single day. The Human Race transformed Nike+ into a global, 3-D, highly participatory billboard for Nike itself. Some 780,000 humans took part the first year, a million the second—12,000 in Seoul; 9,900 in Guangzhou; 7,900 in Singapore; 9,400 in Tel Aviv; 5,100 in Berlin; 1,400 in London; 4,400 in Rio de Janeiro; 11,000 in Buenos Aires; 3,500 in New York; 14,000 in Mexico City. It was a rolling wave of human feet, an endorphin high that rippled across the planet, crossing oceans and continents in time with the sun. City challenged city, country challenged country, and at the end of the day the contestants could feed their photos into the system and get a personalized commemorative book. A magazine in Singapore called it "the day Nike united the world."

Bob Greenberg once wrote in a column in *Adweek* that Nike has moved "from great storytelling to a digital world of customer connections." But that doesn't mean Nike has abandoned stories. "You could argue that Nike+ is a story about running, told through data," said Law. "It's a matrix of stories. It's your own story, and it's brand stories. People jump from one to another, and the doorway to it is your own data." Describing all this, he began to sound like Will Wright on *The Sims*: much as play gives rise to stories in Wright's game, running gives rise to stories on Nike+. "As a brand," Law said, "do you want to create a game environment? Can you compete with Nintendo? There are times when you can—especially when your brand connects with data." Brands become games, and games become stories. "That's why Nike+ works."

11.

The One-Armed Bandit

You wouldn't know to look at it that Hammersmith Hospital is one of the leading medical research centers in the United Kingdom. Located not in Hammersmith itself but in a desultory district of West London known as Wormwood Scrubs ("snake-infested thicket" in Old English), it occupies a mazelike complex of relentlessly institutional buildings hard by the red-brick walls of the old Wormwood Scrubs prison, her majesty's repository for the criminally insane. Deep within the hospital grounds is a brutalist concrete slab that's home to a world-renowned clinical imaging facility. In the upstairs offices, the sterile hum of equipment is randomly punctuated by shrieks and screams from the prison, which has long been notorious for its alternating bouts of rioting and brutality.

For several months in 1997, this cyclotron unit played host to perhaps the most improbable *Battlezone* tournament ever. It was hardly an obvious place to play a vintage Atari arcade game.

But it worked if you were a scientist looking to do the first major brain study of gamers in action.

The gameplay environment was not fun. Lying on their backs, the test subjects were given an intravenous injection of carbon-11, a radioactive isotope of carbon. As the ice-cold liquid shot up their veins, an IV was attached to the other arm to extract blood so the concentration of the isotope could be measured. Once the IV was in, the subjects were slid headfirst into the scanner, where they got to play *Battlezone* with a video screen overhead and one hand on a joystick. Their mission: to maneuver a tank through a battlefield with the joystick, collecting flags and blowing up enemy tanks while trying to avoid destruction themselves. Once they had collected all the flags on the screen, they would advance to a new level where they'd find more flags to collect. For each level they achieved, they'd be paid £7.

The scanner used positron-emission tomography to detect the presence of an agent containing carbon-11 in two different portions of their brains: the cerebellum, which is instrumental in motor control; and the ventral striatum, a critical component of the reward system. The cerebellum was being measured for control purposes; the real focus of the PET scans was the striatum, a U-shaped structure located deep within the brain. There are billions of cells in the brain, but the striatum is loaded with a particular kind of neuron that acts as a receptor for dopamine, the powerful neurotransmitter that's instrumental to our sense of anticipation and reward.

Divining the workings of a living brain requires an extraordinary commitment of resources. This particular experiment had been in the planning stages for three years. The people who devised it were affiliated with Imperial College London, a leading scientific university, and funded by the Medical Research

Council, an agency of the British government. There were nine researchers in total—a psychologist, two mathematicians, a couple neuroscientists, and several psychiatrists. The eight test subjects—all of them male, because you can't inject a woman of child-bearing age with radioactive substances—were mostly students and postdocs at the hospital.

The point of their inquiry was not to study video games. It was to develop imaging techniques that would enable scientists to measure the release of neurochemicals—something that can be done invasively with lab rats and monkeys but not, except in extremely rare circumstances, with humans. The neurochemical most likely to yield results from the technique they were devising was dopamine.

In focusing their attention on dopamine receptors in the striatum, they were homing in on a key component of the brain's reward system—the structure that provides the neural underpinning for human craving, whether for drugs or liquor or french fries. Amphetamines and cocaine had been shown to produce a measurable increase in dopamine, but it was unclear if you could stimulate dopamine production through a cognitive task. Nonetheless, animal studies had shown dopamine to be involved in goal-directed behavior, and games like *Battlezone* are very goal directed—they're all about blowing things up and racking up points. There was heated debate within the research team; after all, gaming had never before been considered worthy of serious research. But in the end, *Battlezone* got the nod.

Carbon-11 has only a 20-minute half-life, so it had to be generated in the unit's underground nuclear accelerator as the men were being readied for the scanner. The moment they were injected, the experiment began. While they played *Battlezone*, the three lead researchers—Matthias Koepp, Andrew Lawrence, and Roger Gunn, all postdocs in their twenties—sat in a nearby control room, watching their progress on a video monitor while munching on bratwurst and sauerkraut.

Koepp supplied the food. A recent graduate of the Free University of Berlin, he was a medical doctor whose own reward system was activated more by skiing than by video games. The gamer in the group was Lawrence, a Cambridge-educated psychologist. He'd been a big fan of arcade games like *Battlezone* and *Pac-Man* as a teenager. Gunn, a top-notch young mathematician, did the bulk of the math that enabled them to convert raw data into meaningful results.

What happens in a PET scan is that positrons—positively charged radioactive particles from the carbon-11—flow through the bloodstream toward the brain. As the positrons decay, the tomograph takes measurements to determine how densely they are binding with receptor neurons in the striatum. The receptor neurons cannot bind with carbon-11 if they bind with dopamine. The readings would tell the researchers where the dopamine was by telling them where the radioactive isotope was not. The experiment, then, would enable them to determine how much dopamine was being released. Only coincidentally would it provide the first real clue about what happens in the brain of a human who's playing a video game.

THROUGHOUT HISTORY, THE BRAIN has been the ultimate mystery box. Not until the second century AD, when the physician Galen observed that Roman gladiators—the football players of their day—lost their mental acuity after suffering brain damage, was the brain even identified as the organ in which thought and consciousness transpired. Some 1,700 years later, around the 1890s, researchers armed with dyes and powerful microscopes began to figure out that the brain is made up of cells—the scientists dubbed them "neurons"—that process information by means of electrochemical stimulus.

In 1953, researchers got their first real insight into how memory works when a young Connecticut man named Henry Molaison—known forever after as patient HM—had part of his brain removed in an experimental surgical procedure. Because the surgery left him unable to form new long-term memories, neuroscientists gained the first real insight into how memory works. (Patient HM also helped inspire Christopher Nolan's deliciously nonlinear thriller *Memento.*) The eighties and nineties saw the development of neuroimaging techniques—PET scans and functional MRIs that enable scientists to peer inside a living brain and try to deduce its workings. Slowly, haltingly, the black box of the brain is giving up its secrets, just as we're inventing a new grammar for storytelling. And unlike the $15 Magic Mystery Box that J. J. Abrams bought as a kid, this one is clearly worth opening.

The groundwork for the Hammersmith Hospital study had been laid in the 1970s and '80s by Wolfram Schultz, a neuroscientist whose research on monkeys provided the first explanations of how the brain's reward system operates. Working in his lab at the University of Fribourg, in a medieval town in the shadow of the Swiss Alps, Schultz had taken to squirting apple juice into the mouths of monkeys while probing their brains with ultrathin electrodes. In a series of experiments, he found that the monkey's brains released dopamine in response to their reward—the apple juice. But the pattern of dopamine release turned out to be more complicated than expected. If the juice was delivered after a tone was sounded, the monkeys would get a dopamine rush not when they tasted the juice itself but earlier, when they heard the tone. If a light came on before the tone, the monkeys would respond to the light. With the pattern of dopamine release as reinforcement, the monkeys were learning when to expect their treat.

Schultz had made a startling discovery. Before his experiments, dopamine was thought to be the brain's way of delivering pleasure. This was the "hedonia hypothesis"—not a Marx Brothers construct but a theory developed in the seventies by Roy Wise, then a psychology professor at Concordia University in Montreal. (Wise now heads the behavioral neuroscience unit at the US National Institute on Drug Abuse.) Yet Schultz's lab monkeys weren't actually responding to the taste of the juice; they were responding to a signal that the juice was about to arrive. What's more, they ceased to respond at all once they learned to expect the juice in a predictable pattern. As Schultz later wrote,

> Dopamine neurons respond to primary rewards only when the reward occurs unpredictably. . . . By contrast, a fully predicted reward does not elicit a response in dopamine neurons.

The implication was clear: dopamine has less to do with pleasure itself than with the drive to seek pleasure.

After Schultz's monkey experiments, neuroscientists looking into the brain's reward system focused mainly on diseases and addiction. Drugs like cocaine and amphetamines, they discovered, deliver an off-the-charts reward by unleashing a flood of dopamine in the striatum and other key areas of the brain. But dopamine itself doesn't provide the sensation of pleasure. As Schultz demonstrated, dopamine regulates our *expectation* of pleasure. Once the anticipated reward becomes commonplace, the dopamine-receptive neurons fail to fire. This doesn't happen with addicts, however. In the currently prevailing view, drugs become addictive because they change the structure of the brain, making the dopamine neurons hypersensitive to the drug in a way that induces craving.

Meanwhile, throughout the 1980s and '90s, people from other disciplines were studying gamers. Cognitive scientists showed gamers to have better peripheral vision, increased hand-eye coordination, superior spatial skills, and quicker reaction time than nongamers. Computer scientists started to wonder how video games could keep someone glued to the screen for hours. But until the Hammersmith Hospital study, scientists had shown little interest in how games affect the brain at the neurochemical level.

As the test subjects were grabbing virtual flags and shooting up virtual tanks, would a sudden dopamine rush prevent the carbon isotope from binding with the receptors in the striatum? The answer turned out to be dramatically yes. "We were amazed," says Andrew Lawrence, now a cognitive neuroscientist at Cardiff University in Wales. "People had said we couldn't do it"—that any dopamine release that occurred would never be large enough to detect. Instead, the scans revealed a massive increase, as much as if the men had injected amphetamines or Ritalin into their veins. And the higher the level they reached in the game, the more dopamine their brains received.

Even though video games were only incidental to the purpose of the experiment, Lawrence and his colleagues were well aware that their findings would be controversial. In documenting a link between video games and the reward system, their research suggested a tie between gaming and addiction. "Companies were threatening to sue us because we were saying games cause addiction," Lawrence recalls. In fact, they were making a much more precise claim. "Addictive drugs hijack the natural reward system," he continues, "and what we showed was that video games hijack it as well." At the same time, the experiment also connected gaming to another behavior—one seemingly quite different, yet equally connected with the role of dopamine in the brain's reward circuitry: learning.

"LEARNING AND ADDICTION ARE very tightly bound together," says Kent Berridge, a prominent neuroscientist at the University of Michigan. "So tightly that they sort of merge." Berridge, head of Michigan's Affective Neuroscience & Biopsychology Lab, is a leader in the burgeoning field of dopamine studies. He thinks about big questions: What causes addiction? Where does pleasure come from? How does the brain decide what's pleasurable and what's not? Learning and addiction are his primary subjects.

Dopamine is clearly the instrument of both. The brain's reward system not only responds to new sensations; it also learns from repeated sensations. Schultz's monkeys learned to expect a squirt of apple juice after the sound of a tone. In a set of experiments involving humans, test subjects learned to draw from one deck of cards and not from another after experiencing repeated losses from a bad deck. Remarkably, however, their learning occurred well before they could provide any conscious explanation of what they had learned or how.

This is the Iowa Gambling Task, an experiment described by Jonah Lehrer in his book *How We Decide* and by Malcolm Gladwell in *Blink*. Put four decks of cards in front of people, two of the decks offering low-risk, low-reward payouts and two offering high-risk, high-reward payouts, and see which ones the subjects pick from more. The results were startling—not because people went for the high-reward decks, but because of how quickly they learned not to.

Designed by a team of neuroscientists from the University of Iowa, the Iowa Gambling Task was intended to find out how humans learn from their mistakes. The players were given $2,000 in pretend money and the four decks of cards. Unbeknownst to them, two of the decks paid out $50 per card and two paid out $100—but randomly interspersed with the payout cards were penalty cards, which were neglible in the low-yield decks but in the higher-yielding decks could cost the player as much as $1,250. The drawing would stop at 100 cards. By that time, anyone who had stuck with the two higher-paying decks would have lost a lot of money.

In addition to the two kinds of decks, there were two kinds of test subjects: "normals," plucked from the general population; and "patients," people suffering from damage to the prefrontal cortex and unable to experience emotions as a result. Subjects in both groups had a finger connected to a device that would give a reading on galvanic skin response—perspiration, a sign of nervousness.

At first, neither the 10 normals nor the 6 patients showed a preference for either set of decks. But the normals quickly began to show an aversion to the high-risk decks. They couldn't explain it in words, but their skin response told the story. By the time they were ready to draw the tenth card, their fingers would start to sweat every time they considered drawing from the punitive decks. Ten cards after that, the sweating continued but they still couldn't explain what was going on. Not until they drew their fiftieth card did most declare they had a "hunch" that something was wrong with the two high-yielding decks, and even then they couldn't actually explain it. By the eightieth card, many of the normals could articulate what was going on. But even the three who couldn't put it into words continued to draw from the lower-yielding decks. Unconsciously, their brains had already learned that the high-paying decks were dangerous.

The patients had a much worse time of it. None of them showed any skin response when contemplating or actually drawing from the bad decks. Three of them eventually got to the point where they could formulate in their heads what was wrong with the bad decks, but they continued to choose from them regardless. Unlike the normals, they never learned—at least, not in any way that mattered.

The Iowa Gambling Task study suggests that there are two very different ways of acquiring knowledge—one conscious and deliberate, the other not. Cognition is the conscious form. It's related to episodic memory, which is the recollection of what happens in your life (what did I do last night?), as well as to semantic memory, which is all about facts and figures (what is the capital of France?). Episodic and semantic memories are thought to be formed through an interaction between the hippocampus, a structure at the base of the brain, and the prefrontal cortex. The type of learning this experiment revealed, on the other hand, has to do with procedural memory (how to ride a bike, how to play the piano). It's learning through repetition, with the brain's reward system as a mediator.

"The dopamine system operates below the cortex," says Berridge. "It's activated by simple Pavlovian learning, not so much by cognitive understanding." Think of it as an extremely sophisticated pattern recognition system that functions beneath the level of conscious thought. We're able to act on it, but if we experience any knowledge of the patterns it recognizes, it comes to us as a feeling, a hunch, rather than anything we can explain. This is learning as an emotional response—one that has nothing to do with logic or reason or linear thought. Which is what makes it so powerful.

One of the mainstays of Brooklyn's indie rock scene is a club in Gowanus called the Bell House. A beacon of nightlife on an otherwise deserted street, it sits surrounded by old, red-brick warehouses that mercifully shield it from the fetid waters of the Gowanus Canal, home to heavy metals and sewer sludge. Most nights the Bell House showcases Brooklyn groups like the National or Elvis Perkins in Dearland, sometimes British imports on the order of Beth Orton. But on a Tuesday night in March 2010, the headliner was a performer of a different genus: Joseph LeDoux, director of the Center for Neural Science (a.k.a. LeDoux Lab) at New York University. He was there to talk about fear.

LeDoux was quite a draw. I got to Gowanus only to find, a block away from the Bell House, groups of club kids heading dejectedly toward the subway, warning latecomers that people were being turned away at the door. Inside, just past the bar that dominates the front room, the doors to the performance space were shut tight. Something about the fire code. Too many people already. Worming my way in through the back room (this is when it pays to be a reporter), I found 450 people standing shoulder to shoulder, drinking beer and learning about their amygdalas. "It's just a really geeky event," explained the guy next to me, a young IT worker who had come with his girlfriend, "and I'm into it."

At 60, LeDoux was a good three decades older than most in

the crowd, but with his regulation jeans and untucked plaid shirt he fit in well enough. After the lecture he would be performing with his "heavy mental" rock band, the Amygdaloids. But now he was talking about the low road and the high road—different pathways for processing information in the brain.

Say you're walking through the woods and you see something long and skinny on the ground. Stick or snake? The information you've received travels from the eye to the cerebral cortex, where it's analyzed and identified. That's the high road. But meanwhile, in a few thousandths of a second, the same information has zipped over to the amygdala, an almond-shaped area near the base of the brain that, like the nearby striatum, is key to learned responses like fear. This is the low road. It's what gives you a start when you see a long, skinny shape on the ground, regardless of what your cortex determines it to be. As LeDoux pointed out, "Better to treat a stick as a snake than vice versa."

Cheers and whistles from the crowd. People banging on the doors to get in. Guards had to use their body weight to make sure the doors stayed shut. Judging from the crowd response, LeDoux seemed to have tapped something almost as primal as fear.

The amygdala, the focus of LeDoux's work, serves a similar function as the dopamine-activated reward system, which includes the striatum and the anterior cingulate cortex, a nearby area that's instrumental in focusing our attention. Together, these areas of the brain are key to much of human and animal motivation.

"If you measure dopamine while an animal is searching, it's very high," LeDoux said later, over lunch at a lower Manhattan café. "But when they find something and consume it, dopamine doesn't register. It's more in the seeking than in the attainment of the goal." If anticipation is so often sweeter than success, dopamine would seem to be the reason why.

This is clearly by nature's design. If the dopamine system is going to motivate us, it needs to keep us focused on whatever will produce the reward. The promise of reward is why we keep going. But rewards can come in different ways. They can come in a predictable fashion—in which case we quickly lose interest. They can come randomly. Or they can come in a way that's neither entirely predictable nor totally random, but somewhere in between. As a motivator, it turns out, this last pattern is more powerful than any other—so powerful that the pattern can become more important than the reward. This would turn out to be crucial in understanding the implications of the Hammersmith Hospital study.

A few years ago, a British neuroscientist gave some schoolkids a test. The neuroscientist was Paul Howard-Jones, who teaches at the University of Bristol in southwestern England. The 50 schoolkids, all around 11 years old, were pupils at an elementary school in Lemesos, a medieval city on the southern coast of Cyprus. They were given a computer-based arithmetic quiz, but instead of a standard scoring system they were told they could be graded either by Mr. Certain or by Mr. Uncertain. If they chose Mr. Certain, they would get no points for an incorrect answer and one point for a correct answer. If they chose Mr. Uncertain, they would still get no points for getting the answer wrong. But if they got it right, they'd have a 50-50 chance of scoring: they might get two points for that question, or they might get none at all. The point of the test was to see which option the children preferred.

The quiz consisted of 30 questions. Of the 50 boys and girls who took part, 30 chose Mr. Uncertain more often than Mr. Certain, with boys showing a greater preference for him than did girls. As the quiz progressed, the pupils' preference for Mr. Uncertain increased. In a subsequent interview, one of them explained why:

> RESEARCHER: Were there instances that made you feel frustrated?
>
> PARTICIPANT: Yes.
>
> RESEARCHER: When?
>
> PARTICIPANT: When I was getting zero points with Mr. Uncertain. I knew my answer was correct but he was giving me no points sometimes.
>
> RESEARCHER: Did that frustration make you want to quit the game?
>
> PARTICIPANT: No . . . no . . . It made me want to try my luck with Mr. Uncertain even more.

"The conventional wisdom is that rewards have to be consistent in the classroom," Howard-Jones told me. "But we found it was more effective if you might or might not get an award."

Howard-Jones's experiment built on a number of studies connecting dopamine release with reward-seeking behavior. To start with, there was the Hammersmith Hospital study of *Battlezone* players. "That's what started the ball rolling with me," he said, sitting in his office in a Georgian building on Bristol's Berkeley Square. "It was a very important paper, because it brought computer games into the frame of neuroscientific understanding. It put them in the same category with a lot of other behaviors that become addictive. There had been addiction studies showing how drugs like cocaine work, and suddenly computer games entered that framework. It clearly showed there's potential to start thinking about a strong motivational mechanism that keeps children glued to their screens."

Shortly after that paper was published, a team at University College London conducted a gambling study in which participants were awarded £1 when they guessed the correct card and penalized £1 when they failed. This, too, caused dopamine levels to rise. Wolfram Schultz was part of a team at the University of Fribourg that found dopamine release in monkeys to be highest when the chance of receiving a reward was about 50-50. Scientists at Concordia University hypothesized that dopamine serves to heighten the brain's focus in response to uncertainty, possibly in an attempt to learn how to predict the reward.

"Dopamine automatically orients our attention," said Howard-Jones. "It's a mechanism we share with other animals. It's part of the animal learning system. And it responds differently depending on how you anticipate the outcome. If you get a signal and you know the reward is coming, you get some dopamine release. If you have no expectation, you get some dopamine release. But the biggest buzz is when it's 50-50."

In other words, nothing gets the seeking system more excited than an unpredictable payoff. The dopamine system makes us vulnerable to anything that schedules rewards this way. We really pay attention when we hit the jackpot, and the next thing we want is to try to hit it again. Slot machine operators and behavioral psychologists have known this for years; it's the idea behind the one-armed bandit (so called because it used to have a lever on one side). It's the same idea that makes government lotteries so tempting, and that made illegal numbers rackets so lucrative that governments began muscling out the Mob. "We're incredibly susceptible," said Howard-Jones. "It's a very powerful thing."

The basic explanation for why unpredictable rewards engage us so much more intensely than predictable ones was provided by Jaak Panksepp, an Estonian-born neuroscientist at Washington State University. Panksepp identifies our fixation on chance results with a behavior that's fundamental to animal survival: foraging—or, as he ultimately dubbed it, "seeking." As he describes it,

> This emotional system . . . makes animals intensely interested in exploring their world and leads them to become excited when they are about to get what they desire. It eventually allows animals to find and eagerly anticipate the things they need for survival, including, of course, food, water, warmth, and their ultimate evolutionary survival need, sex. In other words, when fully aroused, it helps fill the mind with interest and motivates organisms to move . . . in search of the things they need, crave, and desire.

Conventional game mechanics—with their point systems, their leader boards, their levels to be earned—can supply the reward, the bait we think we want. "But I don't think that's what provides the dopamine release," says Howard-Jones. "It's much more about uncertainty. Animal learning systems show an attraction to potentially high gains, and that's very wrapped up in foraging. When you're hunting for food, you need a system that keeps you engaged. We're beginning to learn about gaming, but what we're really doing is learning about foraging."

• • •

Electronic foraging is hardly limited to slot machines and video games. Google is a perfectly designed information-foraging system. The Xerox PARC paper that described Lostpedia as an act of social information foraging was on the money. It's not just users foraging for information; the people who help build Lostpedia are foraging as well. Lostpedia, Wookieepedia, Wikipedia—all are essentially games in which the participants forage for influence, approval, and status. It's the same with social media—YouTube, Flickr, Facebook. Anything that invites us to participate and promises some sort of reward can become a game—including, as participatory media proliferate, storytelling itself.

In a much-noted talk at the 2010 D.I.C.E. Summit, a gaming conference in Las Vegas, Jesse Schell of Carnegie Mellon University issued a callout to Brian Reynolds, the chief designer for Zynga:

> Brian, if you guys do not make a *FarmVille* slot machine where every time you win, you get cash money and every time you lose you get virtual money, then you are stupid! Because that would make you the richest person in the world!

As of this writing, Zynga has not yet installed a slot machine in *FarmVille*. But other participatory media—Twitter, for example—are nothing if not online social slot machines.

The basic game mechanic in Twitter is how many followers you can collect. But the randomness of the Twitter info stream—if you spend two minutes scanning the tweets coming in from the people you follow, what will you find of interest?—makes it inherently a gamble. And then there's the retweet feature: if you see a microstory on Twitter that interests you, you can click a button and send it to all your followers. So Twitter becomes a game in which you see who, if anyone, finds your microstories interesting enough to pass along. There's also the "follow Friday" convention: every Friday, people tweet the user names of other people they find interesting enough to follow. So, will anybody tweet your user name on "follow Friday"? And so on.

It's the same with story-related games such as Dunder Mifflin Infinity: you can collect virtual status symbols for your virtual desk, but will your list of do's and don'ts for special occasions be awarded the grand prize? If you were playing *Why So Serious?*, the alternate reality game for *The Dark Knight*, would you get to the bakery in time to pick up the cake for Robin Banks? And if you did and you followed the instructions to keep your cake phone turned on and charged at all times, when would it ring? What would it tell you to do? In stories like these, surprise and randomness abound. Any narrative that has gamelike aspects—which is to say, any story that invites you into its world—can make an appeal to your foraging instincts. We forage for food, for points, for attention, for friends, for the jackpot, for a happy ending, for closure of any sort.

12.

The Emotion Engine

WE FORAGE, TOO, FOR AN EMOTIONAL CONNECTION—THE kind that stories provide. Fiction is a simulation that gives us a feeling of empathy with characters that seem real, even though we know they're not. We care about the mercenary scribe played by Ewan McGregor in Roman Polanski's *Ghost Writer* because he is so relentlessly human, grit and wit and vulnerability all convincingly wrapped up in a package of flesh and blood, even if we only see it on the movie screen. We care for the "item of mortality" called Oliver Twist because it's nearly impossible not to feel for a character so innocent and plucky in the face of beatings and starvation. Movies, novels, television shows—it doesn't really matter what form the story takes. But games are different. So far, games have tried to tell a story either by taking away the game element, as with Hideo Kojima and his cut scenes, or by providing a setting in which players generate their own stories, as with *The Sims*. If games themselves are ever to tell a satisfying story, they need to engage us emotionally. Which is where Peter Molyneux's dog comes in.

At 51, Molyneux is one of Europe's foremost video game designers, a man who more or less invented the "god game" with the 1989 title *Populous*. (God games are simulations that give players godlike powers over their domain.) Over the years he turned the small town he grew up in—Guildford, in the gently rolling hills 20 miles south of London—into a bustling center of video game development. Settled in Saxon times, sacked in the Norman Conquest of 1066, for centuries a way station for pilgrims bound for Canterbury, Guildford today is a posh suburb boasting corporate offices, good shopping, and a twelfth-century castle. Lionhead Studios, the Microsoft-owned game studio that Molyneux heads, is located in an office park on the outskirts of town on a street called Occam Court. No great surprise, then, that *Fable*, Lionhead's current three-game franchise, should be set in the mythical land of Albion, a locale that resembles medieval England in *Fable I* and the England of the Enlightenment in *Fable II*.

Molyneux's dog is virtual, not real. It first appears at the beginning of *Fable II*, which came out in 2008, and it stays at your side through every adventure, a loyal and adoring companion. Like its predecessor, *Fable II* is a role-playing game, a descendant of *Dungeons & Dragons* that presents you with a series of quests to fulfill while enabling you to explore the countryside, gain wealth, have sex, kill people or save them, and perform many other human-type functions. But near the end of the game, after you've lost your dog and your family, you're presented with a frightful choice: you can bring back your dog and your family, or you can bring back thousands of innocent people who've also been killed during the course of the game. Molyneux got hate mail from players who found the choice too excruciating to make. At one point, picketers appeared outside Lionhead's offices.

A slender gent with receding, close-cropped hair, Molyneux displays a characteristically English blend of reticence, charm, and wit. Yet he seems to delight in putting people in discomforting situations such as this one. "It's a personality test," he told me. "It reflects on what you're really like." In a movie, he added, "you feel empathy for a character, but you very rarely feel guilt. The great thing about computer games is that you're feeling involved—you're feeling guilty yourself." This is not so much true with Japanese players, he's learned: they have no problem playing the bad guy, because they're used to the idea that fantasy can be divorced from reality. (Hence such otaku fixations as lolicon and tentacle porn.) Others, Americans in particular, take a more moralistic approach.

Molyneux is simultaneously admiring and dismissive of Hollywood. He's clearly in awe of filmmakers' storytelling ability: "It's so evident the skill it takes—who are we even to dare to say we have that skill? But the trouble with a lot of Hollywood stuff is—I'm so bored with it! James Bond, Tom Cruise—the character of the hero is locked in concrete. He must have a love interest, they must end up in bed, he never talks under torture. The only surprise is whether they're on top of a cliff or under water. But that's great, because you've got that hero template, and now I can start messing with it. Maybe, just maybe, you'll play *Fable II*, and the next time you go to the cinema you'll see one of these heroes and say, You know what? I'd never be able to do that."

Molyneux's ambition goes beyond challenging the Hollywood hero myth. "If I can make you care about something, then the story will be much more meaningful," he said. "So I wrap the AI"—the software that makes video game characters appear intelligent—"around a dog. He's going to love you, he's cute and fun as a companion, and in tests, people can't help but care about a dog. This is what we can do that books, TV, film cannot."

But if games have the potential to be more emotionally engaging than books or television or movies, they haven't managed it yet. Molyneux may have succeeded in manipulating players emotionally with his dog, but that doesn't mitigate the crudeness of the mechanisms with which the characters themselves express emotion.

Nothing highlights these limitations more than *Fable II*'s "expression wheel," an onscreen device that offers you the opportunity to express your character's feelings by pressing some buttons on the controller. With the expression wheel your character can smile, laugh, fart, flirt, even lead someone to bed. Previously, communication with other characters in games had essentially been limited to talking and shooting. So *Fable II* represented a significant advance: now you could simply dial up the appropriate gesture. But though it was intended as a way of extending the game's emotional range, the expression wheel succeeded mainly in spotlighting how pathetically clunky emotional expression in video games remains.

LIKE THE OTHER BEHAVIORAL components of video games, the characters' emotions are a product of artificial intelligence. Molyneux first began to grasp the potential of game AI when he was leading the development of *Black & White*, a god game that Lionhead released in 2001. One of the more interesting features of *Black & White* is the Creature, an animal the player can teach how to fight or what to eat or any number of things. "The thought was, we've got all this AI stuff—surely we can use it in a more sophisticated way," Molyneux recalled. "So we developed this creature with a mind that learned from the way you dealt with it."

The Creature in *Black & White* was programmed to respond to the feedback it receives: if you reward it for treating your villagers well, it will keep on doing so. But its learning is only as good as the programming it receives in the first place. "The first thing we programmed it for was to search for food," said Molyneux. "It began to feel like this Frankenstein creature. It was midnight when we turned it on, and I'm sure there was a flash of lightning outside. And it started grabbing at its legs. Its mind was programmed to look for the most nutritious thing to eat, and the most nutritious thing to eat was its own legs."

That glitch was easily enough fixed, but it pointed out a much bigger problem, not just with *Black & White* but with AI in general: any system that relies on a programmer to input rules of behavior will eventually run into situations the programmer hasn't thought of. For games, and for many other applications, the workaround has been to severely limit the kinds of situations the system might encounter and to program new rules as needed. The Creature in *Black & White* didn't stop trying to eat its own legs because it had any sense of the dangers of self-mastication—pain, blood loss, infection, difficulty walking, digestive disorders, social rejection, and so on. It stopped only when it was programmed not to eat them.

For all its flaws, *Black & White* was the most impressive of a new spate of games with characters that evinced a modicum of intelligence. *Halo*, *The Sims*, *Grand Theft Auto III*—no longer were game characters total ciphers; now they were able to display some awareness of the situation they were supposed to be in, even show a few basic emotions (like fear). If their commander got shot up, they wouldn't just stand impassively and watch. For games, this represented a huge leap forward. Yet by comparison with movies, for instance, it wasn't impressive at all.

After *Black & White* was finished, Molyneux launched a research project dedicated to developing what he called "emotional AI": technology that would yield a character with such emotional resonance that players would react as if it were real. He called it Project Dimitri, after his godson. The first tangible results appeared in *Fable II*, which came out seven years after *Black & White* and two years after Molyneux sold Lionhead to Microsoft. That was when players were confronted with the loyal-dog dilemma and given the ability to dial up a fart on the expression wheel. But even before the game was released, Molyneux was unhappy with the expression wheel. "I got frustrated," he said. "You pressed a button—it all seemed so trivial. That's not how it's done in real life."

Then, during a design meeting, he had an idea: what if two game characters could touch one another? "When someone is upset, the natural thing to do is to hug them. But game characters are hermetically sealed in a bubble. You rarely see them touch anything. Imagine if I could put touch in the player's control! You could lead a frightened child by the hand to safety. Or you could drag someone to their doom."

It was too late to develop a touch feature for *Fable II*, so Molyneux made it a centerpiece of *Fable III*, released in October 2010. *Fable III* is set several decades after its predecessor, in a Dickensian Albion that bears the scars of the Industrial Revolution. This time you don't just defeat the villain, as in the earlier games; you overthrow the ruler and become king or queen yourself, with all the capacity for good or evil that implies.

Using the touch feature, you're able to virtually touch other characters—to pick up your little daughter, to lead a beggar or a comrade by the hand, to kiss and embrace your spouse, or maybe the governess. By reaching out to other characters, the thinking goes, you'll start to bond with them emotionally. "You have choices, and the choices have consequences," said Molyneux. "And there are characters that are emotionally bound to you. That's what entertainment is all about."

But the real advance in *Fable III* was to have been the sensing system known as Kinect. For nearly two decades, since its early space and flight sims, Microsoft has been working on technology that would watch you play and respond accordingly. That's what Kinect does, using a motion-sensing camera, a microphone, and some very sophisticated software. It recognizes faces. It responds to voices. It sees gestures, and if you want it can imitate them. Ultimately it's intended to replace the game controller, a highly specialized device that works well for gamers but is clearly a barrier to bringing new people into the market. But though Kinect was incorporated into several other games Microsoft released toward the end of 2010, Molyneux announced that August that its implementation in *Fable III* still needed work.

Lionhead's primary showcase for Kinect has been *Milo and Kate*, an outgrowth of Project Dimitri. It features a 10-year-old boy named Milo and his lovable dog Kate. (Don't worry, the dog lives in this one.) Milo can tell from your facial expression if you're happy or sad as you play. If you show him a note—that is, hold it in front of Kinect's camera system—he can read what it says. He responds to your tone of voice. He knows from your tone when you're telling a joke, even if he doesn't exactly understand it.

In fact, Milo doesn't "understand" anything; Molyneux freely admits that his apparent intelligence is a trick, a programming sleight of hand. But at least Milo's not going to start chewing on his own legs. "These characters feel like they are noticing you," he told me, careful to place the emphasis on "feel like." For the moment, that's probably enough. "It completely makes us sweat," he continued. "It puts us completely out of our comfort zone. There are no rules that apply. It feels like somewhere no one has been before." Until this moment, the screen has existed to let the gamer see what's happening. But now, said Molyneux, "it's not a one-way window anymore." The question is, What will the game make of what it sees?

Game designers like Molyneux aren't usually called upon to participate in neuroscience experiments, but this was a special case. Demis Hassabis, a former Molyneux protégé who had become a PhD candidate in neuroscience at University College London, was planning to do fMRI brain scans of people in a virtual reality environment. But first he had to have the environment, so he went to Lionhead and spent six weeks working with Molyneux to modify the graphics engine for *Fable* so it could serve the purpose.

What they came up with was quite simple by video game standards—two virtual rooms, one blue and one green, each 15 meters square, with a small rug in each corner and some furniture so visitors could orient themselves. As subjects for his experiment, Hassabis found four male gamers in their twenties. Their job was to look at a video screen while they were in the MRI chamber and, using a four-button control pad, navigate to different corners of the virtual rooms. Afterward, Hassabis subjected the brain scans to extensive processing. His focus was the hippocampus, a structure deep within the brain that's critical to both memory and spatial orientation. And when he examined the results, something remarkable happened: he was able to tell which part of the virtual rooms the test subjects had navigated to on the basis of activity in their hippocampi. It wasn't mind reading, but it seemed close.

For Hassabis, though, that wasn't really the point. This experiment was a step toward a much bigger goal: to model the human brain so precisely that game designers will be able to create characters that really do have humanlike thoughts and memories and emotions. If Milo is ever to make the leap from parlor trick to virtual human, it will be on the basis of this kind of research.

As a teenage video game designer in the nineties, Hassabis had worked for Molyneux at Bullfrog Productions, an earlier studio he had set up in Guildford. Then he enrolled at the University of Cambridge and earned a degree in computer science. On graduating, he served as the lead AI programmer on *Black & White* before leaving to start his own game studio. A few years and two games later, he began to question what he was doing. The problem seemed very basic. "I felt the AI was holding us back," he told me.

We were sitting in an outdoor café at the Brunswick, a creamy-white shopping center in Bloomsbury. It was a sunny afternoon; the terrace overlooked a row of handsome eighteenth-century townhouses, their sober brick facades marching smartly down the street. Hassabis—his father is from a Greek Cypriot family, his mother an immigrant from Singapore—grew up a few miles from here in the pleasant North London suburb of Finchley. When he was four years old, Hassabis saw his father and his uncle playing chess; he wanted to play too. Within weeks, he was beating them. At 13 he achieved master status. He was 16 when he graduated from the local secondary school.

"There's a reason why games have evolved in the direction of shooters," Hassabis continued, sipping a cappuccino. The alien invaders in *Halo*, the Locust Horde in *Gears of War*—"You're not going to have a conversation. You're not going to show any emotions. You just have to shoot them." He didn't find that very satisfying. Nor was he interested in furthering the kind of "brute-force" AI that went into games like *Black & White*, producing characters that mimic human understanding and emotion because they've been programmed to do so. He didn't want a Creature that had to be told not to eat its own legs.

"AI has been a very stagnant area for a long time," he said. "In terms of human-level, full-spectrum AI, we're not there yet. So I asked myself, can I get it there by staying in the game world? And I decided I had pushed that as far as I could push it."

So Hassabis decided to go back to school, this time to University College London, a top-shelf institution that sprawls across much of Bloomsbury. Its neuroscience department, ranked number one in Europe, is housed in a particularly choice set of buildings on Queen Square, a quiet little park hidden away on back streets a few blocks from the British Museum. After receiving his PhD there, Hassabis stayed on as a postdoc in computational neuroscience—a mashup field that combines neuroscience, cognitive science, and computer science. His goal is to create a digital model of human brain function.

"I'm fascinated by two things," he said. "Can we build an artificial intelligence? And what makes us who we are?" He mentioned seeing an astrophysicist on TV who had said that the most important question is, Are we alone? Uh-uh. "A more important question is, What is intelligence? Because that's the thing that makes our reality."

Obviously, however, our reality wouldn't be good for much if we couldn't remember it. "To me," Hassabis continued, "that is fundamental. Who we are is the sum of our memories. But what is memory? How is it built? Why is it so valuable?"

Hassabis is hardly the only person to have asked these questions, so when he got to UCL in 2005, he read the classic papers on the subject. After a couple of weeks he asked himself, what has everyone missed?

There are two camps when it comes to explaining memory. One holds that memory is like a videotape you play back whenever you need to. On the other side is the reconstructive camp, which holds that memories are assembled by the brain on the fly as we try to summon them up. Hassabis thought the latter explanation made a lot more sense. If memory were like a videotape, it would almost certainly be a lot more reliable than it is.

That's when he saw the missing question. If the reconstructive camp is right—if our brains snap together memories as needed—why wouldn't the same brain mechanisms that go into reconstructing a memory also be involved in constructing new ones? In other words—what if memory and imagination come from the same place?

To Hassabis, the connection between memory and imagination seemed obvious. "It was astounding to me that in 100 years of research, no one had thought to try that," he said. To test his hypothesis, he would need to recruit several memory-impaired test subjects and see how they did at simple visualization tasks—imagining themselves lying on a sandy beach, for example. He had to find people like patient HM—amnesiacs whose brain damage was limited primarily to the hippocampus. People who could not remember what happened to them from one moment to the next. If their powers of imagination were as diminished as their powers of memory, he would prove his point.

The hippocampus is involved with the spatial memory we require to navigate as well as with episodic memory—our memory of what's happened to us. Hassabis's faculty advisor, Eleanor Maguire, was well known for her work in the navigational function. In the late nineties, Maguire conducted a landmark study of London taxi drivers—people who spend two years, on average, learning "The Knowledge" required to find their way across the sprawling metropolis. Maguire performed not functional but structural MRIs—imaging that looked at the brain's structure rather than trying to deduce its function. She found that the posterior hippocampus—the area specifically associated with spatial memory—was significantly larger in taxi drivers than in ordinary people. And the longer they'd been driving, the more overgrown that part of the hippocampus turned out to be.

Maguire has extensive contacts among British neurosurgeons. Through her, Hassabis was able to find five patients suffering from limbic encephalitis—a brain infection that targets the hippocampus, inducing amnesia. One victim was a PhD candidate when he fell ill; another, an industrial biochemist; a third, coincidentally enough, a London taxi driver. Now they all needed full-time care just to get through the day. Hassabis also assembled 10 control subjects. Then he asked each participant to imagine different scenarios: lying on a white, sandy beach on a beautiful tropical bay; standing in the main hall of a museum with many exhibits.

The responses were revelatory. Asked to imagine himself on the beach, the former PhD candidate, now 24, was able to see little more than the color blue. He heard birds, the sound of the sea, and "those ship's hooters." A control subject, given the same task, created a vividly detailed picture—the sun and the sand almost unbearably hot, the sea a gorgeous aquamarine, a row of palm trees behind him, some wooden buildings on a distant point.

Another control subject, asked to picture himself in the museum, described a pillared hall with a domed ceiling and a marble floor, people moving about expectantly, paintings and sculptures all around. A former painter, now suffering from amnesia, got only as far as big doors and huge rooms. Then he admitted, "To be honest, there's not a lot coming."

Hassabis's experiment established a clear connection between memory and imagination. It also provided some insight into what's at work in games and stories. As Hassabis sees it, the brain structures that evolved for memory have also been pressed into service for our imaginative capacity. "We've created the ability to integrate and to imagine, instead of just remembering what happened in the past," he said. Imagination is clearly required for play. It's essential to stories as well, not only for the storyteller but for the recipient. This is why consumers can be said to "co-create" the ads they see, in partnership, so to speak, with marketers. The audience is never entirely passive, even while watching TV. The storyteller invents the characters and spins their tales; the audience fills in the blanks and completes the picture. We're all in this together.

Having recently won a four-year grant from the Wellcome Trust, a £13 billion fund that spends about £600 million each year on medical research, Hassabis is now ready to start building computational models of memory and imagination. "I'm continually looking for algorithms the brain is using so I can reimplement them," he said. That's the point: to reverse-engineer human intelligence.

There are something like 10 trillion neurons in the human brain. The fMRI work Hassabis did in his imagination study gave him a view of a few small bundles of neurons, 10,000 or so in each, in one small area of the brain. Obviously he has quite a long way to go. Nonetheless, he said, "I promised myself I would come back to games once I had done something with AI. What would it really be like to have characters who understand emotions and motivation? That's when games will come into their own."

13.

How to Build a Universe That Doesn't Fall Apart

"Let me bring you official greetings from Disneyland," Philip K. Dick declared one day to an audience in Paris. Or maybe he didn't, since there's nothing to indicate he ever actually delivered this speech. This is the kind of problem you run into all the time with Dick, who concerned himself as a writer with the ultimate ontological question: What is reality? He could be slippery about the answer. But even if this was the best speech he never gave, "How to Build a Universe That Doesn't Fall Apart Two Days Later" was an extraordinary pronouncement. Parts of it show Dick at his most piercingly lucid—the vision-besotted genius of twentieth-century science fiction holding forth on the nature of reality in an increasingly unreal world. Disneyland was just the start.

Yet it was certainly a good start, and not only because Dick at the time (this was 1978) lived in an apartment a couple miles away from the place. The sun-soaked suburbia of Orange County, California, might have appeared unreal by any definition, but what makes it unique, what raises it above the mundane to truly extravagant levels of unreality, is Disneyland. Opened by Walt himself in 1955, when much of the county was still perfumed by orange groves, the so-called "happiest place on earth" transmuted fiction and fantasy into . . . not reality, obviously, but some sort of three-dimensional pseudoreality that Dick was still trying to get straight in his head.

The question of reality is implicit in Dick's fiction, but in this speech, or not-speech, he addressed it directly. He mentioned two of his short stories. One concerned a dog that thinks the garbagemen are stealing food the family has carefully stowed away in metal bins outside the house. The other was about a man who finds out he isn't human. Titled "The Electric Ant," it was published in the *Magazine of Fantasy and Science Fiction* in 1969, when Dick had finally achieved fame, if not literary respectability. (That would come posthumously, when the Library of America collected his best novels in a three-volume set.)

Ever wonder what it would be like to discover you're a mechanical construct? In Dick's story, a businessman named Garson Poole wakes up in a New York hospital room after a traffic accident and is told that he's actually an android—an "electric ant." He's devastated at first—who wouldn't be? But then he grows curious. Realizing that his reality is controlled by a punched tape in his chest (in fact, the same data storage mechanism used in minicomputers at the time Dick wrote the story), he decides to experiment. He punches more holes at random. Suddenly, the room is full of wild ducks. Eventually he cuts the tape, crumples to the floor, and dies. His entire world disappears with him.

What is real? For Garson Poole, it's whatever his "reality tape" says it is. For Dick, it was more complicated:

> I ask, in my writing, What is real? Because unceasingly we are bombarded with pseudo-realities manufactured by very sophisticated people using very sophisticated electronic mechanisms. I do not distrust their motives; I distrust their power. They have a lot of it. And it is an astonishing power: that of creating whole universes, universes of the mind. I ought to know. I do the same thing.

It was Dick's peculiar genius to anticipate by 40 or 50 years the concerns we have today. But whether it's *Do Androids Dream of Electric Sheep?* (the Dick novel that became the basis for the movie *Blade Runner*) or Disneyland, a fictional universe ultimately remains, well . . . fictional. A pretend space. An escape.

That's why we like them. That's why we want to immerse ourselves in *Star Wars* or *Lost* or *The Super Dimension Fortress Macross*. But the lure that fictional worlds exert is balanced by the fear they engender. We are attracted, we are repulsed. And something about Disneyland's artificial snow-covered Matterhorn, across from the imitation Sleeping Beauty Castle, overlooking the ersatz Main Street, U.S.A., appears to have repulsed Dick in particular:

> Fake realities will create fake humans. Or, fake humans will generate fake realities and then sell them to other humans, turning them, eventually, into forgeries of themselves. . . . It is just a very large version of Disneyland. You can have the Pirate Ride or the Lincoln Simulacrum or Mr. Toad's Wild Ride—you can have all of them, but none is true.

So the question remains: What is?

• • •

"THIS IS SURREAL," SEAN BAILEY muttered under his breath. We were standing on a concrete plaza in downtown San Francisco, part of a small crowd gathered for a corporate press conference. The evening was clear and chill, with a stiff breeze blowing in from the bay. Bailey, the recently appointed president of production at Walt Disney Studios, had a long history with the night's speaker—Alan Bradley of Encom International, the giant software and gaming conglomerate.

Bradley, looking every inch the corporate suit, was here to introduce an online game, a resurrected and retooled version of Encom's vintage arcade title, *Space Paranoids*. And to pay tribute to his longtime friend and colleague, Kevin Flynn.

"He always knew the secret before any of us," Bradley declared. "That it wasn't about circuit boards and microchips. It was about people. People whose hopes and dreams he translated into zeros and ones and then right back into pure joy."

"Are we talking about Steve Jobs?" yelled someone from the crowd.

Well, sort of. There is, in fact, no Encom—though it might take you a while to figure that out from its Web site. No Alan Bradley, no Kevin Flynn. But there is a Sean Bailey, and there was, on this Friday evening in April 2010 on a plaza next to the Embarcadero, this gathering. "Alan Bradley," portrayed by Bruce Boxleitner, was speaking about *Space Paranoids Online*, a game that would indeed be available for download a few weeks later, and about "Kevin Flynn," the man who had created the original (but nonexistent) *Space Paranoids*, played by Jeff Bridges in Disney's 1982 cult film *Tron* and again in the 2010 sequel *Tron: Legacy* But the event unfolding before us was no more a press conference than Alan Bradley was a software executive.

Standing in the crowd, a still boyish-looking 40-year-old with a head of dark, curly hair, Bailey looked more or less like everyone around him. There was nothing to suggest he was responsible for all this, both as *Tron: Legacy*'s producer and as the man in charge of Disney's motion picture slate. The entire evening was part of an elaborately scripted fiction for Disney, an alternate reality game devised by 42 Entertainment to familiarize people with the upcoming movie. And while the ostensible point of this event was to introduce *Space Paranoids Online*, the real goal was to introduce the protagonist of the new picture and establish his relationship with his dad.

Set 28 years after the original, which starred Bridges as a brilliant video game designer who gets digitized by a mutinous computer program, *Tron: Legacy* focuses on Kevin Flynn's son, Sam Flynn. In the movie, Sam is a rebellious 27-year-old whose legendary father has disappeared once again—this time, seemingly, for good. Encom has grown to gigantic proportions in his absence, but a tiny band of "Flynn Lives" activists continues to blame the company for failing to mount a serious effort to find him. Sam pretends not to care, but tonight, if all goes well, we'll see that in fact he cares a lot. But things going well was a very big assumption. "This is almost real-time moviemaking," Susan Bonds of 42 had remarked that afternoon in the event's "green room," a hotel suite nearby. And who shoots a movie in one take?

As "Alan Bradley" continued to speak from the stage, Sean Bailey started looking over his shoulder toward the San Francisco–Oakland Bay Bridge. What he knew that others in the crowd did not was that an Encom helicopter was supposed to be headed their way from Oakland International Airport. The flight had been approved by both the Federal Aviation Administration and the Department of Homeland Security. But there had been high winds and rain all afternoon, and it was unclear if conditions would permit the helicopter flight, let alone the stunt they had planned. Oakland was just a 10-minute flight across the bay. But with both a severe weather warning and an air traffic control delay in the mix, there was no helicopter in sight.

Bradley started casting his eyes nervously in the airport's direction. As the minutes ticked on, his speech grew increasingly disjointed. Finally, having reached the end of his script without the expected aerial interruption, he came to a halt and withdrew from the stage. An Encom spokesperson took the mike and apologized for the confusion, blaming "technical difficulties."

The wind was picking up. The crowd, aware that something was supposed to happen but not knowing what, stood expectantly in the chill night air. They had suspended disbelief this far; what was a few extra minutes? The Flynn Lives contingent stormed the stage. They chanted and waved placards in the air for a while, then dispersed.

Only then did the chopper appear, a faraway dot in the sky. It grew closer, closer still. Suddenly it dropped down over the plaza and buzzed the crowd, the red-on-black Encom logo caught in relief by the spotlights. A cheer went up. The chopper swung around and buzzed the plaza again, then rose high into the night sky. As klieg lights played on it from the ground, a single figure stood at the doorway and jumped into the wind. The parachute opened. The figure swung in the sky—first left, then right. Slowly it descended, swinging farther and farther, looking like it might tip over at any moment. Finally, after several agonizing minutes, the jumper landed behind the stage. A waiting SUV scooped him up and disappeared into the city streets. The people on the plaza looked at one another quizzically. What was that about? No matter—it was fun enough. And now, apparently, it was time to go home.

LATER THAT NIGHT, A VIDEO APPEARED on the Flynn Lives Web site that revealed the mystery jumper to be Sam Flynn himself. "Sam Flynn, April 2, 2010," he began, speaking to a handheld camera as he packed up a parachute on the tarmac, the Encom helicopter in the background. "Encom's getting ready to make a big statement. So am I." Subsequent footage showed him flying over San Francisco in the helicopter, jumping out above the plaza, and landing next to the SUV. "Flynn Lives signs and T-shirts are cool," he declared at the end, "but this is the way you really crash a party. Until next time."

The "Sam Flynn" in the video was in fact two people—Garrett Hedlund, the up-and-coming young actor who plays Sam Flynn in the movie, and the stunt man who made the actual jump. The video didn't explain why the helicopter was late. But it did explain what the jump was about, and in more subtle ways it began to lay out Sam's relationship to Encom, to his father, and to Alan Bradley, the Encom programmer-turned-executive who had saved his dad when he got sucked into the computer back in 1982, before Sam was born.

That was in the first *Tron*. It had come out at a time when public fascination with computers was at a peak. IBM had recently introduced its PC, the machine that made personal computers safe for corporate America. *The Soul of a New Machine* had become a best seller on the basis of its portrayal of a swashbuckling engineering team in a cutthroat corporate world. A few months after *Tron* came out, *Time* magazine would change the rules of its "Man of the Year" competition in order to name the computer "Machine of the Year." *Tron* was a movie that promised to actually take you inside a computer—and in a way, it did. At a time when visual effects still meant scale models and optics, *Tron* boasted a Hollywood first: extended sequences of computer-generated imagery.

All this was a big leap for Disney. Walt had been dead since 1966, but the company was still headed by his handpicked successors, among them Ron Miller, his son-in-law. At every juncture they asked themselves, What would Walt have done? Unfortunately, none of them seemed to know. But Miller did want to bring the studio up to date, and to that end he had given control of it to a young Disney PR exec named Tom Wilhite.

Wilhite gave the green light to *Tron*, an outside production—revolutionary for Disney at the time—that had been developed by Steven Lisberger, an independent animator whose big idea had already been turned down by Warner Bros., MGM, and Columbia. Years before William Gibson popularized the concept of cyberspace in *Neuromancer*, Lisberger imagined what it would be like to be digitized—to live inside a computer. In his conception, the digital world was a flat, neon-lit grid that mimicked the look of the wire-frame arcade games of the period—like *Battlezone*, the Atari game that years later would be used in the Hammersmith Hospital study. *Battlezone* was popular on the set. Jeff Bridges played it to psych himself up before his scenes.

While Lisberger was shooting on a soundstage on the lot, Wilhite provided cover. It wasn't that hard: they were spending $20 million to make *Tron*, but the company brass was fixated on the small stuff: Tim Burton, an animation geek who had somehow gotten $60,000 to make a six-minute homage to Vincent Price, the schlock horror-film actor. And John Lasseter, who was so excited by what Lisberger was doing with *Tron* that he started developing his own computer-animated film—an offense for which he was summarily fired. Too bad; Lasseter would go on to make movies like *Toy Story* and *Cars* and ultimately, with Disney's 2006 purchase of Pixar, return to Burbank as the animation division's chief creative officer. And Tim Burton would come back to direct *Alice in Wonderland*, which within months of its March 2010 release would gross more than $1 billion worldwide.

Tron wowed audiences with its unprecedented effects, but it couldn't overcome the uncoolness factor that attached itself at the time to anything Disney. It didn't help that as Kevin Flynn's digital alter ego, Jeff Bridges looked like Buck Rogers in a microchip suit and spouted excruciating lines like "Forget it, mister high-and-mighty Master Control! You aren't making me talk." But there was no competing with Spielberg's *E.T.: The Extra-Terrestrial*, a movie so huge it was number one in the US from early June until Labor Day weekend. At least *Tron* performed better than *Blade Runner*, which came out the same summer and disappeared from theaters five weeks later. But even before it opened, *Tron* was panned by a clueless financial analyst who proclaimed its digital effects "distracting" and hung a sell sign on the company. Soon Disney was locked in a takeover battle with three of the most feared names in finance: Saul Steinberg, Ivan Boesky, and Michael Milken.

Even so, *Tron* was not forgotten. In 1999, Roger Ebert featured it at his first Overlooked Film Festival. Then, some two decades after its initial release, it was screened at the Egyptian Theater in Hollywood. When a top exec's daughter came back raving about it, Disney started to think about somehow reviving the property.

Disney by this time was no longer the sleepy and insular

haven of family values it had been in the early eighties. Led by Roy Disney, Walt's nephew, the company had survived the takeover battle intact, but Ron Miller had been ousted in the process. Michael Eisner took over as CEO and built it into a global media conglomerate—major television networks, a revitalized animation department, a successful live-action film studio, hit shows on Broadway, theme parks across the planet, annual revenues for 2002 of more than $25 billion. Even so, it was far from obvious what to do with *Tron*. By 2005, plans had progressed to the point that the studio announced it was bringing in a pair of writers to script a remake. But nothing clicked until two years after that, when Sean Bailey was brought in to produce it.

BAILEY WAS A PLAYER. A cofounder with Ben Affleck, Matt Damon, and Chris Moore of the production company LivePlanet, he had produced Ridley Scott's *Matchstick Men* for Warner Bros. and, with Affleck and Damon, the television series *Push, Nevada* for ABC. What excited Bailey about *Tron* was the effect it had had on him as a 12-year-old. "I remember looking at the screen thinking I'd never seen anything that looked like that," he said one afternoon, kicking back on a sofa in his office in the Team Disney building—the grandiose Toontown palazzo that serves as corporate headquarters, its monumental pediment supported by the dwarfs from Disney's 1937 classic *Snow White and the Seven Dwarfs*. "The idea of a man going inside his own video game was just mind-blowing. It seemed so futuristic. Steve Lisberger envisioned a world inside the computer—and now look at where we are. It was visionary thinking."

The problem, as Bailey saw it, was that no one had come up with the "big idea" that would make a new *Tron* work. He turned to Adam Horowitz and Eddy Kitsis, the writing duo from *Lost*. "We in no way wanted to do a remake," says Kitsis. "As fans, we wanted to know that everything in the first movie was true." Instead, they proposed a sequel, a father-son story in which the father has been missing for some 20 years. When Sam Flynn goes looking for him, he finds that his father also has a digital offspring—Clu, the program he'd written to hack into the Encom computer system. That's when things start to get complicated.

"I saw the first movie as a kid," says Horowitz. "I remember being completely blown away and not understanding any of it. But it fired my imagination. Is there something inside the computer? What's going on in there?" This was Lisberger's universe—an electronic playing field inside the mystery box that was the computer. The grid was the arena in which humanoid computer programs like Clu and Tron—the electronic creations of their users, Kevin Flynn and Alan Bradley—fought the evil Master Control Program with speeding lightcycles and Frisbee-like flying discs. This was what had wowed 12-year olds a quarter-century earlier—not the dialogue, not the plot.

To give themselves some parameters, Horowitz and Kitsis started to think of *Tron* as a Western. The grid was their frontier. The lightcycles were horses. The disc games were gunslinger showdowns. And they were excited about what Bailey wanted to do with the story—how he wanted to explode it beyond the confines of the movie screen. "We always thought of *Tron* as so much bigger than any one movie," says Horowitz.

"In a movie, you're on only one part of the grid," Kitsis adds. "But there are all these other parts of the story to tell on other grids."

They got a sense of how that could work early on, when Bailey showed them the *Wired* story on the alternate reality game that 42 Entertainment had created with Trent Reznor. Kitsis and Horowitz were dumbfounded. "We were like, they put this in a toilet stall in Lisbon and someone found it? No fucking way!"

Alternate reality games are an evolving story form. With *Year Zero,* which culminated in a secret Nine Inch Nails concert that was broken up by an anti-resistance SWAT team, Bonds and Alex Lieu had created a role for Trent Reznor in his own fiction. With *Why So Serious?*, they had focused on situating *The Dark Knight* within the ongoing saga of Batman, which itself had been evolving since the first comic came out in 1939. Now, with their latest game, *Flynn Lives*, their task was to revive the iconography of *Tron* by showing in real life what it might be like to live inside a computer. For last year's Comic-Con, they'd created a lightcycle. For this year's Comic-Con, they were planning to build the End of Line Club, which in the movie is a nightspot for computer programs. "That's what's great about today," says Kitsis. "You really can live in this world."

To the *Dungeons & Dragons* sensibility Jordan Weisman brought to alternate reality games, Bonds added an Imagineering mind-set. Trained as a systems engineer at Georgia Tech, she's good at complicated things that have a lot of moving parts. In 1984, after a brief stint at Walt Disney World in Orlando, she joined the Skunk Works at Lockheed Martin—the team responsible for the F-117, the slant-sided "stealth" fighter of the eighties. Seven years later she returned to Disney as a creative director in its Imagineering group, building theme park rides like *Indiana Jones Adventure*, which opened in 1995. "People want to be involved in stories," she says. "And Disneyland is about bringing stories to life."

But you could go only so far. Bonds came up against the limitations of theme parks when she was working on the *Mission:*

SPACE ride at Disney World. She wanted to create a ride with multiple endings because, as she puts it, "the generation today wants to be able to control what happens." But how could you do multiple endings on a theme park ride and still achieve a throughput rate of 1,600 people per hour? The whole thing was frustrating. A few years later she found herself at 42, working on *I Love Bees*.

LIKE SUSAN BONDS, BAILEY HAD BEEN working toward this for years. When he helped form LivePlanet in 2000, it was with the idea that they would make movies and television shows that had one foot in the real world. The dot-com bust was just about to hit, but for the moment this was still a heady time for new media enterprises in Hollywood. As a celebrity-fueled Internet something-or-other, LivePlanet was lumped together with such overhyped online video startups as POP.com, which partnered Steven Spielberg and Ron Howard with Microsoft billionaire Paul Allen, and Digital Entertainment Network, which boasted NBC and Microsoft among its investors. In fact, LivePlanet was different. It was based on what Bailey calls the three-ball theory: traditional media, new media, and the real world. To explain the point, he drew a set of circles and pointed to the space where they all overlapped. "Our content lived in all three."

The prototypal LivePlanet project, being readied as Jordan Weisman was running *The Beast* and Electronic Arts was launching *Majestic*, was a show for ABC called *The Runner*. It was essentially a manhunt: For 30 days, a contestant would have to elude capture while traveling cross-country and being tracked by audiences online. If he succeeded, he'd win $1 million; if not, whoever caught him would get the prize. "The folks at ABC are going gaga," Andy Serwer reported in *Fortune*. "Can you imagine the Web traffic? Think about it this way: What if *Survivor* had been a live show and America had cast the final vote?"

That was then. On September 11, 2001, as the show was about to launch, sudden and unexpected events rendered the whole idea inconceivable. A few weeks earlier, as part of a test, Bailey himself had stood atop the World Trade Center, a runner fulfilling his mission. Now the Twin Towers were a smoldering pile of rubble, glowing day and night and reeking of burning plastic and human flesh. A television fugitive trying to avoid capture while sneaking through airports and into skyscrapers? It seemed a relic from another time. *The Runner* was canceled before it began.

But it wasn't just *The Runner*; the whole idea of blurring the line between fiction and real life seemed off-putting. Bailey was a beta subscriber to *Majestic*, the EA game that thrust you into the middle of a government conspiracy. One day his wife, who knew nothing about it, picked up the phone and heard a man say in a threatening voice, "I'm outside the house." That certainly gave her a start. Months later, *Majestic* was kaput. Even other, less ambitious attempts to use the Internet as an entertainment medium—like POP.com, which had already fizzled, and DEN, which had imploded spectacularly amid a boy-sex scandal—were far ahead of their time. In mid-2001, less than 10 percent of US households had broadband, and without broadband Web video was an oxymoron. But more than that, Bailey commented, "I don't think people were ready to immerse themselves in that way."

LivePlanet kept trying. The company's next vehicle was *Push, Nevada*, a show, also developed for ABC, about a nice young Internal Revenue Service agent who goes to the little Nevada town of Push to find out why $1 million has gone missing from a local casino. When he gets there, Agent James A. Prufrock (take that, T. S. Eliot) discovers all kinds of weirdness. Every couple in town, it turns out, has sex at precisely 9:15 every evening. No one has filed an income tax return since 1985. But the weirdness wasn't confined to your TV set. There were puzzles to be solved, and a complex nest of Web sites to explore. When a handoff was supposed to occur in a Las Vegas casino, actors turned up and did a handoff in an actual Las Vegas casino. "You could watch the show alone," Bailey said, "but if you wanted to dig into it, the narrative was happening everywhere."

Television critics loved it—the *New York Times* called the show "inspired"—but audiences were more resistant. They didn't seem to care that the missing $1 million would go to the first person to figure out the clues that were embedded in every episode. It didn't help that the network scheduled it against *CSI*, the country's top-rated drama, and *Will & Grace*, one of the most popular sitcoms on TV. Of 13 planned episodes, ABC ended up airing only 8. And although the prize money was given away in the end, viewers never did learn what the mystery was about—that the whole thing was an experiment by a shadowy company bent on controlling all the media in town. Or that at the end of the series, ABC itself was going to be exposed as the corporate giant behind it all.

LivePlanet was a bit more successful with *Project Greenlight*, a combination reality show/indie filmmaking contest that ran for three seasons between 2001 and 2005. It began to benefit from a shift in attitudes as blogging and Flickr and Wikipedia took hold, aided perhaps by the gradual filtering in of such concepts as otaku and media mix in the wake of the *Pokémon* craze. ABC had an unexpected hit on its hands with *Lost*. NBC showed how television and the Web could reinforce one another with *The*

Office. The Disney Channel—a global business that operates in 32 languages in 163 countries—built a fictional pop idol named Hannah Montana into one of the biggest brands on the planet, available not just on television but in movies, music albums, DVDs, video games, even a line of clothing.

There was also a new way of thinking within Disney itself. During the nineties, before corporate synergy became a bad joke, media conglomerates like Disney had been assembled at enormous cost on the theory that different media platforms—movies, television, books—could reinforce one another. In reality, the merger mania that saw dozens of companies rolled up into a handful of mostly dysfunctional conglomerates had more to do with the egos of the men behind it—people like Eisner at Disney and Jerry Levin, his opposite number at Time Warner—than with any well-thought-out corporate strategy. Disney, News Corp., Sony, Time Warner, Viacom—for all the energy that went into assembling them, each of these companies remained an uneasy coalition of turf-conscious fiefdoms. But now Robert Iger, who had succeeded Eisner as Disney's CEO, was beginning to put forth the idea that movies and television shows might not be just an end in themselves but the focal point in a complex web of stories that could also involve books, comics, video games, alternate reality games, and (of course) theme park attractions. It was as if Iger had stumbled across the media mix strategy that Japanese companies had been employing for years.

In October 2009, Iger unexpectedly named Rich Ross to be the new chairman of Disney Studios. Ross was a television executive, the chief architect of Hannah Montana's success at the Disney Channel. The man he replaced was a seasoned movie executive who enjoyed terrific relationships with agents and talent—long the coin of the realm in Hollywood—but whose approach to the business was decidedly old-school. Ross cleaned house, firing most of the studio's top brass and bringing in people who shared his view of media's future. One of those people was Sean Bailey.

"I've always been interested in how many ways you can touch an entertainment property you love," Bailey told me that afternoon in his office. "I think we're getting closer and closer every day to a wholly immersive experience—something you can touch and feel. A drama that plays out everywhere you go. A dead drop in your local Starbucks. Codes in the newspaper you have to decipher. Somebody's going to nail that." No need to mention that he would very much like to nail it himself.

THERE'S MORE THAN ONE WAY to create a reality. The approach Sean Bailey and Susan Bonds are taking is "to activate the world around you," as Bailey put it. *Flynn Lives*, the alternate reality game for *Tron: Legacy*. *Why So Serious?* for *The Dark Knight*. *I Love Bees* for *Halo 2*. EA's *Majestic*. Or, alternatively, you could retreat from the world around you into some sort of digital head space. Instead of alternate reality, virtual reality: The Metaverse in Neal Stephenson's *Snow Crash*. Or the holodeck in *Star Trek*.

A lot of people in the entertainment business see the holodeck as the holy grail, the definitive if as yet unattainable immersive entertainment experience. Supposedly a product of twenty-fourth-century Starfleet technology, it was presented as the ultimate simulation engine—a special room on the Starship *Enterprise* designed for interactive experiences with life-sized holographic characters. Inside the holodeck, crew members could undergo training, or they could live out a reality of their choosing in the company of virtual humans—constructs as genuinely autonomous as those Demis Hassabis hopes to achieve. You could play detective as Sherlock Holmes or Dr. Watson. You could talk science with Albert Einstein. You could ride the Orient Express or stroll the Champs-Élysées. You could refight the Battle of the Alamo. Story and game, forever and always—world without end.

"Recreation rooms" or "resort rooms" with holodeck-like features were introduced in 1974, both in an animated *Star Trek* series in the US and in *Space Battleship Yamato* in Japan. But the holodeck as we know it was first seen in the premier episode of *Star Trek: The Next Generation*, Gene Roddenberry's 1987 sequel to his series from the sixties. (The original *Star Trek*, which aired on NBC for three seasons between 1966 and 1969, was canceled for poor ratings despite passionate protests from its fans—an early cult hit sacrificed to the economics of mass culture.) In that first episode of *The Next Generation*, the look of wonderment on Commander Riker's face as he steps into a lush holographic forest aboard the *Enterprise* tells us all we need to know about the lure of the holodeck.

But do we really have to wait until 2364, the year the first season of *The Next Generation* was supposed to take place? "The holographic aspect of the holodeck is not particularly far-fetched," Lawrence Krauss observes in *The Physics of Star Trek*. On the other hand, the technology for replicators that could manifest objects you can touch and hold is a bit more problematic. So let's skip the replicators for now. If you were going to solve the other barriers to creating a holodeck, how would you go about it?

Welcome to the Institute for Creative Technologies, a USC lab in Playa Vista. ICT, as it's known, is where science meets fiction. When the lab was formed in 1999, the idea was to put researchers in artificial intelligence and computer graphics together with creative types from Hollywood and video games, with the Pentagon footing the bill. *Star Trek* was the inspiration. "The mantra was, how can we build the holodeck?" said Bill Swartout, the institute's technology director, as we sat in his office. "We're now to the point where digital characters understand what you're saying and can respond with verbal and nonverbal communication. But the ultimate virtual human is a ways off."

Swartout has a friendly, relaxed demeanor. With his deep tan and the shock of white hair that falls across his forehead, he looks more likely to have engineered a really rad surfboard back in the sixties than to be developing virtual humans. Nonetheless, he's been in artificial intelligence for more than 30 years, most of it at USC. As a high school kid in the suburbs of St. Louis, he was torn between becoming a filmmaker and a computer scientist. At Stanford he decided to go into computer science because he liked the idea that he'd be able to put together a set of instructions and have a big machine do his bidding. After grad school at MIT, he spent nearly two decades at USC's Information Sciences Institute, a Pentagon-funded technology think tank that was a key player in the building of the ARPANET—the precursor of the Internet—in the 1970s.

The Institute for Creative Technologies was spun off when people in the Defense Department began to realize that video games were becoming more compelling than their own multimillion-dollar simulators. So they decided to bring in people who understand games and stories. Holography has taken a back seat. In 2007, the institute's graphics lab succeeded in creating a small, 3-D hologram that can be viewed from any angle. It was quite a feat, but what made it work was a mirror spinning at 1,700 revolutions per minute. Scale that up to human size and you'd have a rather dangerous device. Instead, the institute's primary focus has been using life-sized video projections to generate virtual humans—digital agents with the social skills of actual humans. As Swartout put it in a speech at a 2008 army conference in Orlando (a speech that, unlike Philip K. Dick's, he actually gave),

> Imagine a simulated world that's populated with simulated characters that are almost human in their performance. . . . They're reasoning by themselves using artificial intelligence, figuring out what to do, based on things that have happened in the simulation. They understand the environment they're in. They perceive the people who are communicating with them. And they use the full range of communications skills that we as people use.

"We can create environments where people will react to a virtual human as if it were a real person," Swartout told me. "The characters don't even have to be photo-real. It's amazing—we are very anthropomorphic. We try to see people in all kinds of things." Even, as the researchers behind the 1944 study of Massachusetts college students discovered, in two triangles and a circle.

The bigger challenge has been the problem Peter Molyneux and Demis Hassabis have run up against: AI, and emotion in particular. "We realized people were going to ascribe emotions to our characters whether we wanted it or not," Swartout said. "But we thought emotion would be an overlay on behavior—something to make them more believable. Now, characters are making decisions based on emotions. Characters are not only behaving more believably, but emotions are becoming part of their cognitive reasoning. So understanding emotion turns out to be one of the real keys to creating truly intelligent characters."

HERE'S THE SCENARIO. It's the 1880s and you're in a lawless little town in the Wild West. You walk into a darkened saloon. You see Utah, the bartender, standing behind the bar, and Harmony, the bar girl, sitting nervously in a corner. They're not saying much. Lurking in the back room is Rio Laine, the notorious gunslinger. You've got a six-shooter in your holster and a badge pinned to your chest. What do you do?

If you're like a lot of people, you just freak.

You've stepped into *Gunslinger*, a Skunk Works holodeck in a nondescript brick building a few blocks from the lab's black glass headquarters. It's essentially a stage set, the fourth wall open. The props you see—the rough-hewn bar, the unpainted walls, the splintered wooden floor—are real. Utah, Harmony, and Rio are life-sized figures on video screens—in Utah's case, a screen behind the bar. Imagine the giant, mesmerizing televisors in Ray Bradbury's *Fahrenheit 451* and you get the general idea.

"People get very, very emotionally involved," said Kim LeMasters, ICT's creative director. "They know from the media how the good guy is supposed to behave. But they're also afraid of Rio."

With his full, ruddy face and no-bullshit grin, LeMasters looks more than a little like William Shatner, the original series' redoubtable Captain Kirk, in his post–*Star Trek* years. As a CBS programming exec in the 1970s and '80s, LeMasters had a hand in hits like *Dallas*, *Knots Landing*, *The Dukes of Hazzard*, and *Murphy Brown*. Later he was an executive producer on Barry Sonnenfeld's *Wild Wild West*. Now he represents the entertainment side at ICT.

From his years in Hollywood, LeMasters had assumed that if he told you to go in and arrest Rio Laine, you'd play by the rules as laid down in hundreds of Westerns: You'd say, "Rio, you're coming with me." Or "Rio, I want you to surrender." Or something of the sort. Not so. Some people simply announced they didn't want to fight. About 40 percent tried to plug Rio straight away, on the theory that if they didn't shoot first, they wouldn't have a second chance. Bad move: try to outdraw Rio and you won't get out alive—but you won't know that until it's too late. Other people simply ran out of things to say. *Gunslinger* relies on the same "brute force" AI that video games do: its virtual humans are programmed with 6,000 responses, but they have no actual knowledge. If the certifiable human doesn't give them something to respond to, the exchange stalls out.

Still, it's not the machines LeMasters finds frustrating. "How do you get a human being to behave the way you wish them to behave?" he demanded. "In a normal story, I have complete control over all our characters. In this story, I have control of only three characters. The other character has a human brain."

"GUNSLINGER" MAY BE an appropriate name for a technology that feels like the lawless frontier of entertainment, but the Pentagon isn't funding ICT to the tune of millions of dollars per year to get a life-sized, interactive Western. "We did *Gunslinger* to show how far virtual humans have come," said LeMasters. Now the task is to put these virtual humans to work.

In *Star Trek*, the holodeck is used for training as well as for entertainment, and so it is with the military. Several years ago, General James "Mad Dog" Mattis of the Marine Corps asked for a real-life holodeck to train his people—a life-sized, interactive, and completely immersive training facility. At the time, Mattis was commander of the First Marine Expeditionary Force, which has seen action in every US engagement in the Middle East since the 1991 Iraq invasion. The result was the Infantry Immersion Trainer, which opened in late 2007 at the unit's home base, Camp Pendleton, a vast and mostly empty stretch of land on the Pacific coast just north of San Diego.

Pendleton has been a major training center ever since it was set up in World War II, but it's been a while since the US Marines had to practice invading Pacific islands. So Swartout and LeMasters created a virtual Iraqi village inside a disused 30,000-square-foot tomato-sorting shed on the base. Their prototype Infantry Immersion Trainer combined real-life props—furniture, rooms, entire buildings—with startlingly realistic sound effects and life-sized, high-resolution digital video projected onto the walls.

Inside the immersion trainer, anything can happen, most of it bad. You might open a door and find a virtual insurgent wielding an AK-47. A marine fires; an instant later, bullet holes blossom on the opposite wall. Or you could be going down the street in a jeep when it's hit by a rocket-propelled grenade, killing a fellow marine and wounding an Iraqi woman. With the woman covered in blood and screaming, insurgents start firing on your squad. You duck into a room and find women and children inside. An insurgent pops up with an AK-47. Declaring you don't want to fight is not an option.

But as immersive as the Infantry Immersion Trainer can be, its virtual Iraqis are essentially pop-up figures. They can't speak, they can't hear. The next-generation immersion trainer, which was scheduled to be ready in fall 2010, is much more holodeck-like. Called CHAOS—short for Combat Hunter Action Observation and Simulation—it builds on a Marine Corps training program known as Combat Hunter that involves actual Afghanis who speak through an interpreter in Pashto. Also spearheaded by General Mattis, Combat Hunter was designed to inculcate American Millennials with "primal skills" like tracking and hunting that "we evolved out of," in the words of Colonel Clarke Lethin, the unit's former chief of staff. But there are only so many Afghanis the Pentagon can deploy to US training bases. Hence the call for CHAOS.

CHAOS is as sophisticated as *Gunslinger*. That makes it suitable for more delicate lessons—negotiating, for example. "The idea is to figure out how to observe situations and pick up clues," said LeMasters. Suppose a squad leader is talking to an Afghani who has a generator—obviously a leading figure in the community, since having a generator makes him the local electricity provider. Once again, the conversation is being conducted through an interpreter in Pashto. Everybody except the squad leader is a video projection. The Afghani claims he knows nothing about recent Taliban activity. "But if you're observant," said LeMasters, "you see he has a garage door opener on a table. What's that for? Well, if you want to blow up an IED, it's a really useful device."

The technology that goes into these systems is extraordinary—speech recognition, natural language processing, speech synthesis, dialogue management, emotion modeling. But because everything they say or do has to be scripted by their programmers, they remain a very long way from the computer-generated humanoids (or fake humans, if you prefer) anticipated in *Star Trek*. The ultimate simulacrum, the *Star Trek* projection, Disneyland in a box—that's still years away. But eventually, who knows? Even in *Star Trek*, the holodeck is shown to be dangerously immersive. Witness Lieutenant Reginald Barclay, a brilliant engineer and pathetic milquetoast who was introduced in season 3 of *The Next Generation*. Barclay, the prototypal nerd, leads a life of glory within the holodeck's confines—and not surprisingly, he spends as much time there as possible. Wouldn't you?

YEARS AGO, I WENT TO Sleeping Beauty's castle. Not the one at Disneyland but the—well, I was going to say the real one, but who's to say what's "real" about a fairy-tale castle? Anyway, there is an actual castle in France that once upon a time, in a manner of speaking, was Sleeping Beauty's. It's the Château d'Ussé, in the Loire valley, and I came upon it at the end of a half-day hike through the woods. "La Belle au bois dormant," as she's known in France, turns out to have had quite the enchanted castle.

Constructed in the fifteenth and sixteenth centuries, grandly adorned with towers and turrets and terraces, the Château d'Ussé is a storybook blend of medieval castle and Renaissance château. Across a flat plain before it flow the River Indre and the Loire itself; behind it rises a steep hillside covered in woods so dense and forbidding they look as if they might creep down and envelop the château overnight. This is the Forêt de Chinon, a strangely gloomy woodland whose gnarled and twisted trees stretch southward for miles. According to legend, it was as a guest at the château that Charles Perrault was inspired to write "Sleeping Beauty."

A prominent literary figure and government official during the reign of Louis XIV, Perrault was well into his sixties when he wrote the tale of a princess who falls into a 100-year sleep before her Prince Charming finds her amid a dense and overgrown forest. Perrault based the story on an ancient European folktale that had already been written down in a 1634 Italian collection and before that in an anonymous fourteenth-century manuscript. He published his version in 1696, and a year later he included it with "Cinderella," "Little Red Riding Hood," and six other stories he'd written down in a collection called *Tales of Mother Goose*. ("Mère l'oye" was a common term for nanny at the time.) Walt Disney put his movie version into production some 250 years later, and a couple years after that the Sleeping Beauty Castle began to rise above the orange groves surrounding the mammoth construction site that was Disneyland.

Sleeping Beauty was a disaster when it hit movie screens in 1959, eviscerated by critics and largely ignored by audiences. More than 20 years had passed since Disney's triumph with *Snow White and the Seven Dwarfs*, and in the interim, Disneyfication had curdled into self-parody. Yet today, some 16 million people per year tour Disneyland's Sleeping Beauty Castle, where they view Disney dioramas of Perrault's fairy tale. As for the Château d'Ussé, it's one of the less popular attractions of the Loire, its fusty Sleeping Beauty waxworks notwithstanding.

And why should things be any different? The château, for all its glories, is a creaky old palace that over the centuries has been home to some of France's leading families, one of which happened more than 300 years ago to host an esteemed writer with a keen interest in folktales. The Sleeping Beauty Castle at Disneyland is narrative architecture purpose-built to provide an immersive experience of a 1950s interpretation of one of those tales. At the château, a story that had been passed down over the centuries by oral tradition was transmuted into written form for a society that was just then making the transition to the linear progression of print. The theme park castle processed that story into something every suburban mom and pop could stand in line with the kids to experience.

Disney, of course, never intended his castle to be a faithful replica of the Château d'Ussé. It was partly inspired by the châteaux of the Loire, but it was also heavily influenced by several Bavarian castles—in particular Schloss Neuschwanstein, the flamboyantly theatrical nineteenth-century confection built in the foothills of the Alps by King Ludwig II. Conceptualized by a stage designer for Richard Wagner, Neuschwanstein was itself a fantasia inspired by medieval castles in Germany and France. So Disney's Sleeping Beauty Castle is a simulacrum of a simulacrum. Which raises the question, Do two simulacra make an authentic?

People today are experiencing an authenticity crisis, and with good reason. Value is a function of scarcity, and in a time of scripted reality TV and Photoshop everywhere, authenticity is a scarce commodity. But what is authenticity, exactly? Or as Philip K. Dick would put it, what is real? Being who or what you claim to be is part of it, but at a deeper level, authenticity means being true to yourself—a quicksilver concept if ever there was one, especially when it's applied not to humans but to things. Thus we have *Authenticity* the book, published in 2007 by Harvard Business School Press, a how-to for marketers that helpfully draws the distinction between "real fake" and "fake real." We had Stolichnaya's 2007 "Choose Authenticity" advertising campaign, which used faux-constructivist graphics to promote Stoli as real (unlike, say, Grey Goose, the rival brand whose creators devised the marketing first and the vodka second). And of course we have those who can't resist the temptation to fake it altogether—like the folks at Wal-Mart who in 2006 launched the Hub, an agonizingly unhip and blatantly promotional "social networking" site for teenagers.

Authenticity issues have surfaced before. "I just want to say one word to you. Just one word," said the family friend to the bright young man in *The Graduate*. "*Plastics*." That was in 1967. Authenticity then may have harked back to some preindustrial ideal, but the quest for it now is a pure product of technology. We live in a high-speed, always-on world in which identity is always suspect, but we also have the media savvy to sniff out fakery and the tools to spread the word. Technology makes authenticity suspect, and technology gives us the wherewithal to demand it—if that's what we really want.

Except, of course, that it's not what we want. It's what we think we want. What we really want—many of us, anyway—is the holodeck. We want to be sucked inside the computer like Jeff Bridges in *Tron*. We want to be immersed in something that's not real at all.

Which is exactly what Walt wanted to do. Disney had long dreamed of building an entirely new type of amusement park—a place where he could re-create, in idealized form, the little Missouri town where he'd grown up (Main Street USA) and the settings for all those characters he'd created or appropriated (Sleeping Beauty). He called his creation "the happiest place on Earth." It was a fully, indeed obsessively immersive environment, kept cleaner than clean and staffed with a cadre of young men and women who were trained to smile as if their jobs depended on it (which in fact they did). In *The Disney Version*, his landmark biography, Richard Schickel found Disney semihysterical when explaining the philosophy that underlay all this:

> "I don't like depressing pictures," he growled. . . . "I don't like pestholes. I don't like pictures that are dirty. I don't ever go out and pay money for studies in abnormality. I don't have depressed moods and I don't want to have any. I'm happy, just very, very happy."

Disney was as enamored of technology as anyone in Hollywood today. His version of immersive entertainment combined the real-world environment of Disneyland with his own iteration of virtual humans—not holograms or video projections but robots, mechanical figures powered by hydraulics and controlled electronically by magnetic tape. Audio-Animatronics, he called it. He had started working on this in the mid-1940s with miniature figures that were controlled by punched tape, not unlike the "reality tape" that Garson Poole discovers in his chest in "The Electric Ant." By 1964 the technology had progressed to the point that he was able to stage an exhibit called "Great Moments with Mr. Lincoln" at the Illinois Pavilion in the New York World's Fair. The "Lincoln Simulacrum," as Dick dubbed it, was a mechanical construct of the sixteenth president, a life-sized and astonishingly lifelike figure that spouted platitudes lifted from the great man's speeches. After the World's Fair ran its course, the exhibit was installed in Disneyland, where it resides to this day. Schickel saw it as a horror, "the dehumanization of art in its final extremity, paradoxically achieved . . . after a lifetime search for a perfect means of reproducing the reality of human life." Others just call it creepy.

It was Dick's peculiar fate to live a mile or two from this world, in one of the apartment complexes that were slapped together after the freeways went through and the orange groves were ripped out. Disneyland went too far—too far for Dick, anyway. But though the revulsion he felt at its fakery was instinctual, it was clearly compounded by a sense of complicity. "I do not know how much of my writing is true, or which parts (if any) are true," he admitted in the speech he gave/did not give in Paris. "We have fiction mimicking truth, and truth mimicking fiction. We have a dangerous overlap, a dangerous blur."

The fictional reality Disney built out of bricks and ambition became the foundation for a global media empire that in its most recent fiscal year took in $36 billion. Dick wrote for peanuts, but the worlds he imagined now command top dollar in Hollywood, where they've given rise to such movies as Ridley Scott's *Blade Runner* and Spielberg's *Minority Report*. In the end it comes down to sensibility. Whose pseudoreality would you rather live in—Dick's or Disney's?

I'll say this for Dick: at least he didn't manifest a deep-seated need to paper over his insecurities with false happiness; nor did he share Disney's obsessive need for control. Quite the opposite, as he pointed out in the same speech:

> It is my job to create universes, as the basis of one novel after another. And I have to build them in such a way that they do not fall apart two days later. Or at least that is what my editors hope. However, I will reveal a secret to you: I like to build universes which do fall apart. I like to see them come unglued, and I like to see how the characters in the novels cope with this problem. I have a secret love of chaos. There should be more of it.

We fear the fictional even as we long to immerse ourselves in it. But from *Robinson Crusoe* to *Lost*, any fiction worth experiencing has been immersive. Books, movies, television, virtual worlds—century after century, we port our willing suspension of disbelief to whatever new and more immersive medium appears. So, what do we do when the universe this latest medium spins for us begins to fall apart—as inevitably it will? It's not just the characters that have to respond, after all; it's us. How do we cope when the fictional bleeds into the real, and vice versa? How do we handle the blur?

In *Inception*, the Christopher Nolan film that followed *The Dark Knight*, Leonardo DiCaprio plays a thief in dream space who keeps a tiny, spinning top that will topple over only if he isn't dreaming—that is, if he's in the real world. It's the one sure cue that will tell him what state he's in. At this point in history, it's impossible to say how immersive these story worlds we're building—*Avatar, Tron*, the holodeck—will actually become. But if the blur ever does get out of control, a spinning top might be very handy to have.

Notes

Prologue

1 *landmark 1944 study:* Fritz Heider and Marianne Simmel, "An Experimental Study of Apparent Behavior," *American Journal of Psychology,* 57, no. 2 (April 1944): 243–47.
4 *Spending on music in 1999:* International Federation of the Phonographic Industry, "2000 Recording Industry World Sales" (IFPI, April 2001), 8.
4 *sank to $25 billion in 2009:* Andrew Paine, "Global Recorded Music Market Down 7.2%," *Billboard,* April 28, 2010.
5 *"What we're doing is fucking with the rules":* Peter Biskind, *Easy Riders, Raging Bulls* (New York: Simon & Schuster, 1998), 45.
6 *The couch potato:* David Blum, "Couch Potatoes: The New Nightlife," *New York,* July 20, 1987.
7 *"An artistic movement":* David Shields, *Reality Hunger: A Manifesto* (New York: Knopf, 2010), 5.

Chapter 1: The Dyslexic Storyteller

11 *Christopher Nolan on* The Dark Knight *footage:* John Campea, "Description of First 6 Minutes of New Batman Film," theMovieblog.com, December 4, 2007.

17 *"Here was entertainment"*: Frank Rose, "And Now, a Game from Our Sponsors," *Wired*, January 2008, 155–56.
23 *"What we're doing is a giant extrapolation"*: Ibid., 157.
24 *"interactive, immersive and invasive"*: Janelle Brown, "Paranoia for Fun and Profit," Salon.com, August 10, 2001.
25 *"a noble experiment that failed"*: David Kushner, "So What, Exactly, Do Online Gamers Want?" *New York Times*, March 7, 2002.
27 *"So I started thinking"*: Rose, "And Now, a Game," 154.

Chapter 2: Fear of Fiction

32 *"If ever the Story"*: Daniel Defoe, *Robinson Crusoe* (Cambridge: Cambridge University Press, 1900), xii.
32 *novels were judged by their "truth to individual experience"*: Ian Watt, *The Rise of the Novel: Studies in Defoe, Richardson, and Fielding* (Berkeley: University of California Press, 1957), 13.
33 *"There never was a time"*: Samuel Johnson, *The Adventurer*, no. 115 (December 11, 1753), quoted in Watt, *Rise of the Novel*, 58.
33 *"impression of life"*: Henry James, "The Art of Fiction," *Longman's Magazine*, September 1884, quoted in Raymond A. Mar and Keith Oatley, "The Function of Fiction Is the Abstraction and Simulation of Social Experience," *Perspectives on Psychological Science*, 3, no. 3 (2008), 175.
33 *"Life is monstrous"*: Robert Louis Stevenson, "A Humble Remonstrance," *Longman's Magazine*, December 1884, quoted in Mar and Oatley, "Function of Fiction," 175.
34 *the proscenium arch shot*: Roberta E. Pearson and Philip Simpson, eds., *Critical Dictionary of Film and Television Theory* (London: Taylor & Francis, 2001), 5.
36 *soaking up all the free time*: Clay Shirky, "Gin, Television, and Social Surplus," Herecomeseverybody .org, April 26, 2008.
36 *Every new medium*: Janet H. Murray, *Hamlet on the Holodeck: The Future of Narrative in Cyberspace* (Cambridge, Mass.: MIT Press, 1997), 18–21.
36 *"Thank God for that"*: Ray Bradbury, *Fahrenheit 451* (New York: Simon & Schuster, 1993), 112.
37 *"Suddenly, dazzling"*: Aldous Huxley, *Brave New World* (New York: Harper & Row, 1946), 200.

38 *"[He] so buried himself in his books"*: Miguel de Cervantes, *Don Quixote*, trans. Burton Raffel (New York: Norton, 1995), 10.
38 *"A consensual hallucination"*: William Gibson, *Neuromancer* (New York: Ace, 2000), 51.
39 *"pathological-techno-fetishist-with-social-deficit"*: William Gibson, *Idoru* (New York: Berkley, 1997), 115.
40 *"Understanding otaku-hood"*: William Gibson, "Modern Boys and Mobile Girls," *Observer*, April 1, 2001.
40 *Murakami traces the origins of otaku*: Takashi Murakami, "Impotence Culture-Anime," in *My Reality: Contemporary Art and the Culture of Japanese Animation* (Des Moines, Iowa: Des Moines Art Center, 2001), 60.
40 *"otaku" used to address other characters*: Lawrence Eng, "The Origins of 'Otaku,'" CJAS.org, November 4, 2003.
43 *tacit understanding with fans*: Daniel H. Pink, "Japan, Ink," *Wired*, November 2007, 219–21.
44 *"For the casual consumer"*: Henry Jenkins, *Convergence Culture: Where Old and New Media Collide* (New York: New York University Press, 2006), 131.

Chapter 3: Deeper

65 *"I couldn't tell what was real"*: Josh Quittner, "Are 3-D Movies Ready for Their Closeup?" *Time*, March 19, 2009.
66 *"The Big Mac is all about the thrill"*: Brian Quinton, "McDonald's Is Latest Augmented Reality Convert with 'Avatar' Campaign," Promomagazine.com, December 15, 2009.
67 *"authentic and exclusive content"*: "Coke Zero Immerses Itself in 'Avatar,'" *BrandWeek*, November 25, 2009.
67 *"There wasn't a common ground"*: "Video: Avatar Producer Jon Landau Speech at 3D Gaming Summit," G4TV.com/thefeed, April 23, 2010.

Chapter 4: Control

84 *Wesch at the Library of Congress*: Michael Wesch, "An Anthropological Introduction to YouTube" (speech, Library of Congress, June 23, 2008).

85 *"You aren't going to turn"*: Kevin Kelly, "We Are the Web," *Wired*, August 2005, 95.

87 *the twentieth-century approach to advertising had it all wrong:* Anca Cristina Micu and Joseph T. Plummer, "On the Road to a New Effectiveness Model: Measuring Emotional Responses to Television Advertising," ARF White Paper, Advertising Research Foundation, March 2007.

89 *industrialization causing appalling conditions:* Steven Johnson, *The Ghost Map* (New York: Riverhead, 2006), 34–35.

90 *Thomas Hardy and* A Pair of Blue Eyes: Andrew Radford, *Thomas Hardy and the Survivals of Time* (Aldershot, England: Ashgate, 2003), 49–51.

91 *"Is Little Nell dead?"*: Edgar Johnson, *Charles Dickens: His Triumph and Tragedy*, vol. 1 (New York: Simon & Schuster, 1952), 303–4.

91 *A century and a half later*: "On the Use of Mr. Dickens's *Our Mutual Friend* in *Lost*," *The London Review*, November 1865.

91 *"Through serial publication"*: John Butt and Kathleen Tillotson, *Dickens at Work* (London: Methuen, 1957), 16.

92 *"The drawbacks of adhering"*: E. D. H. Johnson, *Charles Dickens: An Introduction to His Novels* (New York: Random House, 1969), 67.

92 *"The form of publication"*: Quoted in Jennifer Hayward, *Consuming Pleasures: Active Audiences and Serial Fictions from Dickens to Soap Opera* (Lexington: University of Kentucky Press, 1997), 26.

95 *"They attacked a whole bunch of kids"*: Henry Jenkins, *Convergence Culture: Where Old and New Media Collide* (New York: New York University Press, 2006), 195.

96 *"We believe"*: "Our Mission," Dprophet.com/dada.

96 *call the whole thing a "miscommunication"*: Jenkins, *Convergence Culture*, 196.

97 *"Has Disney decided"*: Dave Kehr, "O, Prince! How Clear You Are on Blu-ray," *New York Times*, October 14, 2008.

99 *"I am a little scared"*: News Reel, Wim-wenders.com, October 2002.

99 *"the least imitative of authors"*: William Gibson, "God's Little Toys," *Wired*, July 2005, 118–119.

100 *piracy among American college students*: "RIAA Continues College Deterrence Campaign into 2008" (press release, Recording Industry Association of America, January 10, 2008).

100 *piracy among UK youths:* David Bahanovich and Dennis Collopy, "Music Experience and Behavior in Young People" (UK Music, 2009).

101 *"When I was a boy"*: Quoted in Lawrence Lessig, *Remix: Making Art and Commerce Thrive in the Hybrid Economy* (New York: Penguin, 2008), 24–25.

Chapter 5: Forking Paths

105 *"moronic and offensive"*: Roger Ebert, "Mr. Payback," *Chicago Sun-Times*, February 17, 1995.

105 *"That's why you have a director"*: William Grimes, "When the Film Audience Controls the Plot," *New York Times*, January 13, 1993.

106 *"What are the scientists to do next?"*: Vannevar Bush, "As We May Think," *Atlantic Monthly*, July 1945, 101–8.

108 *"Attention Deficit Disorder"*: Gary Wolf, "The Curse of Xanadu," *Wired*, June 1995, 140.

109 *"Only Nelson's ignorance"*: Ibid., 143.

110 *"corridor gossip"*: Tim Berners-Lee, "Information Management: A Proposal," W3.org, March 1989/May 1990.

110 *"I had (and still have)"*: Tim Berners-Lee, "Hypertext and Our Collective Destiny" (lecture, Vannevar Bush Symposium, MIT, October 12, 1995).

111 *2002 study at UC Berkeley*: Peter Lyman and Hal R. Varian, "How Much Information? 2003" (School of Information Management and Systems, University of California, Berkeley, October 30, 2003, 1–2).

112 *"Even when I'm not working"*: Nicholas Carr, "Is Google Making Us Stupid?" *Atlantic*, July/August 2008, 56–63.

112 *books encourage forgetfulness*: Jonah Lehrer, "Our Cluttered Minds," *New York Times Book Review*, June 6, 2010.

113 *"stopped worrying"*: Alissa Quart, "Networked: Don Roos and 'Happy Endings,'" *Film Comment*, July/August 2005, 48–51.

113 *"irony of ironies, I've lost the link"*: Roger Ebert, "*Syriana*," *Chicago Sun-Times*, December 9, 2005.

114 *"But surely, Monsieur Godard"*: Susan Sontag, *Styles of Radical Will* (New York: Picador, 2002), 157.

115 *"In all fictional works"*: Jorge Luis Borges, *Labyrinths* (New York: New Directions, 1964), 26.

117 *"a post-Freudian, pulp-fiction fever dream"*: Stephen Holden, "*Mulholland Drive*," *New York Times*, October 6, 2001.

118 *"about murder, money, and success"*: Jean Tang, "All You Have to Do Is Dream," Salon.com, November 7, 2001.
119 *"The greatest of all reversals"*: Marshall McLuhan, *Understanding Media* (Cambridge, Mass.: MIT Press, 1994), 12.
119 *"the illusion of perspective"*: Ibid., 13.

Chapter 6: Open Worlds

122 *"at times reminiscent"*: Ralph Lombreglia, "Dispelled," theAtlantic.com, November 19, 1997.
122 *"a kind of puzzle box"*: Jon Carroll, "Guerillas in the Myst," *Wired*, August 1994, 69–73.
124 *"When I examine issues of* Wired*"*: Kevin Kelly, "We Are the Web," *Wired*, August 2005, 95, 99.
125 *"when a man industriously"*: Francis Bacon, *The Essays* (London: Penguin, 1985), 77.
130 *"established the principles"*: Tom Bissell, "The Grammar of Fun: Cliffy B and the World of the Video Game," *The New Yorker*, November 3, 2008.
135 *"stealing the innocence of our children"*: John Seabrook, "Game Master," *The New Yorker*, November 6, 2006.
138 *" 'You must be joking!' "*: Stanislaw Lem, *The Cyberiad* (New York: Seabury, 1974), 166.
141 *"a kind of thought experiment"*: Steven Pinker, "Toward a Consilient Description of Literature," *Philosophy and Literature* 31 (2007), 161–77.
142 *"that readers understand a story"*: Nicole K. Speer, Jeremy R. Reynolds, Khena M. Swallow, and Jeffrey M. Zacks, "Reading Stories Activates Neural Representations of Visual and Motor Experiences," *Psychological Science* 20, no. 8 (August 2009), 989–99.

Chapter 7: The Hive Mind and the Mystery Box

150 *"If we're pregnant enough"*: James B. Stewart, *Disney War* (New York: Simon & Schuster, 2005), 485–87.
151 *"I realized I haven't opened it"*: J. J. Abrams, "The Mystery Box: J.J. Abrams on TED.com," Blog.ted.com, January 10, 2008.

153 "Lost *may not be interactive directly*": Peter Pirolli, "A Probabilistic Model of Semantics in Social Information Foraging." Paper presented at the AAAI 2008 Spring Symposia, Stanford University, March 26–28, 2008.
155 *another scholarly essay:* Jason Mittell, "Sites of Participation: Wiki Fandom and the Case of Lostpedia," Journal.transformativeworks.org, 3 (2009).
166 *urged upon Dickens by Bulwer-Lytton:* E. D. H. Johnson, *Charles Dickens: An Introduction to His Novels* (New York: Random House, 1969), 71.
167 *a condition of their staying:* Josef Adalian, "'Lost' Set for Three More Years," *Variety*, May 6, 2007.

Chapter 8: Television: The Game

178 *"The idea that ten years from now"*: Frank Rose, "The End of TV as We Know It," *Fortune*, December 23, 1996.
183 *"We've heard the complaints"*: Jeff Jensen, "'Heroes' Creator Apologizes to Fans," *Entertainment Weekly*, November 7, 2007.
185 *get someone to write back:* Joshua Davis, "The Secret World of Lonelygirl," *Wired*, December 2006, 232–9.
188 *average price for a prime-time ":30"*: Tim Arango, "Broadcast TV Faces Struggle to Stay Viable," *New York Times*, February 28, 2009.
188 *the worth of NBC Universal:* Diane Mermigas, "GE Says No NBC Sale, but 2009 Could Change Everything," Mediapost.com, March 25, 2008.
192 *"Viewers who pay attention"*: Brian Steinberg, "Viewer-Engagement Rankings Signal Change for TV Industry," Adage.com, May 10, 2010.
193 *"Four million people"*: James Poniewozik, "Saving Chuck: Don't Applaud, Throw Money," Tunedin.blogs.time.com, April 23, 2009.
196 *The placement was so brazen:* Brian Steinberg, "Subway Places More Than Just Product in NBC's 'Chuck,'" Adage.com, April 16, 2009.
196 *"The demand for* Chuck*"*: Sarah Rabil, "NBC's 'Chuck' TV Series Saved by Subway Sponsorship," Bloomberg.com, May 19, 2009.

Chapter 9: Twitter and Nothingness

200 *"Half a billion is a nice number"*: Mark Zuckerberg, "500 Million Stories," Blog.facebook.com, July 21, 2010.

200 *a Nielsen survey found:* "Led by Facebook, Twitter, Global Time Spent on Social Media Sites up 82% Year over Year," Blog.nielsen.com, January 22, 2010.
203 *"seem vaguely 'out there' ":* Stanley Milgram, "The Small World Problem," *Psychology Today* 1 (1967), 61–67.
204 *"Each of us is part":* Albert-László Barabási, *Linked: The New Science of Networks* (Cambridge, Mass.: Perseus, 2002), 30.
204 *"We attend to one another compulsively":* Brian Boyd, *On the Origin of Stories: Evolution, Cognition and Fiction* (Cambridge, Mass.: Belknap, 2009), 164.
205 *"In the long run":* Ibid., 171.
207 *empathy among college students:* "Empathy: College Students Don't Have as Much as They Used to, Study Finds," *ScienceDaily*, May 29, 2010.
208 *brain researchers at the University of Parma:* Daniel Goleman, *Social Intelligence: The New Science of Human Relationships* (New York: Bantam, 2006), 41.
208 *when the monkey watched a person:* Giuseppe di Pellegrino, Luciano Fadiga, Leonardo Fogassi, Vittorio Gallese, and Giacomo Rizzolatti, "Understanding Motor Events: A Neurophysiological Study," *Experimental Brain Research* 91, no. 1 (October 1992), 176–80.
208 *1999 study at UCLA:* Marco Iacoboni, Roger P. Woods, Marcel Brass, Harold Bekkering, John C. Mazziotta, and Giacomo Rizzolatti, "Cortical Mechanisms of Human Imitation," *Science* 286 (December 24, 1999), 2526–28.
209 *"enable social connectedness":* Vittorio Gallese, "Mirror Neurons, Embodied Simulation, and the Neural Basis of Social Identification," *Psychoanalytic Dialogues* 19 (2009), 519–36.
209 *fMRI study at University College London:* Tania Singer, Ben Seymour, John O'Doherty, Holger Kaube, Raymond J. Dolan, and Chris D. Frith, "Empathy for Pain Involves the Affective but Not Sensory Components of Pain," *Science* 303 (February 20, 2004), 1157–62.
209 *The same team:* Tania Singer, Ben Seymour, John P. O'Doherty, Klaas E. Stephan, Raymond J. Dolan, and Chris D. Frith, "Empathic Neural Responses Are Modulated by the Perceived Fairness of Others," *Nature* 439 (January 2006), 466–69.
209 *a team at the University of Toronto:* W. D. Hutchison, K. D. Davis, A. M. Lozano, R. R. Tasker, and J. O. Dostrovsky, "Pain-Related Neurons in the Human Cingulate Cortex," *Nature Neuroscience* 2 (1999), 403–5.
210 *too freaked out to function:* Jean Decety and Philip L. Jackson, "A

Social-Neuroscience Perspective on Empathy," *Current Directions in Psychological Science* 15, no. 2 (May 2006), 54–58.
212 *the blog population had reached a few thousand*: Rebecca Mead, "You've Got Blog," *The New Yorker*, November 13, 2000.
212 *Blogger alone had 600,000 users*: Max Chafkin, "Anything Could Happen," *Inc.*, March 2008.
215 *"The qualities that make Twitter"*: Brad Stone and Noam Cohen, "Social Networks Spread Defiance Online," *New York Times*, June 15, 2009.
217 *"not just a practitioner"*: Chafkin, "Anything Could Happen."
217 *50 million tweets*: Kevin Weil, "Measuring Tweets," Twitter.com, February 22, 2010.
218 *"But as we add more links"*: Barabási, *Linked*, 34–35.
218 *revenues of only $25 million*: Spencer E. Ante, "Twitter Is Said to Be Profitable after Making Search Agreements," Bloomberg.com, December 21, 2009.
219 *"Check Twitter!" came the retort*: Daniel Terdiman, "Journalist Becomes the Story at Mark Zuckerberg SXSWi Keynote," Cnet.com, March 9, 2008.

Chapter 10: This Is Your Brand on YouTube

225 *"These networks comprise"*: Brian Morrissey, "Carl's Jr. Makes New Kind of Network Buy," *Adweek*, June 1, 2009.
227 *"In the midst of all this"*: Rosser Reeves, *Reality in Advertising* (New York: Knopf, 1961), 50–52.
227 *spent years not talking to one another*: Randall Rothenberg, *Where the Suckers Moon: An Advertising Story* (New York: Knopf, 1994), 62.
228 *minutes are worth millions*: Frank Rose, "The Lost Boys," *Wired*, August 2004, 116–19.
229 *the networks crowed in triumph*: Bill Carter, "Young Men Are Back Watching TV. But Did They Ever Leave?" *New York Times*, August 9, 2004.
229 *"Where are we going?"*: "Steve Heyer's Manifesto for a New Age of Marketing," Adage.com, February 6, 2003.
230 *television's share of Coca-Cola's US ad budget*: Bradley Johnson, "TV Still Rules, but the Net Is Showing Gains," *Advertising Age*, June 25, 2007.
230 *"There must be"*: Angelo Fernando, "Creating Buzz: New Media Tactics Have Changed the PR and Advertising Game," *Communication World*, 21 no. 6 (November–December 2004): 10–11.

230 *"Used to be, TV was the answer":* Jean Halliday, "Poor Results Spark Cut: GM Zaps $40 Mil in Upfront Buys," *Advertising Age*, February 16, 2004.
231 *hiring actors to shout slogans at the screen:* Stuart Elliott, "Under an Audacious Campaign, the Chatter before the Movie Starts Might Just Be about a Nissan," *New York Times*, November 6, 2003.
231 *"This is the first time we've used foreheads":* Lisa Sanders, "Selling Scions with Forehead Ads," *Advertising Age*, April 7, 2004.
232 *Publicis Groupe study of Second Life:* Frank Rose, "Lonely Planet," *Wired*, August 2007, 140–44.
232 FarmVille *product integration:* Elizabeth Olson, "For FarmVille Players, a Crop from a Real Organic Farm," *New York Times*, July 14, 2010.
233 *"Fragmentation has decimated audiences":* Bob Garfield, *The Chaos Scenario* (New York: Stielstra, 2009), 31.
233 *Millward Brown research:* Erik du Plessis, "Digital Video Recorders and Inadvertent Advertising Exposure," *Journal of Advertising Research*, 49, no. 2 (June 2009): 236–39.
233 *dismissed this argument as "idiotic":* Garfield, *Chaos Scenario*, 35.
234 *study of eight UK homes:* Sarah Pearson and Patrick Barwise, "PVRs and Advertising Exposure: A Video Ethnographic Study," *Qualitative Market Research* 11, no. 4 (2008): 386–99.
235 *some dude wearing a chicken outfit:* Rose, "Lost Boys."
236 *"Signals that evolve through competition":* Brian Boyd, *On the Origin of Stories: Evolution, Cognition and Fiction* (Cambridge, Mass.: Belknap, 2009), 160–61.
237 *"The 'Subservient Chicken' campaign":* Frank Rose, "And Now, a Word from Our Customers," *Wired*, December 2006, 228–31.
239 *"there's quite a few arms raised":* Scott Donaton, "How to Thrive in New World of User-Created Content: Let Go," *Advertising Age*, May 1, 2006.
240 *"I was like, This song is too perfect":* Chris Cadelago, "Forget MTV—Apple's iPod Ads Are the New Music-Star Makers," *San Francisco Chronicle*, November 24, 2007.
240 *on the air by the end of October:* Stuart Elliott, "Student's Ad Gets a Remake, and Makes the Big Time," *New York Times*, October 26, 2007.
241 Ad Age *bemoaned the arrival:* Brian Steinberg, "Don't Like Product Placements? Here's Why It's Your Fault," Adage.com, February 11, 2010.
247 *Jonathan Mildenhall on the Happiness Factory:* Steve Barrett, "Happiness Factory Offers a Vision of Media's Future," Mediaweek.co.uk, May 20, 2008.

252 *"Just Do It" emerged:* "Nike's 'Just Do It' Advertising Campaign," CFAR.com, January 1999.
254 *"the day Nike united the world":* Ajeeja Limbu, "The Day Nike United the World," theUrbanWire.com, October 28, 2009.
254 *"from great storytelling to a digital world":* Bob Greenberg, "The Runner's High," *Adweek*, April 30, 2007.

Chapter 11: The One-Armed Bandit

260 *the brain of a human who's playing a video game:* M. J. Koepp, R. N. Gunn, A. D. Lawrence, V. J. Cunningham, A. Dagher, T. Jones, D. J. Brooks, C. J. Bench, and P. M. Grasby, "Evidence for Striatal Dopamine Release during a Videogame," *Nature* 393 (May 21, 1998), 266–68.
262 *when to expect their treat:* Jonah Lehrer, *How We Decide* (Boston: Houghton Mifflin Harcourt, 2009), 36–37.
262 *expect the juice in a predictable pattern:* Kent Berridge, "The Debate over Dopamine's Role in Reward: The Case for Incentive Salience," *Psychopharmacology* 191 (2007), 391–431.
262 *"Dopamine neurons respond":* Wolfram Schultz, "Dopamine Neurons and Their Role in Reward Mechanisms," *Current Opinion in Neurobiology* 7 (1997), 191–97.
263 *drugs become addictive because:* Terry Robinson and Kent Berridge, "The Psychology and Neurobiology of Addiction: An Incentive–Sensitization View," *Addiction* 95 (2000), S91–S117.
263 *injected amphetamines or Ritalin:* Koepp et al., "Evidence for Striatal Dopamine Release," 266–67.
265 *stuck with the two higher-paying decks:* Lehrer, *How We Decide*, 46–47.
266 *Unlike the normals:* Antoine Berchera, Hanna Damasio, Daniel Tranel, and Antonio R. Damasio, "Deciding Advantageously before Knowing the Advantageous Strategy," *Science* 275 (February 28, 1997), 1293–95.
269 *Mr. Certain and Mr. Uncertain:* Paul Howard-Jones and Skevi Demetriou, "Uncertainty and Engagement with Learning Games," *Instructional Science* 37, no. 6 (November 2009), 519–36.
270 *"Researcher: Were there instances":* Ibid.
271 *University College London gambling study:* Rebecca Elliott, Karl J. Friston, and Raymond J. Dolan, "Dissociable Neural Responses in Human Reward Systems," *Journal of Neuroscience* 20, no. 16 (August 15, 2000), 6159–65.

271 *Schultz on dopamine release in monkeys:* Christopher D. Fiorillo, Philippe N. Tobler, and Wolfram Schultz, "Discrete Coding of Reward Probability and Uncertainty by Dopamine Neurons," *Science* 299 (2003), 1898–1902.
271 *Scientists at Concordia:* Peter Shizgal and Andreas Arvanitogiannis, "Gambling on Dopamine," *Science* 299 (2003), 1856–58.
272 *"This emotional system":* Jaak Panksepp, *Affective Neuroscience: The Foundations of Human and Animal Emotions* (Oxford: Oxford University Press, 1998), 52–53.
273 *"Brian, if you guys do not make":* "DICE 2010: 'Design Outside the Box' Presentation," G4TV.com, February 18, 2010.

Chapter 12: The Emotion Engine

282 *Hassabis experiment:* Demis Hassabis, Carlton Chu, Geraint Rees, Nikolaus Weiskopf, Peter D. Molyneux, and Eleanor Maguire, "Decoding Neuronal Ensembles in the Human Hippocampus," *Current Biology* 19 (April 14, 2009), 546–54.
286 *study of London taxi drivers:* Eleanor A. Maguire, David G. Gadian, Ingrid S. Johnsrude, Catriona D. Good, John Ashburner, Richard S.J. Frackowiak, and Christopher D. Frith, "Navigation-Related Structural Change in the Hippocampi of Taxi Drivers," *Proceedings of the National Academy of Sciences of the USA* 97, no. 8 (April 11, 2000), 4398–4403.
287 *"To be honest, there's not a lot coming":* Demis Hassabis, Dharshan Kumaran, Seralynne D. Vann, and Eleanor A. Maguire, "Patients with Hippocampal Amnesia Cannot Imagine New Experiences," *Proceedings of the National Academy of Sciences of the USA* 104, no. 5 (January 30, 2007), 1726–31.

Chapter 13: How to Build a Universe That Doesn't Fall Apart

289 *"Let me bring you official greetings":* Philip K. Dick, "How to Build a Universe That Doesn't Fall Apart Two Days Later," in Lawrence Sutin (ed.), *The Shifting Realities of Philip K. Dick: Selected Literary and Philosophical Writings* (New York: Vintage, 1995), 262.

290 *he's actually an android:* Philip K. Dick, "The Electric Ant," in *Selected Stories of Philip K. Dick* (New York: Pantheon, 2002), 382–400.
291 *"I ask, in my writing, What is real?":* Dick, "How to Build a Universe," 262.
291 *"Fake realities will create fake humans":* Ibid., 263–64.
296 *developed by Steven Lisberger:* John Culhane, "Special Effects Are Revolutionizing Film," *New York Times*, July 4, 1982.
297 *most feared names in finance:* John Taylor, *Storming the Magic Kingdom* (New York: Knopf, 1987), 23–24.
298 *bringing in a pair of writers to script a remake:* Cathy Dunkley and Michael Fleming, "Mouse Uploads 'Tron' Redo," *Variety*, January 12, 2005.
301 *"The folks at ABC are going gaga":* Andy Serwer, "What Do These Guys Know about the Internet?" *Fortune*, October 9, 2000.
302 *10 percent of US households had broadband:* US Department of Commerce, "A Nation Online: Entering the Broadband Age," NTIA.doc.gov, September 2004.
306 *"The holographic aspect of the holodeck":* Lawrence Krauss, *The Physics of Star Trek* (New York: Basic Books, 2007), 138–39.
308 *"Imagine a simulated world":* "Dr. William Swartout—Immersive Environments," Video.google.com.
311 *Inside the immersion trainer:* Jim Garamone, "Simulation Brings Combat's Chaos to Pendleton Facility," American Forces Press Service, Defense.gov/news, February 20, 2008.
312 *inculcate American Millennials with "primal skills":* Rick Rogers, "Teaching Marines to Be like Hunters," *San Diego Union-Tribune*, February 29, 2008.
317 *" 'I don't like depressing pictures' ":* Richard Schickel, *The Disney Version* (New York: Simon & Schuster, 1968), 354.
317 *"the dehumanization of art":* Ibid., 335–37.
318 *"I do not know how much of my writing is true":* Dick, "How To Build a Universe," 266.
318 *"It is my job to create universes":* Ibid., 262.

Acknowledgments

This book would have been impossible without years of reporting for *Wired*. For that opportunity I owe a debt of gratitude to Chris Anderson, *Wired*'s editor, as well as to his predecessor, Katrina Heron, who brought me in. Working with the *Wired* team—among them John Abell, Chris Baker, Bob Cohn, Evan Hansen, Nancy Miller, Susan Murcko, Mark Robinson, and Nicholas Thompson—was a rewarding experience, and one I count myself lucky to have had.

I was equally lucky to have had a top-notch team at Norton. I'd like to give special thanks to my editor, Brendan Curry, and to the others who have made this happen: Steve Colca, Elisabeth Kerr, Ingsu Liu, Jeannie Luciano, Anna Oler, Nancy Palmquist, Tabitha Pelly, Jessica Purcell, and Bill Rusin. I'd also like to thank my agent, James Levine; my copyeditor, Stephanie Hiebert; and Jason Booher, whose remarkable cover design conveys in a single image what it took me three hundred pages to say.

Many people were generous enough to spend time explaining to me what to them may have seemed obvious. Among those I owe special thanks to are Susan Bonds and Michael Borys, whose contributions you may stumble across as you read the book. For their help and encouragement at crucial moments, I'd also like to thank Melanie Cornwell, Julie Crabill, Jeff Howe, and Kit Rachlis. I received invaluable assistance from Marianne Do, Katie Drummond, and Erik Malinowski; and without Peter Saczkowski I'd probably still be trying to figure out what a QTE is. And finally, for their support both professional and personal, I'd like to thank my friend Susan Kamil and my wife, Beth Rashbaum.

Index